EGGS Y'ALL

EGG GG

SHOP

THE COOKBOOK

NICK KORBEE

WM

WILLIAM MORROW
An Imprint of HarperCollinsPublishers

HarperCollins books may be purchased for educational, business, or sales promotional use. For information please e-mail the Special Markets Department at SPsales@harpercollins.com.

FIRST EDITION

Designed by Suet Yee Chong
Photography by David Malosh

Library of Congress Cataloging-in-Publication Data has been applied for.

ISBN 978-0-06-247661-6

17 18 19 20 21   ID/QDG   10 9 8 7 6 5 4 3 2 1

FOR AMANDA,
THE WATER FLOWING UNDERGROUND

CONTENTS

FOREWORD

HATCHING EGG SHOP

by founders Sarah Schneider and Demetri Makoulis

New York City has a way of making all things feel possible . . .

In the beginning, we would talk about our "Egg Shop" idea constantly to friends. It was part of our small talk—a party trick, really. But it was secretly becoming a big part of our lives. It began as a simple question, with a not so simple answer: "How can two people obsessed with egg sandwiches, but with *no* background in the kitchen or the food industry, create a restaurant dedicated entirely to them?" We needed help, and our longtime friend and now fellow Egg Shop managing partner, Florian Schutz, was the person to ask. Flo was a hotel general manager with loads of experience. Famously, Flo said, "Sarah, Demetri, you know I love you guys, but I'm so sick of hearing about the egg place. Can you find a chef and work out a business plan already?!" Ding ding ding.

When a friend introduced us to Nick Korbee, the executive chef at Smith & Mills in Tribeca, we got more than a little anxious. Smith & Mills was not only one of our favorite restaurants, but it was universally beloved by critics and New Yorkers alike. Nick was the guy who created the meatball dish for Smith & Mills that *BlackBook* had referred to as a "rich mouthful of velvety succulence." This is getting real, Flo!

Also, Nick was pairing his food with cocktails crafted by partners from Employees Only, which had been named World's Best Bar at Tales of the Cocktail. I mean, he was the guy who was on the cover of the *Daily News* and quoted saying, "[Diners] don't need to know what we went through for that dish, and that's what makes it a labor of love." As outsiders to this business, we were hyperaware that we could be viewed as posers with just another idea for an eatery, so to actually be sitting with a *proper* chef from one of the most beloved restaurants in New York City . . . well, let's just say we thought about canceling our meeting more than once.

We met Nick for lunch in Brooklyn. It may have been the rosé, but there was an immediate kinship between us. We laid out our vague idea—Egg Shop would be a casual eatery with a full bar that served the very best egg sandwiches and Bloody Marys all day and late into the night. That was it. Our menu concept was to be simple and concise. But, as the conversation developed, we realized it could be so much more—"all eggs, all the time."

Nick has a *strong* poker face by nature. He listened and asked a few questions that didn't give us any sense of whether he thought it could work, whether he liked it, whether he wanted to help . . . basically, anything. We left it at "thanks so much for your time and let's stay in touch," expecting never to hear from him again. One week later Nick called back to say, in his now familiar, measured tone, "I think this can be great. I have a ton of ideas I want to talk to you about, and I want to be a part of this with you." And Flo said he was in too!

So, with a meticulously anal-retentive, conservative-on-the-verge-of-paranoia business model in the works, we began our two-year journey to see how far our ovo-centric vision quest could go!

Our first tasting of potential dishes for the restaurant was life-changing. Nick was nailing it on both a micro and macro level, approaching each dish with the mind-set of a chef at any Michelin-starred restaurant. Integrity of ingredients, importance of technique, and true flavor development were the foundation for creating each item. The bacon, egg, and cheese was insane, with a sweet/savory tomato jam, fresh rice vinegar–pickled jalapeños, and an array of local sharp cheddar cheeses, bacon, and jamón served in rotation. Nick brought an arsenal we never could have imagined: unforgettable dishes like a French toast made with premium chocolate milk from local dairy Ronnybrook Farm, garnished with white nectarines, perfectly ripe golden Italian sugar plums, and crispy Serrano ham, or the *tamagoyaki musubi,* with its folded-to-perfection Japanese omelet, pickled heirloom carrots, and sweet ponzu reduction, wrapped in warm sushi rice and toasted nori. It was the moment we knew our restaurant could truly be a temple to the egg.

As we developed our menu, there were two camps emerging. One preferred dishes with what we called *lurp:* buttery rolls with melty, gooey fromage; fatty cured, smoked, or roasted meats; and the perfect sauce—items that you just can't resist but probably shouldn't eat, at least not on the daily. The other camp preferred dishes that were carbless, gluten-free, veg-heavy, and left you with a sense of having done something right by your body. Finding balance was the key. If the essence of a dish was lurptastic lurpiness, like a traditional Eggs Benedict or a Mexican breakfast platter, we would find a way to offer the flavor and decadence without the unnecessary calories, preservatives, fats, or sugars. Our eggs Benedict became gluten-free, and instead of hollandaise we developed a lemony yogurt-based citronette that has since developed quite the following. The Mexican breakfast became our El Camino (page 163), allowing beautifully slow-cooked pork and a perfectly poached egg to take center stage over any kind of refried beans, melted cheese, or large-looming tortilla.

This process of decadent refinement was how our Break' Bowl culture was born. It was simple— we wanted to give customers the option of eating our dishes without the bread or on the go.

Whether the bowl is light, low-cal, and delicate, or saucy, rich, and protein heavy, the idea was thoughtful food for busy people to eat while on the run from work, to life, to the gym, to the kids, to the lurp, to the party, to the morning after the party, back to work, back to the party, back to the gym, and home again. It was much more than an egg in a bowl, it was a vibe. Sometimes you need Tom Petty and the Heartbreakers, Otis Redding, and the Beach Boys and other times call for Three 6 Mafia, Geto Boys, and Raekwon. They all get you through. They all lift you up.

Today the two camps live in harmony. A diner craving an egg salad sandwich with a juicy piece of hot honey-drizzled fried chicken on a just-baked buttermilk biscuit happily shares a table with someone enjoying a miso quinoa bowl with ribbons of quick-pickled organic carrots, ripe avocado, baby kale, and a perfectly poached egg. No matter the mood or momentary need, our dishes were calibrated to be both satisfying and fuss-free.

When we opened our doors in August 2014, we had no clue how our concept would be received. But the first weekend we were in business, we had a two-hour wait. While two-hour waits are still very much a staple of our weekend, the most satisfying moment is still when a guest passes us at the door and whispers, "This was worth the wait and the best breakfast/brunch/lunch/dinner I've ever had." And it's been nothing but a soft scramble ever since.

INTRODUCTION

This book is here help you get the Egg Shop experience—whether it's breakfast for one or a boozy brunch for twenty of your closest friends—without having to wait two hours, or travel to New York City, for the food. Though we served more than 150,000 people in our first year alone, chances are we have yet to serve you and your family. Transforming your home kitchen into a sexy new egg-atorium doesn't require a visit from a pseudo celeb with a tool belt, or even a break in the space/time continuum, but a simple understanding of our approach to cooking. The goal in the Egg Shop kitchen is to take things further, balancing creativity and controlled experimentation, and editing our work only in the final dish that we present. We offer the insights gleaned from our experiments in the pages that follow, but more important, we offer all of our delicious results.

Beyond the playfulness and bold flavors that color our creative expression, this book is guided by one very simple principle: *You must know how to begin, and what you desire in the end.*

At Egg Shop, we begin with quality ingredients, so we start here with a guide to making strong choices no matter where you're shopping or how hands-on you want to be in the kitchen. Whether you live around the corner from the best bacon smoker in the world or you've always wanted to try doing it yourself, a dedication to quality and integrity is imperative. We introduce you to our purveyors, offer DIY recipes for the adventure seekers, and most important, work to create a common language to help you source in your area.

Next we build the knowledge base of egg cookery that will improve your egg game across the board, whether you're cooking from this book or creating your own recipes. We work through the most common and useful egg cooking techniques, plus some new and underutilized techniques like coddling eggs in mason jars full of truffle oil and basting eggs with coffee-infused compound bacon butter . . . excited yet? We do it all while highlighting the tricks and tips we've learned from crackin' it 365 days a year.

Each of the recipes in the Eggs in Space! chapter is complete and delicious in its own right, from the most basic soft scramble technique to the more complex Italian meringue. But these recipes stand as the keys to unlocking gastronomic glory to come; sandwiches and bowls alike reference back to these basic egg cooking techniques while adding their own flair.

So this is how we begin. And what do we want in the end? Love. It's all anybody wants, and according to the Beatles it's all we need. The recipes that complete the book are all the dishes we truly love to cook, and that our guests love to eat—and even some we wish we had the menu space to feature, or will be featuring soon! Each recipe presents a complete dish, assembled from several components that you'll find to be as versatile as the egg itself. This unique pantry of flavors and condiments can be adapted, as you'll see, to complement and change a dish and even help inspire new ideas. The pickling brine from the carrots makes a great base for a hot sauce, the chili pulp from the hot sauce makes an incredible sweet chili paste, the tomato juice from the confit makes a killer salad dressing, day-old rice long-simmers for congee. And so it goes, on and on.

On first flip, check out the components and prepare a few that pique your interest. As you work through the book you'll find your fridge and pantry full of things to play with in your own cooking and in your own timeframe.

In sharing these recipes with you, we share the love story that is our collective time and adventures in New York City. Eggs are messy. Love, it's messy. Living a joyful life is perhaps the messiest thing of all. So with that we hope you find this book informative, inspiring, beautiful, funny, and delicious—but above all else, we hope you make a great big mess.

—NK

QUALITY INGREDIENTS

Let's get this one thing straight: Good ingredients make good food. We've made that a starting point at Egg Shop, and it can be far easier than you think to do it in your own cooking, too. In this chapter we define what "good" ingredients mean to us and how to go about sourcing them wherever you may live.

It's one thing to hop, step, or jump onto one's New York City or So-Cal pedestal and speak down to everyone about such localistic esoterica as a curated selection of hand-foraged, single-origin native species of pregerminated, paleo-Babylonian endosperm-only tri-colored pasta that Chef has prepared specifically for your party. It's another thing to talk about the human interactions that our current super-duper-market culture deprives us of on the regular. We're after the latter, and it's simple: Go directly to the people who grow or make the thing you want to eat. Talk to them, shake their hands, ask them questions, and take their advice. That one ingredient you're after, that one thing—that may be their entire life. Do not disrespect, and you will be greeted in an edible Valhalla!

EGGS

Chicken farming practices have been a hot topic in recent years, but it seems to have been more about branding than public education—an effort to name and rename minute differences in farming practices to give one dozen an edge over the next on the grocery shelf. Seeing through the smoke and mirrors is as simple as going to your local farmers' market and asking a few questions, then cultivating a basic understanding of the chicken. Here's our take: If you consume an animal product of any kind, you must be comfortable consuming everything that animal consumes, as well as any chemical or preservative that the FDA deems necessary in processing that animal product before it's called safe for consumption by the mass market. At Egg Shop we can do without the chemicals, antibiotics, and radiation. It doesn't freak us out that pasture-raised chickens consume the occasional insect in addition to organic feed and other vegetation. In fact, considering this is a helpful exercise in understanding where flavor, color, and texture differences come from in different types, brands, and sources of eggs. We want you to make your best choice for you, your family, and, of course, for the hens, too.

WHERE DO EGGS COME FROM?

Many birds and other creatures lay eggs, from the Galapagos turtle and Nile crocodile to those fierce, fluffy emus your creepy neighbor has running around his backyard. In this book we focus on the hen's egg, with a duck or quail egg thrown (gently) in here and there. Where do those eggs come from? *News flash: They come from a chicken's butt!* Not really, but yeah, they sort of do; a hen's reproductive and excretory system have a single output, the cloaca. (Pretty polite way of saying that, don't you think?)

And those chickens are busy. While the human reproductive cycle works on a monthly basis, a chicken has a cycle in the course of a single day, and egg output is deeply impacted by the time between a single sunrise and sunset; the longer the period of sunlight, the more likely a hen is to lay an egg. All species want to reproduce, but chickens are really going for it! Sun's out, gun's out in constant hope of fertilization. Another factor is the chicken's desire to develop what is known as a "clutch." This is not a strapless handbag but rather a roost or nest full of up to twelve eggs to protect and keep warm until the (theoretical) chicks hatch. Biology has tuned the chicken to increase its odds for success by attempting to lay eggs until they have a big pile (clutch). Removing eggs from a roost on a daily basis, or as they are laid, increases the hen's imperative to produce.

Another factor in egg production is diet. The amount of protein, calcium, and other nutrients that go into producing a single egg is astounding. If the total weight of an egg is 60 grams, the chicken needs at least 20 grams of protein alone to produce it! That's a lot. To put it into perspective, that is 2 percent of a 3-pound chicken's body weight. A 150-pound human would need to eat 3 pounds of protein a day to produce a similar egg. Laying eggs is an amazing process, and hens deserve a hand! Which is why we prefer to source eggs from farmers who don't tax their hens by forcing overproduction. Give credit where credit is due—appreciate the animal and appreciate the egg.

WHAT DO THE LABELS MEAN?

CAGE FREE: This USDA-designated label means only that the hens were not raised in cages. It says nothing else about their conditions, which may not be particularly luxurious.

FREE RANGE: This means the hens have "access to the outdoors" (a space not covered by a roof). This is occasionally an enclosed dirt or concrete yard similar to a parking lot.

PASTURE RAISED: This term is legally unregulated, but a step in the right direction for those who uphold the ethos. Though HFAC and its Certified Humane initiative requires 108 square feet of rotated pasture per bird with a maximum of two weeks' annual allowance of indoor living in periods in inclement weather. Other qualifying standards dictate that the pasture must provide a high percentage of nutrition in the form of insects and grasses and other vegetation for the hens to forage. Pasture does not equal parking lot. Very *bueno,* dude!

ORGANIC: This is where the USDA gets the most specific, although regulations change from state to state. The baseline is as follows: The hens are given "organic feed," which is free of pesticides, antibiotics, and other farming chemicals; they are allowed "free range;" and if the outdoor area is not pasture, they must be fed fresh plant feed on a daily basis. Pretty decent.

ANTIBIOTIC FREE: No antibiotics are given to the hens, either in the feed or in other supplements. It isn't a USDA-certified term, but farms can be audited for false advertising.

OMEGA-3 FORTIFIED: The typical organic/pasture egg already contains about 30 milligrams of omega-3 fatty acids! This is because the hens are typically given a feed that is high in omega-3s, such as fish-based meal, alginates, and even flaxseed and flax oil. The feed does significantly increase the amount of fatty acids present in the egg, but it's not USDA regulated, so it's more of a marketing tool than anything else. Long hair, don't care about this one.

VEGETARIAN FED: This isn't regulated by the USDA, so if you're buying "vegetarian-fed" eggs in a supermarket, you're basically trusting that someone isn't lying to you. The only way to know for sure is to buy direct from a farmer or a source you trust. Hens are often fed bone meal that could contain anything from ground oyster shells to pig trotters. If vegetarian-fed eggs are important to you, you'd better ask somebody!

WHAT SHOULD YOU ASK AN EGG FARMER?

HOW MANY BIRDS DO YOU HAVE?

The size of the flock usually affects the quality of production and the freshness of the eggs. Fewer birds usually get more attention and have a wide range of diet, as there is less competition for the tasty bits around the pasture. With fewer birds, the farmer can't stockpile eggs to bring to market. While this means superior freshness, eggs will be scarce or unavailable during the winter months. Fewer than fifty hens is a hobby farm; fifty to one hundred is a very small commercial size, but up to five hundred would still fall in the realm of a family farm.

WHAT KIND OF ACCESS DO THEY HAVE TO THE OUTSIDE?

This is an important question! Is the terroir of the eggs a parking lot or a pasture? I often follow up with questions about parts of the pasture and types of grasses and bugs their birds seem to really enjoy. Ideally the hens can come and go as they like, free to roam around a diverse and verdant pasture, and return to their coop to roost and lay as they please. This will obviously be affected by colder temperatures and inclement weather, as birds don't like to be out in the cold or rain.

DO YOU USE HORMONES OR ANTIBIOTICS? WHAT DO YOUR HENS EAT?

If anyone raising chickens ever tells you they are experimenting with or using hormones, please report them to the USDA. It's against the law. But the use of antibiotics is a more nuanced issue. Using low-dose antibiotic feed is not a good policy, but an antibiotic supplement for a sick hen is not the end of the world. The consistent use of nontherapeutic low-dose antibiotics can result in resistant strains of bacteria that have the potential to comprise the entire flock. When you have a sick bird in a sizable flock, it does no good to treat the single hen, as the bacteria have likely already been spread like wildfire. So farmers get in the habit of treating the whole flock, even as a preventative measure. This is the dangerous bit, because consistent illness implies poor conditions. Go deep on this one. If your farmer says yes to antibiotics, ask what kind of antibiotics and how often they're administered. The answer you are looking for is "We use only antibiotics that are not used in human medicine to treat specific illness under the direction of our vet." You have a right to know, and good farmers will be proud to tell you. You are not annoying, you are interested.

Hens need protein to lay (about 20 grams per day to produce an egg, as mentioned). They do not need pesticides, chemicals, GMO grain by-products, or mixed bone meal. However, 100 percent vegetarian-fed isn't necessarily a goal, and frankly it isn't possible for true pasture-raised hens, which eat a fair amount of insects. Ask the question, and you decide if you're comfortable consuming the answer.

HOW ARE YOUR EGGS PREPARED FOR MARKET?

This should get an interesting response. The USDA says that eggs must be treated with water 20 degrees warmer than the interior temperature of the egg, a foodsafe detergent, a chlorine-based sanitizer (think bleach), a second rinse, and an approved drying process. It's important that you run away if someone tells you they give the eggs a good "soak." The shell is *porous,* and water draws bacteria through the shell to the egg! Most small farmers take pride in very clean eggs and will proudly tell you their eggs are brushed to remove only the surface debris, or they have a specialized (very expensive) egg washer. Just be cautious—the shell will always contain more bacteria than the inside of the egg, so please refrain from licking the shells of farm-fresh eggs and you should be in the clear. *Note: It's the breed and diet of the chicken that dictate the color of the shell, not a mechanized bleaching process. Organic eggs can also be white.*

BREAD

Bread baking is an art form. Like most artists, bread bakers are total weirdos (in the most adoring sense of the word)! Think of people so dedicated to their craft that they're willing to reverse their circadian rhythm by working through the night. Think of people so talented, confident, and self-sufficient that they rarely see their products into the hands of happy customers. For a baker, it's enough to leave a rack of perfect bread cooling in the morning breeze and peace out until the next moon.

My favorite weirdo is my friend and neighbor Josh Shuffman. I can't begin to work on a recipe for a bread product without visiting his home kitchen. Bread is ancient, and the wisdom that surrounds its many processes is vast and varied. It takes an expert to get to the bottom of it. Josh isn't an expert. He's Merlin, MacGyver, and McGee all in one dude. When we hang out and talk bread, I'm able to glimpse the bread life and briefly be a part of a world where wild yeast can be cultivated from thin air and time is counted in the hours and days of fermentation, proof, and rise. If Zen is for surfers and motorcycle mechanics, then Bread is for paranormal researchers and blues guitar players. We know the truth is out there, and we meet at the crossroads.

THE TRUTH

We define "good bread" as artisan breads, handmade in small batches from fresh-milled local flour and organic ingredients. We work with precision, using a scale and the metric system. We prefer wild yeast to commercial whenever time allows.

THE CROSSROADS

You will succeed at these recipes, and you will have commercial-quality bread from your home oven, but you will become obsessed with making it again, and making it better. It's a soul contract.

BREAD STARTER

100 grams organic flour (organic is important, as the flour will bring some of its own wild yeast to the table)   100%
100 grams tepid water   100%
Plus another 50 grams flour and 50 grams water for the first feeding

1. In a clear container (preferably a glass bowl or wide-mouth mason jar), mix the flour and water together. Be sure to use your hands to mix the starter, as wild yeast exists even on the surface of your skin. Use a spatula or bowl scraper to clean the sides of your container and remove any remaining cling-ons from your hands. These little bits can go back into the starter—no reason to wash them down the drain! Cover loosely with cheesecloth; even a tea towel or napkin will do.

2. Let the mixture ferment in a cool place in your kitchen for 48 hours. By this time you should be able to see some tiny bubbles on the sides of the container and the mixture will have a slightly funky, overripe fruit aroma. If this doesn't happen after 48 hours, simply let the mixture ferment a little longer, up to 4 days if necessary.

3. Give the mixture a good stir and discard about 80 percent of it. This doesn't have to be exact; simply dump a good deal of the mixture. Now, add another 50 grams flour and 50 grams water to the remaining mixture and incorporate by hand. This step is the first feeding and is how you can judge the strength of the yeast cultures in your starter. If the cultures are strong and active at this point, you will notice the starter bubble and rise within 2 to 4 hours after feeding and then fall. If it takes longer to notice these signs of fermentation, not to worry—just wait and take note of how much time passed before the rise and fall. This will help you understand when your starter is ready to use in making the leaven for your dough. When the starter is rising in the 2-hour range after feeding, it's ready to make bread, and that 2-hour mark after a feeding is exactly when you want to use it in the future.

Here are a few guidelines for working with and taking care of your new starter.

› Store the starter covered in a cool place or in the fridge.

› Always bring your starter up to room temperature before feeding.

› Feed the starter on a regular once-a-day schedule with equal parts water and flour.

› When feeding, discard at least 20 percent of the starter (this helps keep your amount of starter under control and also keeps the acidity in check).

› Use the starter only after feeding.

So . . . you've got a starter and we're speaking the same language. Now let's make bread. The recipes that follow offer a safety net in the form of active dry (commercial) yeast. If you're feeling at all intimidated, try the recipes first with commercial yeast to build your confidence. When you're ready to use your starter for these recipes, remember to use a well-fed starter about 2 hours after feeding. As a general rule any recipe that calls for commercial yeast can be made with natural leaven by using twice as much well-fed starter as commercial yeast. For example most of our recipes call for 7 grams active dry yeast, and that would convert to roughly 14 grams well-fed starter. In theory, using starter should not impact the baker's percentage of your recipe as long as you always feed the starter equal parts flour to water.

REAL BREAD NOW!

The recipes that follow are presented using metric measurements because they're the international language of bread baking. Whether you are bro-ing out hardcore with Chad Robertson in NorCal, rolling Retrodor baguettes like cigarettes in Paris, or whispering *"lievito madre"* into an ancient stone oven with Shuffman in the hills northwest of Firenze, learning this language is the first step. The reasoning is simple. Working with metric measure allows the baker to:

1. Scale production from a small batch to a large batch by simply multiplying the ingredients.
2. Uniformly portion and scale dough, resulting in a more consistent end product.
3. (Most important) Understand that all bread recipes function as the ratio of liquid ingredients to flour. This is known as *hydration percentage,* wherein flour represents the constant, 100 percent. These percentages are listed in the ingredients list for Panini Roll (page 13).

Now let's get real. Real bread is made from real yeast, the wild yeast that exists on the surface of almost all organic matter and drifts in the air all around us. Cultivating this wild yeast in the form of a bread starter is Dark Ages–level easy. While there are many creative twists and turns to adding character and depth of flavor to a starter, it's best to understand the basics first, then move on to variations.

COCKTAIL PARTY TERMS:
AUTOLYSE, PRE-FERMENT, AND POOLISH

Then, without notice, she leaned in, and with the hushed tone of a true professional, whispered, "Why don't we blow this pop stand and make poolish?"

But he wasn't ready. Not for her, not that night.

"Sorry, sugar, I never pre-ferment on the first date."

In that moment, there was no saxophone solo, no pull of the primal tide, and had there been fireworks they would most certainly have been obscured by skyscrapers and the passing shadow of storm clouds.

The two politely finished their drinks over the course of a thirty-second eternity. Hardly making eye contact, barely shifting in their seats, they knew they were in autolyse—their collective human protein and starch strengthened by hydration and fed by a distinct inactivity.

Great bread is like a tawdry romance and involves a particular kind of angst and playing hard to get. Developing flavor and texture is a courtship ritual among starch, gluten, and yeast. This is what separates real bread from milk toast. That developing relationship hinges as much upon fermentation as on the ingredients in a particular recipe. To the novice, naturally leavened or "real" bread is stuck in the category of "sourdough" and qualified simply as having a slightly sour aftertaste. But real bread in the hands of an experienced baker can express flavor notes as varied as any other fermented or cultured product—wine, beer, cheese, and so on. In the recipes that follow we pre-ferment and autolyse our doughs in order to hydrate the flour and give the gluten formation a necessary head start. As the yeast cultures feed on the starch, they release several by-products: acetic and lactic acids, alcohol, and carbon dioxide. As the starch (complex sugars) of a flour is consumed, the gluten proteins are strengthened and then stretched into longer strands by the released carbon dioxide. The interplay of these acids and the ingredients of a particular recipe create depth of flavor over time. Though the art is in the balancing, as fermentation continues, alcohol and acetic acid levels rise, and if left unchecked they kill off the yeast cultures and disintegrate the gluten proteins.

STAGES OF BREAD BAKING

These are the basics. While not every recipe will follow each of these steps, the steps themselves are guideposts in the process of making great bread, and eventually making your own recipe adaptations. If you don't play by the rules, just don't play the fool.

PRE-FERMENT: This flavor development stage can involve various techniques known as poolish (page 15), levain, biga, and so on. It's as simple as mixing flour with liquid and letting time do the work. Gluten is strengthened and acids develop.

MIX/AUTOLYSE/MIX: These steps involve combining all the ingredients in three stages. First, the pre-ferment/yeasts are mixed with liquid ingredients, fats/sugars, and flours. (Each time you add a new item for measure, you will have to tare—that is, balance the scale; when you measure ingredients in a bowl, it's important to tare the empty bowl first because you want to weigh only the ingredients, not the bowl itself.) Next comes autolyse, a resting period of 30 minutes to 2 hours that allows the yeast to become active and the flour to begin to hydrate, which in turn begins gluten formation. Finally, salt is added and the dough gets a final mix before kneading.

KNEAD: This can be done in a mixer using a dough hook or by hand on a floured surface. Kneading develops gluten strands in the dough by physically pushing and stretching the dough.

BULK FERMENT: This step further strengthens gluten development and completes flavor development by letting the yeasts further feed on the starch and release carbon dioxide, which creates rise in the dough as it is trapped like air in a balloon of tightly woven strands of gluten proteins.

SCALE/DIVIDE: Here we portion uniform pieces of dough using a scale to make sure each piece is the same exact weight.

PRESHAPE: This step coaxes the portioned dough into its eventual form, providing a structure that the gluten proteins will relax into.

BENCH REST: This allows the tight gluten proteins to relax enough to be shaped into the bread's final form.

SHAPE: This is when the dough is given its final shape and truly begins to resemble the end product. It's the shaping stage that's responsible for making a dough into a baguette, a boule, a dinner roll, or a braided challah.

PROOF: The final rise of the fully shaped dough, during which yeasts continue to release carbon dioxide and the well-shaped bread will puff up. Proofing can occur in the fridge, at room temperature, or near a warm oven, depending on your timetable. Proofing is finished when the dough has nearly doubled in size and no longer springs back when gently poked with your finger.

SCORE/WASH: Scoring is making a cut in the surface of the bread with a razor, lame (pronounced *laaahhm*), or very sharp knife. It's both aesthetic and functional, as the cut gives bread room to expand as moisture escapes during the baking process. Washing is a mostly aesthetic final step that involves painting the surface of a baked good with a liquid or fat, typically beaten egg, milk, cream, or honey syrup.

BAKE: This step will show you all the results of the hard work you've already put into your bread. It's important to make sure your oven is at the proper temperature and all of the steps of a given recipe are followed to the letter. Typically a product is baked to the desired color and checked by giving the bread a light flick on the bottom. If it makes a hollow thump, feels light in the hand, and is the color you want it, you're done. For pan loaves in particular, it's also helpful to check the internal temperature: A fully baked loaf should register between 195° to 205°F.

COOL/CONSUME/STORE: Bread products are unbelievable when just cool enough to eat. But chances are you won't be able to eat your entire batch in one sitting! In that case, cool the bread on a rack and store as directed in the particular recipe, as certain breads stale at different rates under different conditions. In general, if you've worked hard to achieve an excellent crisp crust, avoid storing in an airtight container or the fridge; a paper bag or an old-school bread box is best.

NOTES ON PROOFING: I generally bring the oven up to temperature farther in advance than you might expect, which allows you to accomplish two things. First, you raise the ambient temperature of your entire kitchen, which allows for a more even and timely proof and lets you make large batches, if desired. Next, this offers an insurance policy that the oven will be fully up to temperature the moment you're ready to bake. Should your oven not be up to temperature, the consequence of the waiting game is most often "overproofed dough." What goes up must inevitably come down, and that's exactly what happens when something is "overproofed." Your beautiful rolls will fall either during the bake, or before you ever get them in the oven! Be vigilant, be prepared.

A

B

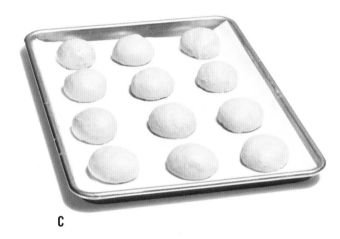

C

D

E

F

PANINI ROLL

MAKES 1 DOZEN
70-GRAM ROLLS

500 grams all-purpose
flour (plus more for
rolling)   100%

250 grams cool water 50%

50 grams whole milk   10%

50 grams vegetable
oil (plus more for the
bowl)   10%

60 grams whole egg*   12%

10 grams pure cane
sugar   2%

20 grams wildflower
or other floral honey   4%

7 grams active dry
yeast   2%

15 grams kosher salt 2.5%

50 grams heavy cream, for
brushing the rolls

This hybrid recipe came from testing variations of Parker House rolls and challah hamburger buns. We wanted something eggy yet super light and not too sweet. The goal was a dough that would stand up to a couple days in the fridge or even freezer, in order to make it an option at home, not just a party trick.

1. Put the bowl of a stand mixer on a scale and weigh all the ingredients *except the salt* into the bowl (salt, acid, heat, and cold are the enemies of yeast).

2. Attach the dough hook, set the bowl in the mixer, and mix the dough on the lowest speed for 5 minutes. When the dough begins to pull away from the sides of the bowl, sprinkle in the salt. Mix for another 7 minutes. You should have a smooth dough that pulls away from the bowl and clings slightly to the dough hook.

3. Oil a medium bowl and place the dough in the bowl. Cover tightly with plastic wrap and let rise (bulk ferment) for 45 minutes at room temperature (70° to 72°F). The dough will double in size. (A)

4. Turn the dough out onto a lightly floured surface and portion into one dozen 70-gram pieces. (B)

5. Cover the pieces with plastic wrap on the table as you work to prevent any drying. Form each piece into a ball by rolling against the table in the cup of your palm. To do this, pinch your thumb and forefinger together as if you were holding an invisible pencil and form a cup with the rest of your fingers. Hide the dough in the cup of your hand and trace tiny circles on the table with that invisible pencil. Don't lift the base of your palm from the table or the dough might escape!

6. Place the rolls on a parchment-lined baking sheet, brush lightly with oil, and cover with plastic wrap. (C)

7. If you plan on baking the rolls later (up to 2 days from now), you can refrigerate the tray. To bake them now, preheat the oven to 375°F and let the rolls proof nearby for 2 hours, or until they have doubled in size and do not spring back when gently poked. (D)

8. Brush the rolls with the cream (E) and bake for 24 minutes, rotating the baking sheet halfway through the baking process. When the rolls are ready to rock, they will have a deep, golden-brown crust with a slight sheen and will feel quite light in the hand. (F) Cool, then store appropriately.

* Crack an egg, whisk it, and then weigh the whisked yolk/white. For 60 grams, start with 1 egg.

FRENCH HERO

MAKES 12 HEROES

POOLISH

150 grams water

150 grams all-purpose flour

1 gram active dry yeast

DOUGH

330 grams water

7 grams active dry yeast

285 grams poolish (be sure to weigh it!)

550 grams all-purpose flour, plus more for shaping

15 grams kosher salt

Vegetable oil, for the bowl

A sandwich-size baguette with a crisp crust and an airy crumb. You better believe you made it yourself! The depth of flavor here is the direct result of the one-night stand known as poolish, the most basic kind of pre-ferment (see page 10). It involves mixing equal parts flour and water with the tiniest bit of yeast culture and fermenting for 8 to 12 hours. This draws out just the right amount of acid to give your final product a subtle bit of sour while giving gluten development a kick in the pants.

1. To make the poolish, the night before you're baking the bread, in a medium bowl, combine the water, flour, and yeast and use your hands to mix until as shaggy and thick as a vagrant's beard; there won't be anything uniform or clean about it. Wrap with plastic and go to sleep.

2. To make the dough, in the morning, measure the water and yeast into the bowl of a stand mixer fitted with the dough hook. Add the poolish and mix by hand with the water until the water is thoroughly cloudy and the poolish is completely saturated. Measure the flour into the bowl, turn the mixer to the lowest speed, and mix for about 1 minute, or until the flour is mostly incorporated. Cover the mixer bowl with plastic and let the dough rest for 20 to 60 minutes.

This step is called autolyse and provides the basis for gluten formation by slowly hydrating the flour and giving the yeasts a head start at feeding on all the sugars present in the flour.

3. Turn the mixer to a slightly higher speed, in the 2 or 3 range of a KitchenAid mixer, and mix the dough for about 5 minutes, until the dough clears the side of the bowl and begins to climb the dough hook.

4. Oil a medium bowl and place the dough in the bowl. Turn the dough into the bowl and cover with plastic. (A) Let the dough rise for at least 1 hour, until doubled in size. (If you don't intend to bake the bread immediately, you can refrigerate the dough after that initial bulk fermentation for up to 5 hours.)

5. Fold the dough onto itself in the bowl, stretching one side over the other from the bottom of the dough up and over the top. Do this 3 times to develop the gluten in the dough and remove some of the air that has developed in the dough (this is known as punching down, but I find this term indelicate and dangerous when taken literally). Cover the dough with plastic and let it rest for 30 minutes. (B)

6. Turn the dough out onto a lightly floured surface and gently press it into a rectangular shape. Fold it in half so that both top and bottom of the dough are

A

B

C

lightly floured. Now, use a bench scraper or chef's knife to cut the dough into 100-gram pieces (weighing each piece on a scale as you go), covering them in plastic as you work to keep a skin from forming. The shape of each piece isn't important at this stage; it's all about the weight, and it's perfectly fine to add a tiny scrap of dough as you cut to make sure you measure a perfect 100 grams. With practice you'll be able to cut consistent 100-gram pieces, but hitting it on the nose every time is highly unlikely.

7. Shape each hero by pressing the piece of dough into a rough triangle, with the tip pointing away from you. Fold the tip toward the center and press down, then fold both upper sides (shoulders) in to meet the tip. Gently roll the entire form toward you and use the heel of your hand to press the seam closed against your work surface. The final shape should be a cylinder that's about 2 inches wide and 5 inches long. (C) Dust the cylinders with flour, cover them loosely with plastic, and let them rest for 30 minutes.

8. On a floured work surface, place a cylinder seam side up and horizontally in front of you. Press gently to deflate it and form a rectangle. (D) With open palms facing you, touch the tips of your little fingers together and use that edge of your hands to fold the top edge of the rectangle toward the center.

9. As the dough touches down, lightly push down into the table and away from yourself to seal the deal. Repeat this folding/rolling process one more time. (E)

10. Next, imagine your left thumb is a tiny surfer and the cylinder is a breaking wave. Your thumb is about to shoot the tube from the right side to the left and you'll use your fingertips to fold the dough over your thumb like the breaking of the wave. (F)

11. Work from right to left, folding the back side of the dough wave all the way over to touch the work surface, all the while keeping your tiny thumb surfer just ahead of the break. This will create a seam in the cylinder. (G)

12. Use the heel of your hand to tap and press across the length of the dough to seal the seam. (H)

13. With the seam down and the cylinder resting on the table, put your hands together over the dough with palms down and index fingers joined side by side, as if you had one big eight-fingered hand. Center your index fingers on the cylinder, letting your fingertips touch the work surface and the cylinder rest between your fingertips and the pad of your knuckles. (I)

14. Gently wiggle the cylinder back and forth while separating your hands. (J)

15. This separating/rolling action will stretch the hero just shy of its final length of 7 inches. In this rolling/separating position, make sure your fingertips and the heel of your hands are always in contact with the work surface. Repeat to make the rest of the heroes. (K)

16. Line two baking sheets with parchment paper and dust with flour. Place 6 heroes on each baking sheet with about 2 inches in between, dust them lightly with flour or a light spray of olive oil, and cover them loosely with plastic. (L)

17. Let them proof for 1 hour at room temperature. *But*—and it's a big but!— if you have the time, proofing for 2 hours in the fridge first (before the 1-hour room-temperature proof) makes a world of difference in the crust. This is a little truth bomb that will give you fish-eye blisters, the little round bubbles

L

M

N

that appear on the crust of really well-made crusty breads of all kinds. (You can achieve this texture and aesthetic by doing this cold proofing, but professionals often use a steam-injected oven; M)

18. The heroes are proofed when you can lightly press them and leave an indentation without the dough springing back.

19. Place a cast-iron pan on the oven floor and a rack in the center of the oven. Preheat the oven to 450°F.

20. Just before baking, using a lame, razor blade, or extra-sharp paring knife, Score each hero lengthwise in one fluid motion, doing your best to begin and end 1 inch from either end and cutting one-third of the way through the hero. (N)

21. Place the baking sheet on the rack and pour 1 cup hot tap water into the hot pan on the oven floor to create steam. Bake for 25 minutes, or until the heroes are deep brown and sound hollow when thumped lightly with your finger. Let the heroes cool for 10 to 15 minutes before serving, and let them cool completely before storing in a paper or cloth bag. Storing in an airtight container will prolong the shelf life, but it will also kill any crust you worked so hard to develop. (If you are a crust fanatic and prefer to use a pizza stone for extra-crispy, crusty heroes, place the parchment paper on an inverted baking sheet so you can use it as a pizza peel and slide the shaped, proofed, and scored heroes onto the stone, parchment and all.)

HOT SEEDED RYE

MAKES 1 LOAF

RYE PRE-FERMENT

0.5 gram yeast (pro tip: substitute sourdough starter)

75 grams water (pro tip: substitute beer of your choice)

50 grams medium rye flour

40 grams all-purpose flour

DOUGH

60 grams water

7 grams dry active yeast

30 grams medium rye flour

275 grams all-purpose flour, plus more for kneading

60 grams labneh

10 grams fine sea salt

1 tablespoon pickled jalapeño seeds

1 tablespoon caraway seeds

40 grams jalapeño pickle juice

Vegetable oil, for the bowl

This is the classic New York breakfast staple that reminds me of the old Lower East Side, but done with a slight jalapeño kick as a nod to the neighborhood's more recent past. Like the French Hero, this bread involves a pre-ferment to aid in flavor development. This time we are changing the hydration percentage a bit by increasing the all-purpose flour, as rye has an extremely low gluten content and mixing straight rye flour tends to make your dough sticky and unmanageable. We also let the pre-ferment go a full 24 hours, to fully hydrate the bulk of the rye flour and develop a rich, sweet rye funk that could otherwise be buried by the all-purpose flour. This recipe also assumes you have accumulated an Egg Shop "cabinet of curiosities," because it incorporates pickle juice and the seeds from the bottom of your jar of Fresh Pickled Jalapeños (page 223).

1. To prepare the pre-ferment, in a medium bowl disperse the yeast in the water, then add the flours and stir with your hands until the flour is incorporated and the mix is as shaggy as a vagrant's beard. Scrape the sides of the bowl, cover loosely with plastic, and set aside for 24 hours.

To make the dough, measure the water into the bowl of a stand mixer fitted with the dough hook. Add the yeast and the pre-ferment and stir to disperse the pre-ferment evenly in the water. Add the flours and labneh and mix 2 minutes on the lowest speed to incorporate the ingredients. Finish by hand and scrape down the bowl with a bowl scraper or rubber spatula. Cover and let the dough rest (autolyse) for 30 minutes.

2. Sprinkle the dough with the salt, jalapeño seeds, and caraway seeds. Add the pickle juice and mix on speed 1 (low speed) for 5 to 7 minutes, until the dough begins to pull away from the sides of the bowl and appears less tacky.

3. Oil a medium bowl and place the dough in the bowl. (A) Turn the dough into the bowl and cover with plastic wrap. Let the dough rise about 1 hour, or until doubled in size. (B)

4. Turn the dough out onto a well-floured surface and press gently with well-floured hands to slightly deflate. Shape the dough into a rounded boule shape by cupping with both hands and gently rounding against the work surface. Try to keep the outer edge of your hands (from the tip of your little finger to the heel of your hand) in contact with the work surface as you move the dough in a very subtle circular motion against the work surface. The dough will end up in

A

B

C

D

E

F

a rounded dome shape or a ball with a slightly flat bottom, with a smooth outer surface. Lightly dust with flour and cover loosely with plastic wrap or a towel. Let rest for 30 minutes.

5. Preheat the oven to 425°F. Grease a 9 x 4-inch metal loaf pan.

6. Shape the dough as for the pre-shape of the French Hero (page 15, steps 7 and 8) and place seam-side down in the pan. (C)

7. Let the loaf proof for 1 hour under well-oiled plastic wrap. (D)

8. The loaf is ready to bake when the dough no longer springs back when pressed gently. Score the loaf with one long slash, or make two x shapes using a sharp knife or lame and bake for 30 minutes. (E)

9. Reduce the oven temperature to 350°F and bake for another 15 to 20 minutes, until the outer crust is lightly browned and the internal temperature of the bread reaches 200°F. Cool the loaf 10 to 15 minutes in the pan, then remove it to a rack and let it cool to room temperature. (F)

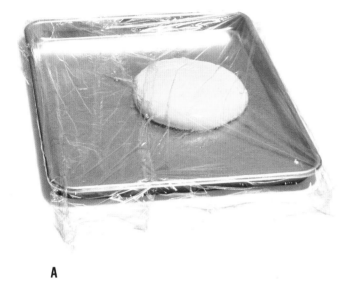

A

B

C

D

PIZZA BIANCA FOCACCIA

MAKES 1 HALF SHEET

275 grams + 25 grams water

7 grams active dry yeast

25 grams + 15 grams olive oil, plus more for greasing the pan

550 grams all-purpose flour

7 grams pure cane sugar

10 grams kosher salt

20 grams dried oregano

2 tablespoons chopped fresh rosemary leaves

1 tablespoon wild fennel pollen (optional)

1 tablespoon Maldon salt, or any fancy salt of your choice

This pizza-style focaccia is by far the easiest of our bread recipes and an extremely adaptable dough for topping however you like for weeknight at-home pizza parties. We speed it up a bit by using a mixer rather than a no-knead method, and we up your chance of home-baking success by using a baking sheet. This recipe is the backbone of our Green Eggs and Ham (page 137).

---

1. Measure 275 grams of water into the bowl of a stand mixer fitted with the dough hook and add the yeast. Disperse with your hand, then add 25 grams olive oil, the flour, and sugar. Mix briefly on low speed to combine the ingredients, then let rest (autolyse), covered, for 20 minutes.

Sprinkle with the kosher salt and add the remaining 25 grams water. Mix on speed 1 (low speed) for 5 to 7 minutes, until the dough begins to pull from the sides of the bowl and appears shiny and smooth.

2. Turn the dough out onto the greased baking sheet and cover loosely with well-oiled plastic. (The easiest way to oil a sheet of plastic is simply to drag it across the greased baking sheet; A)

3. Let the dough rise for 1 hour; it will be quite puffy and fill nearly three-fourths of the sheet pan. (This first rise on the baking sheet uses gravity to help spread and stretch the dough.)

4. Gently remove the plastic and use well-oiled fingertips to poke the dough and stretch to fill the pan. (This step fulfills the same purpose as a punch down or pre-shape in some of our other breads. You're taking away some of the gas while encouraging the dough to take its final shape; B)

5. Preheat the oven to 425°F. Cover the focaccia with well-oiled plastic, and let it proof for 45 to 60 minutes, or until the dough fills the entire pan. (C)

6. Gently remove the plastic and give the dough one last well-oiled poke. Sprinkle with the oregano, rosemary, and fennel pollen (if using). Drizzle with the remaining 15 grams olive oil. Bake for 25 minutes, or until golden brown. Sprinkle with the Maldon salt and cool on a wire rack. (D)

GREENS AND REDS

Buying local, incredibly fresh produce gets you closest to eating "right off the vine" or "fresh picked." Truly, nothing is better! It's admittedly Birkenstocks-and-socks-level naturalism to speak of these things in terms of absorbing energy, but there's something inarguable about the freshness of munching greens that were happily growing moments ago. Your best bet is buying from a local farmers' market or joining a CSA or farmshare of some kind. Yes, that's easier said than done if farmers' markets are scarce in your community or the growing season is brief. Even so, you have some options to facilitate your quest for fresh: Grow your own and buy smart. It does little good to stock your fridge with beautiful "fresh" produce that will wilt or dehydrate in a day or two, much less buy low-quality, underripe, and out-of-season produce! Do not settle! A tomato should smell like a tomato, a peach should be tender and pungently fragrant, a carrot should be relatively slender and vibrantly colored. No one will blame you if you don't maintain strict seasonality, but if you ignore your own standards for choosing fruits and veggies, you can only blame yourself.

But chances are good that you usually do your shopping to last through the week, and that you can't rely on local produce for all your fruits and vegetables all year long. So it's important to know the role of hearty, durable fruits and veggies that can function as staples while you treat yourself to more delicate seasonal items when you can, to add interest to your cooking. The following fruits and vegetables last: kale, carrots, sweet potatoes, cabbage, bok choy, green beans, bell peppers, broccoli, apples, bananas, citrus, some berries, cauliflower, leeks, squash. These don't: tomatoes, soft herbs, melons, most salad greens, fresh figs, avocados, cucumbers, sprouts, spring or young varietal veggies, and so on.

Our plan for success in enjoying the best produce is threefold: (1) Develop your standards and stick to them when buying. (2) Know what's in season in your area. (3) Grow whatever you can manage, starting with herbs, and try something new every season. If you give a damn, your food will taste better (whatever your level of cooking skill) and everyone will notice.

THE ART OF THE HERB SALAD

An herb salad is a simple easy way to enhance any sandwich, salad, or whatevs-dish that would otherwise merit a few conventional green leaves. When we compose an herb salad, we consider all the following factors and tend to roll with a mix that is one-third fines herbes, one-third extra Italian parsley, one-sixth a combination of herbs in the mint/basil family, and one-sixth dill. For the most part, dressing an herb salad is unnecessary and can cause the herbs to wilt or otherwise be weighed down and lose texture. We don't want to mask the individual flavors in any way, but rather find balance where each herb has its chance to explode on the palate. Here's how we do it.

1. Italian parsley is your workhorse because it's readily available, has a larger leaf than other herbs, and has a distinctly verdant flavor that tends to blend well without overpowering. But parsley can be slightly bitter, so try to use parsley-heavy herb salads to balance sweet and acidic recipes. Bitter on bitter makes me bitter.

2. Don't overdo any one flavor profile. For example, basil, tarragon, mint, and chervil done together would overwhelm the palate, as they all carry a mild anise flavor.

3. Fines herbes, the classic combination of parsley, chives, tarragon, and chervil used in French cuisine, exists for a reason. It's a good combo that won't overwhelm the palate served.

4. Pick, don't chop! For salad purposes, pick where the leaf meets the stem (as opposed to general cooking, in which herbs may be chopped, stems and all, then mixed into a sauce or with many other ingredients). For a perfect herb salad, never pick midleaf or chop (how gauche!).

5. Herb flowers are excellent and edible; include them whenever possible.

NOTE: Always wash leafy herbs and greens with ice cold water and be sure to give them at least 2 or 3 good soaks, then lightly towel them dry or spin them in a salad spinner if you have one.

YEAR-ROUND EGG SHOP HERB GARDEN

No matter your level of DIY enthusiasm, you can have an herb garden. Most herbs can thrive in a sunny window or by virtue of a minimal grow light. For an instant garden, begin with plants rather than seeds, and experiment with placement. Usually south-facing windows or areas are best for any plants that require full to moderate sun. Be sure to give plants adequate space if planting in a window box or a single pot. If your light or outdoor space is limited, consider growing in individual containers, which will make it easier to move the plants around to catch light or bring inside on a chilly night. Adequate drainage is also very important, as roots will rot if left to soak in water. Once your plants are thriving (sending up new leaves and shoots), it's often helpful to sow a few seeds in the pot in order to keep plants growing in rotation. As the new plants mature, you can exhaust the older plants and let the young plants take their place.

FULL SUN/PARTIAL SHADE:
CILANTRO, PARSLEY, DILL, MINT, OREGANO, THYME

These plants like a fair amount of sun and can thrive at moderate room temperature (68° to 75°F), and some enjoy colder temps. Cilantro, for instance, is surprisingly strong in the fall and early spring. Be sure to give parsley, dill, and cilantro plenty of space. Oregano, mint, and thyme are shorter plants and can do well with less room to grow. However, mint can be quite a garden mooch, so be sure to plant in a container to avoid that herbin' sprawl. When cutting, never harvest more than one-third of the plant, and try to cut stems closer to the bottom of the plant.

FULL SUN:
ROSEMARY, CHIVES, BASIL

These plants are like fat cats or a big old dog. They like to spread out in the sun. They thrive in warmer climates and can do with a little less water than the more shade-tolerant herbs. Give them plenty of space and plenty of sun, but otherwise the same rules apply. If growing indoors, light and temperature are key, and it will likely be worth investing in an unobtrusive grow light and doing a makeshift greenhouse by tenting the plant in clear plastic (a basic painter's plastic works wonders in the winter to maintain finicky basil).

NOTE FOR THE ADVENTURE SEEKERS: If you want to take this further, try starting with a raised bed for lettuces, then move on to more complicated fruits and veggies like tomatoes, carrots, peppers, and cucumbers.

Succumb to the idea that the odds are against you for perfection. Be happy with achieving a certain ratio of what you thought it would be. —César Vega

COFFEE

To say César Vega is a smart or talented guy is an understatement. César Vega is a dangerous person, tuned in to something much, much bigger than himself or the products he sells. He's dangerous because he backs his tremendous skill and knowledge base with a childlike curiosity and love for the plant he refers to as that "bizarre shrub." These two rules are his constants: only Nicaraguan coffee, and only direct from farmers. This dedication to source and terroir allows a level of focus on the coffee that transcends quality norms and creates a web of understanding that runs as deep as the roots of a family tree, quite literally. He's from there.

When we talk about coffee, we might talk about a bass note, or the treble present in an acidic finish, or even the washed-out, lingering retronasal sunshine of pure aroma. But just as numbers can add up to nothing, so does an obsession with flavor alone. That's for roasters and boasters. Deep down, this dude is trying to do right by the people he admires most: his mother and those who work the land.

At Egg Shop we use Dulcinea, the one and only blend by César Vega's Café Integral. While other importers and roasting companies may make numerous blends in different styles (French roast, holiday spice, orange mocha frappuccino), César treats his Dulcinea more like a Meritage wine or field blend than a marketing tool. His blend is seasonal, balancing different coffee varietals and specific lots for a consistently unique balance that is still approachable. As César puts it, "You want something different from coffee through the seasons. There are times of year when coffee tastes awesome; coffee in the fall is the best. The heat of the summer isn't clawing up your nose. We focus on flavor and aroma in spring and fall because, as drinkers, we're ready to soak it in. Winter is a much dimmer time for the senses— you want more body, more sugar, more bass. You almost want the mulled wine of coffee; it's kind of dumb but it's intensely satisfying. In the summer we get light and think about acid and aromatics."

This is life on the ground. For César, atypical of small roasters and coffee brands, the process of sourcing coffee is intensely personal. He isn't going door to door asking for Juan Valdez. He is building lasting relationships with growers by partnering from harvest all the way to sale. This benefits the growers most of all, by engaging them in the market at large and encouraging a higher standard of quality and consistency from year to year. This is true fair trade/direct trade. This is our favorite coffee. This is Café Integral.

THE PERFECT CUP

Perfect. I'm reminded of the Lou Reed song every time I use the word. His perfect day would have been one of the worst days of my life. Perfect is personal and entirely subjective. In order to find a common sense of perfect, focus on the objective qualities of brewing a cup of coffee.

GRIND

The grind of the coffee impacts depth of flavor in relation to brew time. Making filtered coffee, whether it's pour-over, aeropress, or more traditional drip, involves an extended brew time of 1 minute or more per cup, so a medium grind is in order. For a cold-brewed coffee that involves hours of contact with water, a coarse grind is best.

WATER TEMPERATURE AND QUALITY

Use filtered water if possible, but at the very least develop an awareness of what you taste directly from the tap. Next, water temperature is key to releasing the coffee's soluble flavor components and essential oils in a short amount of time. *196° to 206°F is the ideal range.* Either use a digital thermometer in your kettle or bring the water to a boil, then remove it from the heat for 2 minutes before using.

FILTRATION, EQUIPMENT, AND STORAGE

Please try using a scale and thermometer. Accuracy does produce a more delicious cup of coffee. A small, narrow spout kettle is best for controlling the pour of hot water. The AeroPress is an excellent piece of equipment that can yield something approaching espresso quality at home. Storage is important. Grind freshly roasted whole beans only as needed, and always store them in an airtight container in your pantry.

BEST CUP: AEROPRESS

MAKES 1 CUP

8 ounces filtered water at 196° to 206°F

17 grams freshly ground coffee

2 MINUTES TOTAL BREW TIME

Using the AeroPress either inverted or filter-side down, pour a little of the water over the paper filter, then add the grounds and half the remaining water. Give one light stir to make sure the grounds are evenly dispersed in the water. Rest 30 seconds, then add the remaining water. Rest 1 minute, then stir a few times vigorously. Press the coffee directly into your cup or other brewing vessel. The AeroPress does require about 30 pounds of pressure, so be sure to press into a sturdy vessel on an even surface. This cup will drink like a well-made Americano.

RED-EYE CHAI

So, you're coming to terms with the fact that you might be an overachiever. It's cool, me too. This recipe is for us, fam'. A well-made chai is a thing of beauty that is lauded in Ayurvedic circles for its health benefits, from aiding digestion to regulating blood pressure and soothing depression and anxiety. But you don't have to subscribe to this philosophy to appreciate chai as a delicious way to accentuate well-made coffee!

RED-EYE CHAI

MAKES 1 CUP

17 grams medium-grind coffee

2 ounces (¼ cup) water

4 ounces (½ cup) Chai Concentrate (recipe follows)

4 ounces (½ cup) That's So Nut Milk (page 35)

Prepare the AeroPress as if you were going to make the Best Cup (see page 30), by placing the coffee in the press and heating the water. Then STOP!

Simmer the chai concentrate and milk together in a saucepan or kettle.

Pour the water over the coffee in the AeroPress and give it a stir to disperse the grounds. Let it rest 30 seconds, then pour the chai/milk into the press. Let it rest 1 minute, stir vigorously, and press. Serve immediately.

CHAI CONCENTRATE

MAKES ENOUGH FOR 8 TO 10 CUPS

7 cups water

1 cup pure cane sugar

½ cup roughly chopped fresh ginger

20 green cardamom pods

5 cinnamon sticks

2 tablespoons freshly ground black pepper

1 tablespoon whole cloves

6 star anise pods

3 tablespoons high-quality black tea
(preferably Darjeeling, or your favorite)

In a medium saucepan, combine the water, sugar, ginger, cardamom, cinnamon, pepper, cloves, and star anise and bring to a simmer over medium heat. Simmer until the mixture is reduced by one-third, 30 to 45 minutes, stirring often to dissolve the sugar. Add the tea and remove from the heat. Steep for 15 minutes, then strain out the solids and let the liquid cool completely. Store in an airtight container in the fridge for up to 2 weeks.

COLD BREW

Making cold brew at home is extremely cost effective. Cold brew is a two- or three-times-a-day thing for New Yorkers in the summer, and if you live or work anywhere near a coffee shop, you can easily drop up to four bucks a cup for cold-brew deliciousness. Yes, we're an overly caffeinated bunch, but that can really add up!

All you need to make pro-level cold brew at home is a glass or nonreactive container, your trusty nut milk bag (or Toddy mesh), and a large paper coffee filter.

HOME COLD-BREW CONCENTRATE

MAKES 7 CUPS

¼ pound coffee, coarsely ground
8 cups cold filtered water

1. Line a large glass or nonreactive container with a Toddy mesh or nut milk bag, then place a large paper filter inside the bag. Add the coffee to the paper filter. Working in stages, pour the cold water over the coffee, taking care to keep the coffee grounds from spilling over the filter. As the water level rises, pull the Toddy mesh over the lip of the container to keep the coffee above the water level. This will prevent cloudiness later.

2. When all the water is added, gather the edges of the paper filter and gently tie the bag closed with kitchen twine or a bit of plastic wrap (you're making a giant coffee "tea bag"). Knot the mesh/bag at the open end to enclose the coffee filter bag. Lower the bag into the container.

3. Let the coffee steep 12 hours at room temperature or 24 hours in the fridge. Note: The longer and colder you brew (e.g., in the fridge for 24 hours or more), the more concentrated the cold brew will be.

4. Remove the bag slowly and gently squeeze out any liquid trapped inside. It's important to do this as slowly and gently as possible, and even quit while you're ahead, or you risk a cloudy cold brew with a lot of sediment.

5. The cold brew will keep in the fridge for a week or more before it loses some of its thunder. To serve, either pour over ice and drink straight or dilute with a little water if you find the brew too strong for your taste.

MILK VIBES

We talk a lot about good vibes, hi-vibes, and things being "vibey." It's a way of saying something has character, or that an inanimate object or space seems to have an inherent power, mood, or agenda. It's not real. We don't believe it. It's simply common parlance for the newfangled spiritualism of overly intellectual creative superdorks. Being the nerd-lords that we are, we wanted the vibiest milk money could buy!

The only problem is you can't, like, just buy vibes, man! *You make them!*

Of course, on the daily at Egg Shop, we love fresh, local, single-dairy cow's milk for its unrivaled creaminess and noticeable terroir, and you should seek it out and use the best quality available both in your coffee and your cooking. But, what's more vibey than paying homage to your bovine homies without taxing the collective world teat? With this recipe we set out to have some fun and create something different: an uber-milk that balanced all the things we enjoy about single-base alternative milks while giving us something comparable in texture and flavor to our go-to high-quality fresh cow's milk. We use almond and coconut milk for their distinct flavor and sweetness. These two also have the power to trick the palate into experiencing a creaminess that isn't necessarily there. We add cashews and macadamia nuts to access the slight floral qualities of each, and to harness their high fat content and fill the gap on the previous palate trick. Medjool dates play an interesting part in this formula by providing both natural sweetness and the slight fermentation necessary to mimic the lactic acid of cow's milk. Adding the dates to the soak is similar to feeding a sourdough starter with flour (complex sugars) at the beginning of the fermentation process. Most good bacteria feed on sugars, both simple and complex, and leave behind a distinct acidified by-product. Vibes achieved. Enjoy.

THAT'S SO NUT MILK

MAKES 6 CUPS

TOOLS: 8-cup glass or nonreactive container, Vitamix or other high-powered blender, and nut milk bag

½ cup each organic raw almonds, cashews, macadamia nuts, dried coconut
3 organic Medjool dates, pitted
9 cups cold filtered water
Pinch of Himalayan sea salt
1 tablespoon chyawanprash (optional; see Note)

1. In a large glass or nonreactive container, combine the nuts, coconut, dates, and 4 cups of the water. Cover the container loosely with plastic wrap and let soak at room temperature for 24 hours. Time and temperature are the key factors here to developing the slight sour of fermentation. (Most recipes say to soak nuts overnight or for up to 8 hours. This is great for softening the nuts so they can be pureed, but taking this a little further yields more complex flavor development.)

2. Drain the mixture in a colander (discard the soaking water), then transfer the nut mixture to a high-powered blender (Vitamix or similar). Add the remaining 5 cups water, sea salt, and chyawanprash (if using). Now, let her rip!

3. When you no longer hear the sounds of nuts hitting the blender blade and the puree appears evenly white and frothy, you're ready to strain. Stretch the nut milk bag over a large pitcher or bowl and pour the mixture into the bag. A good deal of liquid will pass through immediately, but you will have to *squeeeeeze* the bag repeatedly to extract as much vibes as possible.

4. That's it. Store in the fridge for up to 4 days in an airtight, nonreactive container.

NOTE: Chyawanprash is an ancient Ayurvedic combination of nutritive herbs and fruits that tastes like an earthy, sweet jam. Yes, it's vibey, but it's also ultra-deluxe-super-good-for-you-to-the-max!

MEATS

"Hello, Pino's."

"Hi, who's this?"

"This, Pino!"

It's safe to say Pino is in his late sixties, but nobody really knows. Not even his wife. Even over the phone you can tell the guy was born with a knife in his hand, but all suspicions are confirmed upon entering Pino's Prime Meat Market on Sullivan Street. The meaty funk of aging prime beefsteak hangs in the air like antique boxing gloves longing for the days of busted lips and cauliflower ears. Long before Pino took over 149 Sullivan Street from his paesano, Mario Merino (who famously sold his shop to Pino so he could finally buy a brand new Cadillac), long before the Coupe de Ville even, there had been a butcher in this room since 1904! Today, same as years ago, patient smiles greet customers making their very particular orders for chicken cutlets and holiday roasts as the chest-high display case hides bloody aprons with its array of marbled cuts. All the while Italian opera plays in the background. Pino and his sons, Sal and Leo, are my guys, and in New York everybody needs their guys.

At Egg Shop we serve more than eggs and bacon. We slow-roast hundreds of pounds of pork butt, shave and grill tons of grass-fed beef tenderloin, fry copious amounts of chicken, and make burgers and sausage from Pino's expert grinds. We would never have time to break down the amount of meat we serve, let alone develop a mastery of the butchering trade. It's about trust and an understanding of quality. Fortunately, the butchering trade is having a boutique resurgence all over the country, and developing that trust with your local butcher is just a few questions away.

Hey, Pino—

HOW DO YOU GRADE PRIME?

You see the stamp? Yeah, they put the stamp, but it doesn't mean nothing. You have to be a butcher. It's about the grain of the meat and the fats. The marble. Look at this, this is Kobe beef. Fat everywhere. Now this, tomahawk rib steak, you see the marble? It's different, but still prime because the fat goes with the grain and look, a little over here, a big piece here, a big piece there, more little fat in the grain. To me this is prime. I have been looking at this from 1971 to now, every day.

WHERE AND HOW DO YOU BUY YOUR MEATS?

It depends on the customer. I can get beautiful meats right here, from upstate, from across the river, local Berkshire pork, organic chicken; now is the time for good lamb from Colorado. I like to buy local whole beef for our dry age; I like the Piedmontese beef for grass-fed. It depends on the customer and the size of the order. We work for you. To say only this, or always that, it's impossible. You tell me, "Pino, I want this, can you get it for me?" I say, "I have a guy who has the best for thirty years."

WHAT SHOULD I MAKE FOR DINNER?

You know, when I first moved to open this store, I had an old customer hire a private investigator to find me. He would ask me twice a week, "Pino, what's good? What's for dinner?" When I moved, it took a while but my old customers found me. This guy with the investigator, when he found my new store he came in with bottles of Champagne and his wife, and we drank, then he asked me . . . you know.

So, you ever cook the cotechino? It's good, my nephew makes this. Or, you see the German sausage? [Me: Is that Weisswurst, white brat?] Yes, my son Salvatore is making this. I want you to try this and tell me what you think, and the dry-aged burger blend is very good, mostly short rib with some chuck and rib-eye. It's a nice day, like summer, so burgers for you.

NOTE: If your butcher's answers don't resemble Pino's, take down those boxing gloves and sock this hack in the kisser. (Don't worry if he chases you with a knife, because he obviously doesn't know how to use it!) Repeat after me as you run: *Not my guy.*

LET'S TALK BACON!

In our world there are three kinds of bacon: smoky, sweet, and funky.

There can be crossovers, of course. Funky bacon, which is funky because it isn't necessarily made of pork, or it's cured or seasoned in a prominent way, can also be sweet or intensely smoky.

Smoky and sweet bacons are more straightforward. A smoky bacon *can* be sweet, but a sweet bacon is qualified both by its sweetness and a lack of overall smokiness.

ALL BACON

› Should be salty, without allowing the salt to overpower.
› Should be cut in a way that's appropriate to its use and the bacon's own fat-to-meat ratio.

FAT-TO-MEAT RATIO

Great bacon starts with great pork. Yet, discussing heritage breeds has been done. Lauding the multisensory experience that is enjoying these breeds' distinct and varied creamy bits has become as annoying as hearing someone overpronounce the word "Mangalitsa." (It makes me want to Mangal-eat-some anxiety medication.)

When it comes to bacon, it's not about the breed. It's all about the fat-to-meat ratio. *You are looking for just over the perfect 1:1 balance of fat to meat, one that errs on the fatty side.* A 60 percent fat to 40 percent meat ratio is the limit of acceptability for a standard bacon slice (cut from $\frac{1}{16}$ to $\frac{1}{8}$ inch thick). If you're looking at a slab of quality bacon with a higher fat content, it's best to hand-cut a thick slice, up to $\frac{1}{4}$ or $\frac{1}{2}$ inch thick, to allow time to cook the bacon to the point of crisp on the outside while allowing the interior fat to soften and end up with a texture reminiscent of braised pork belly.

CRISP TESTS

We got serious about bacon while planning the menu at Egg Shop and found that all bacon was not created equal when it came to achieving our desired result: supreme crispiness. We obsessed about why certain cuts crisped perfectly so you could apply our insights, from source to sizzle.

It was this over-the-top attention to detail that helped us find the perfect bacon for our Egg Shop B.E.C (page 115). If you are microfocused on the quality of an ingredient, you must be microfocused on how you prepare it! When performing bacon-specific experiments, it's as simple as doing the math. To determine the fat-to-meat ratio, you dissect your ideal strip, separating fat from meat, and then weigh each. This is your starting ratio. Measuring surface area and volume can also factor in when it comes to achieving proportional bacon coverage on a sandwich or other dish, but those measurements are overly complicated and time consuming, as you can see in figure 1a on page 40.

To run your experiments, you'll need to control the cooking time, temperature, and equipment (e.g., if you're comparing three types of bacon, you need to cook them exactly the same way). Everyone prefers their bacon cooked to a slightly different definition of crispiness, so let your own standard tell you when the bacon is ready. At Egg Shop we cook $\frac{1}{16}$-inch-thick bacon in a 350°F convection oven for exactly 19 minutes, then drain and cool. To serve, it's later grilled at a high temperature

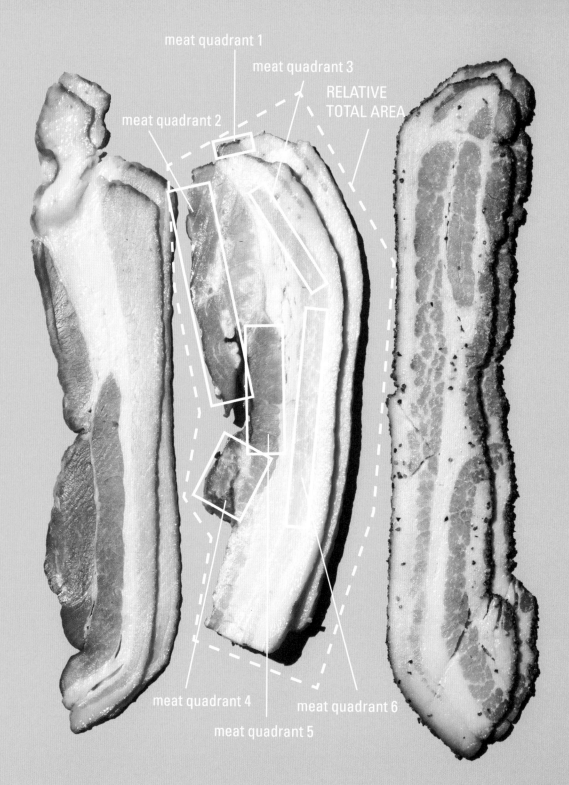

meat quadrant 1

meat quadrant 3

RELATIVE TOTAL AREA

meat quadrant 2

meat quadrant 4

meat quadrant 5

meat quadrant 6

Figure 1A
Total area: sum meat quad 1–6 = Fat
Meat : Fat ratio = sum meat quad 1–6/Fat %

for 30 seconds to finish crisping to our standard. We found that our favorite bacon maintained a very similar fat-to-meat ratio from start to crisp. Measure twice, cook once!

MAKIN' BACON

It's more than a euphemism—it's an impressive skill! The experience of making your own bacon is a great introductory lesson to curing meats of all kinds. The method here will yield naturally cured bacon that might prevent you from buying bacon ever again. And you'll be hard-pressed to believe how easy it is!

HOME SWEET HOMEMADE BACON

This recipe produces fully cooked bacon. The curing salts aren't mandatory, but they do help keep possibly harmful bacteria from forming, and they preserve the pink/red color of the pork all the way through the cooking process. If you leave it out, the bacon will still taste great, but it will look more like cooked pork belly than bacon.

MAKES ABOUT 5 POUNDS

3 tablespoons juniper berries

2 tablespoons coriander seeds

1 tablespoon black peppercorns

1 tablespoon dried marjoram

1½ teaspoons curing salt

¼ cup kosher salt

5 pounds pork belly, preferably local

¼ cup molasses (or dark brown sugar)

This is a waiting game. First, crack the juniper berries, coriander seeds, and peppercorns slightly with a mortar and pestle or in a spice grinder. Then combine the spice mixture, marjoram, and salts and rub this cure into the pork belly, covering all sides. Drizzle the pork belly evenly with molasses (or sprinkle it with the brown sugar) and pack it in an airtight container or a plastic brining bag. Cure the pork belly for 7 days in the fridge, taking care to give it a flip every day to disperse the cure and any resulting liquid evenly.

After 7 days, rinse the bacon to remove any excess cure. At this point, either slow-smoke the pork belly over hardwood (such as applewood) coals at 200° to 250°F for 3 hours or, if you don't have access to a smoker, lay the pork belly on a rack set into a rimmed baking sheet and bake at 300°F for 2 hours.

CHEESE

Many an egg sandwich experience has been ruined by sad juggernauts of melted goo or some such accidental string-cheese beardnet. To ensure this never happened at Egg Shop, we enlisted our friend and neighbor Anne Saxelby to do more than just sell us fromage perfecto, but also educate us on the hows and whys of cheese in the wild. Saxelby Cheesemongers was founded in 2006 with the goal of bridging the gap between America's artisan dairy producers and their consumers. Today Anne and her business partner Benoit Breal are known for championing the farmstead movement with pure enthusiasm, deep knowledge, expert curation, and an amazing lack of pretension.

"Farmstead cheese" by definition, is made on the farm where the milk comes from, as opposed to a cheesemaking facility that buys milk from a number of local farms to make a range of products. The phrase can apply to goat's, cow's, and sheep's milk cheeses. This movement and tradition is important for a number of reasons. First, it leads to more interesting cheese, with distinct terroir. But farmstead cheese production also helps the family farm. Over the course of the last century, dairy farming in particular has been deeply affected by price-setting on the part of the federal government, making it nearly impossible to break even on a small dairy farm.

The options are pretty clear: (1) Sell milk in the broad market for little money. (2) Cut out the middleman and bring your own milk to market, where prices are also limited. (3) Turn your delicious milk into amazing cheese and sell direct, so that pricing is limited only by the quality and skill behind the product. *No brainer.*

That said, it is important to support the farmstead movement in your area beyond just cheese by buying local dairy products whenever possible. Both farmstead and premium locally produced cheeses and dairy give value to farming efforts that stimulate your local economy.

SOUNDS A LITTLE INTIMIDATING. HOW DO I GET INTO CHEESE?

Much like wine, farmstead cheese is about the land, and it's all in. Your opinion is your own! As you taste different cheeses, simply think about what you are tasting and then develop your palate by activating your sense memory. Sound esoteric? It isn't! It's a nosh-makes-perfect concept— the more cheese you chomp, the more cheese you know. Using a cheese flavor wheel is also big help for the adjectives that are commonly ascribed to cheese tasting.

I'LL STOP THE WORLD AND _____ WITH YOU . . .

What makes a cheese perfect for melting? This question nearly made my head explode when I was developing the Egg Shop B.E.C. (page 115). I wanted the perfect cheddar cheese, and I wanted it to melt without becoming oily or stringy, and I refused to use an overly stabilized block cheese from no-man's land, or some such fromunda.

I narrowed my selection—Red Rock from Wisconsin, Cabot Clothbound from Vermont, and Shelburne from Vermont—and stopped the world to melt with them. After ten minutes under the glow of a commercial heat lamp, Red Rock was bubbly and oily, Cabot was quickly dropping globular strands, and Shelburne oozed in single elegant sheets without becoming oily. But why?

The answer is that everything factors into it: fat and moisture content, acidity, and cheesemaking style all impact how casein proteins and calcium combine in a single cheese, and thus how the cheese performs when heated. Fat and moisture have impact, but acidity and pH really make all the difference. Here are the deets: The higher the pH, the more the cheese will melt into a puddle of goo (Brie and blue). The lower the pH, the less likely the cheese is to melt at all (ricotta, feta, halloumi). But, right in the middle, in the 4.9 to 5.5 pH range, you have Salvador Dali's cheese plate. Our big winner is just on the edge of reason at a pH level of 5.5.

NOTE: To go full nerd on your perfect melting project, contact the cheesemaker directly and ask for the moisture content, fat content, and pH.

LET'S TALK ABOUT OUR BFF: CHEDDAR

Cheddar is both a noun and a verb, and our cheese of choice when it comes to making a perfect egg sandwich. As a noun, Cheddar is the name of a cheese as well as a town in England. But, during cheesemaking, the curds undergo a process called "cheddaring," in which they acidify in a vat before the whey is drained. In order to understand this step you have to have a basic understanding of cheesemaking in general.

It's time for *Cheesemaking 101*! Yay!

HOW CHEESE HAPPENS

1. Add a culture to warm milk. The bacteria eats the lactic acid.
2. Add rennet and stir. (Rennet is an enzyme that coagulates the liquid. Rennet comes from the fourth stomach of a baby ruminate animal, but there are also synthetic vegetarian rennets available.) The liquid changes to a solid curd.
3. Cut the curd and expel the whey (to get a tofu consistency).
4. Place the curd into a cheese form.
5. Age or finish the cheese as dictated by the style you are making.

To make cheddar, cheesemakers cook the curd to toughen it up somewhere between steps 2 and 3. When the whey is drained, these hot curds sit at the bottom of the tank and begin to knit together. Then cheesemakers cut the curd into blocks that are stacked and flipped over and over again to up the acidity. The blocks are then put through a cheddar mill (a woodchipper for cheese; this is where those squeaky cheese curds come from). The squeaky curds are put into a form and pressed, typically by hydraulic force. Then the cheese is packed and aged. The aging process is a slight continuation of the acidification process, but aging primarily leads to breakdown of fat and protein, which leads to flavor development, not heightened acidity.

Most cheddars are aged between one and two years, and mostly in Cryovac plastic packaging to retain moisture, rather than in the open air to develop as a natural rind cheese. But there are regional traditions in packing. For instance, a Cabot Clothbound Cheddar from Vermont is making use of an English tradition of wrapping with muslin and painting with lard to make the cloth stick.

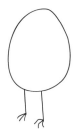

EGGS IN SPACE!

What's in an egg? Where does it begin? Where does it end? If you were a yolk suspended in the albumen of time, how many light years would it take to define the timeless abyss of your inner thoughts?

First things first, eggs are weird. Almost as weird as the previous paragraph. They come from a chicken's *cloaca!* They are embryonic slime. They are synonymous with all things dorky—eggheads, Eggbert, Humpty freakin' Dumpty! If you expect to work with eggs and stay clean and cute and wear a little paper hat around the holidays, then buy Martha's book. This is not that. Remember, we embrace the creative mess. We let the whites ooze through our fingers when we separate yolks, and we revel in irregular amorphous meringues, fissured, crisp, and sweet. Our eggs can be delicate or lurpy, modern or rustic, but we let the kitchen ego go away, and we begin our journey to the stratosphere of flavor with cookery's most versatile ingredient: *The Egg.*

POACHED EGGS

In the case of the traditional Eggs Benedict, the poached egg is a thing of beauty, a balancing act between just-set white, liquid yolk, and a 90 percent fat emulsion known to most as hollandaise, all laid to rest on that culinary bed of nails: the English muffin. (Nothing deflates a poachy like those naughty nooks and crannies.)

While it may sound daunting, the Benedict provides the perfect context in which to discuss the delicate nature of egg poaching, and to offer solutions for when things go south. The way hollandaise complements the poached egg is uncanny. Both are precarious and delicate, at their best on the verge of breaking. Mastering classic hollandaise is the best possible inroad to making consistent poached eggs, because it teaches respect for the yolk and a mastery of heat and motion, both in the hand of the cook and the simmer of the water. The goal here is for you to learn how to make hollandaise over the same pot of water you're using to poach your eggs . . . in under 5 minutes. Beauty and speed are the name of the game—the faster you can do it, the more you'll want to make it.

It all starts with preparing the poaching pot and sending your fears downstream on a lotus leaf. Namaste, poaching phobia. Nama'go make some hollandaise!

OUR POACHING PRACTICE

6 to 8 cups water

6 tablespoons light vinegar (white, Champagne, cider, rice, and so on)

1 teaspoon sea salt

As many eggs as you desire (poaching a few at time)

1. In a medium or large saucepan (not a shallow pan), combine the water, vinegar, and salt and bring to a rapid simmer (*not* rapidly boiling and *not* lukewarm) over medium heat.

2. Release the egg(s) close to the surface of the water, one at a time. If you have temperature-resistant fingertips, just crack and go, or crack each egg into a small bowl and gently release it into the water.

3. The egg will fall to the bottom, then quickly be turned over by the motion of the simmering water as the white sets. As the egg begins to become more buoyant, and almost floats toward the surface, use a slotted spoon to lift it out of the water. Poke it, jiggle it, test it. . . . If it seems like the white will split as you lift it, or the white is still obviously not set, let the egg cook a bit more. Don't be afraid to keep testing—just don't forget about your egg. A gentle poke with tell you when the white is set but the yolk is still liquid, and you're done!

4. Great news—you can poach eggs up to 24 hours in advance! Immediately submerge the poached eggs in ice water and refrigerate them. To reheat, simply take the par-poached eggs from the water/ice bath and dunk them in simmering water for 30 to 45 seconds. This is best done a few eggs at a time.

CLASSIC EGGS BENEDICT

MAKES 2 SERVINGS

4 slices Canadian bacon or ham of your choice

1 tablespoon unsalted butter

2 English muffins

4 poached eggs (page 49)

Classic Hollandaise (page 52)

Fresh flat-leaf parsley leaves and minced chives, for garnish

The creamy dreamy overlord of brunch—Canadian bacon and all. The dish is most commonly attributed to Oscar Tschirky, the maître d'hôtel of the Waldorf Hotel in New York City, who responded to a patron's request for the combination as a cure for his turn-of-the-century hangover.

1. In a medium cast-iron skillet, cook the Canadian bacon in the butter over medium heat until hot and nicely browned in places. Set aside in a warm place.

2. Open the English muffins and toast them in the pan with the browned butter and rendered fat from the meat.

3. Build the Benedicts by stacking as follows: English muffin half, Canadian bacon, poached egg. Top with hollandaise and finish with fresh herbs.

FOUR BENEDICT VARIATIONS

NORWEGIAN BENEDICT: Replace the Canadian bacon with either Cognac-Cured Gravlax (page 127) or a Smoked Whitefish Schmear (page 128).

FLORENTINE BENEDICT WITH CREAMY SPINACH: Replace the Canadian bacon with sautéed spinach finished with a bit of labneh (use your newfound *monter au beurre* skills, page 59).

COUNTRY HAM BENEDICT WITH RED-EYE GRAVY: Use shaved country ham in place of thick Canadian bacon and stir a shot of espresso into your hollandaise. Finish with a copious amount of "That's Hot!" Hot Sauce (page 150).

LOBSTER ROLL BENEDICT: In place of the Canadian bacon, buy or steam and pick your own fresh lobster meat (Dungeness crab works great, too) and sauté it in melted butter. Toss in minced, fresh chives and tarragon. (The Blood Orange Hollandaise [page 53] is great with this!)

CLASSIC HOLLANDAISE

MAKES ABOUT 2 CUPS

2 egg yolks

Juice of 1 lemon

1 cup Clarified Butter
(recipe follows)

Sea salt

Pinch of cayenne pepper,
or to taste

This is a skill sauce. At its best, hollandaise is an extremely light emulsion rich with the flavor of clarified butter and bright with the acid of freshly squeezed lemon. Practice this classic technique in a medium stainless bowl over the pot of simmering water you've prepared for poaching eggs.

1. Set a pan half full of water on the stove and bring to a simmer over medium-high heat. You'll also need a stainless steel bowl that fits over the pan without touching the water. Whisk the egg yolks and lemon juice in the stainless steel bowl and place it on top of the simmering water. Whisk the yolks vigorously until they are light, thick, and pale yellow. This is called the sabayon or ribbon stage, as the egg mixture should leaved ribbon-like traces and briefly stand on itself when drizzled from the whisk. (Once you've got the hang of this recipe, this is when you should drop the poached eggs in the water to make Eggs Benedict.)

2. As you continue to whisk, drizzle in the clarified butter one ladleful at a time, or pour it in a thin stream from a measuring cup. Control the heat at this stage by incorporating some butter on the heat and some off the heat. The sauce is complete when it has thickened slightly but doubled in volume and the vast majority of the butter is incorporated. Season with salt to taste and the cayenne. Reserve in a warm place until ready to serve. (If holding for an extended period of time, it's best to cover the bowl with plastic wrap.)

CLARIFIED BUTTER

MAKES ABOUT 1½ CUPS

2 pounds (8 sticks)
unsalted butter

The clarified butter lasts up to 30 days in the fridge and can be used for sautéing as you would olive oil, and it's the most perfect poaching medium for fish and shellfish in the event you want to blow minds. . . . Just sayin'.

In a small saucepan, melt the butter over low heat and let it rest 2 minutes. *Do not boil that butter, baby.* Using a ladle, skim the milk solids from the surface of the butter and discard. Clean the ladle of any residue, then ladle the clarified butter into a container. When you near the bottom of the pan, you'll see the milky white water content of the butter settled at the bottom. Avoid disrupting it as you ladle out the remaining clarified butter. Discard the water.

HOLLANDAISE RESCUE: So, your hollandaise broke and looks like curdled, oily goop. It's okay, simply start over with new yolks and lemon and use the broken sauce in place of the clarified butter. If your sauce is on the verge of breaking, use a few drops of cold water to resuscitate it at any point in the process. Try. Fail. Try again. You'll get it. You're golden, you're a star.

HOLLANDAISE VARIATIONS

You got the skills to pay the bills! Now let's show off!

HOLLANDAISE IN A BLENDER: Same ratio of ingredients, except you put the yolks and juice in a blender and crank it. Slowly add ¼ cup hot water, then drizzle in the clarified butter. Done in 2 minutes.

SRIRACHA HOLLANDAISE: Beat 1 tablespoon Sriracha sauce or your favorite chili paste (such as Sweet Chili Paste, page 151) into the egg yolks with the lemon juice.

BLOOD ORANGE HOLLANDAISE: Simply replace the lemon juice with fresh blood orange juice for a slightly sweet orange-flavored hollandaise.

BASIL AND TOMATO WATER HOLLANDAISE: First, infuse the clarified butter with delicious fresh basil leaves, either as you melt the butter or when you reheat reserved butter. Next, substitute tomato water for the lemon juice (see the Crystal Bloody Vodka, page 315).

SCRAMBLED EGGS

What does it mean to be "scrambled"? You can scramble quickly between places or tasks. In military surveillance terms, you can mess up communications or coded signals. But when the term applies to eggs, there can be no mistake; a perfect scrambled egg begins with careful attention to the method and the end result.

At Egg Shop, soft scrambled eggs are delicately folded upon themselves over medium heat. The pan is turned and a spatula shapes the eggs to resemble a rose, a winding mountain road, or an elegantly terraced hillside. A "French-style" soft scramble entails stirring and folding eggs with butter over the gentlest heat until the eggs are cooked but still entirely pourable. There are many roads to your perfect scramble, but it starts with what you want in the end. Is this scramble a structural component to a sandwich? Is it a textural complement to high-quality caviar? Is it breakfast for a toddler who is not yet fork savvy?

But whatever you desire from a scramble, please, please, please *do not* overcook. The goal is *not* a flat yellow mass dotted with brown spots, lacking sheen and reminiscent of cheap foam rubber. Remember the first time someone made scrambled eggs for you just right, just the way you liked them? You can get there. All you have to know to be dangerous are these three points:

1. The ratio is 2 eggs to 1 tablespoon of fat (however you're defining the fat).
2. Use a bowl and fork; a whisk tends to incorporate too much air.
3. Start with a hot pan. Whether it's a perfectly seasoned cast-iron, a nonstick, a copper, or the hood of your DeLorean, if you can hold your hand an inch from the cooking surface comfortably for 30 seconds, it's not hot enough! Nicely sizzling fat will put you on the path to mastering your own egg destiny.

Okay, scramblers, let's get scrambling!

CLASSIC FRENCH SOFT SCRAMBLE

MAKES 1 SERVING

2 tablespoons unsalted butter

2 eggs, lightly beaten

Sea salt

This yields an ultracreamy, buttery, decadent, and entirely pourable scrambled egg. This is an exercise in patience. On one hand the smell of melting butter is almost too good to resist, on the other you realize that if you can just hold out and keep the heat low, your eggs will be the stuff of convulsion-inducing culinary genius!

1. Bring about 2 cups of water to a simmer in a small saucepan, then set a medium stainless steel bowl over the pan to function as a double boiler. Add 1 tablespoon of the butter to the bowl. When the butter is fully melted, add the eggs and stir. Keep stirring. When the . . . no, keep stirring. Okay you're developing some small curds of cooked eggs. Keep stirring. The eggs appear to be able to stand on themselves like a quality risotto. Keep stirring just a little more . . .

2. *Now!* Remove the bowl from the heat, add the remaining 1 tablespoon butter, and stir gently until the butter is completely melted. Season to taste with sea salt and pour the eggs on whomever you like.

MICROHUEVOS

MAKES 1 SERVING

1 tablespoon cold unsalted butter

2 eggs

Sea salt

This technique uses a microwave to create scrambled eggs with a texture that would make even Julia Child salivate. A respectable scramble from demon technology is hard to come by, but we'll show you how.

1. Use a bit of the butter to grease the inside of a 2-cup glass measuring cup as if it were a muffin tin. Reserve the remaining butter.

2. Crack the eggs into the measuring cup and scramble well with a fork. Set the microwave power to 50 percent. Cook the eggs in 30-second intervals, scrambling thoroughly with a fork after each interval, until the eggs are the consistency of a Classic French Soft Scramble (previous recipe).

3. Mix in the rest of the butter until fully melted. Season to taste with salt and serve, or eat right out of the measuring cup like a boss.

THE EGG SHOP SCRAMBLE

MAKES 1 SERVING

2 eggs

1 tablespoon heavy cream

1 teaspoon olive oil

Sea salt

"That's Hot!" Hot Sauce
(page 150)

This is the standard method we use at Egg Shop. The result is a beautifully light and barely set rosette-shaped scramble.

1. In a small bowl, gently whip the eggs with the heavy cream.

2. Heat a small nonstick or cast-iron pan over medium heat. Add the olive oil and swirl to evenly coat the bottom. When the pan is hot, pour in the eggs. They should sizzle and bubble a little bit. Wait about 20 seconds for the eggs to set, then, keeping a heat-resistant (silicone or rubber) spatula vertical, pull the eggs across the pan in one motion from front/nose to the back/handle. Tilt the pan forward at a 45-degree angle to let the loose eggs fill the other side of the pan. Repeat the motion with the spatula, this time from back to front. You should have eggs that look like the floppy ears of a basset hound. Now, keeping the spatula vertical, turn one ear in to the center of the pan, then do the same with the other ear. Hold the eggs together with the spatula and gently swirl the pan to allow any liquid eggs to run to the center of the pan and fill in any cracks. You're done, you did it! Season to taste with a bit of sea salt, serve, and pass the hot sauce.

COFFEE SHOP SCRAMBLE

MAKES 2 SERVINGS

TOOLS
espresso machine with a steam
wand and a ceramic pitcher,
or an electric milk frother and
heater (see Note)

4 eggs

2 tablespoons heavy cream

1 tablespoon unsalted
butter

Sea salt

This method is both an ingenious use of limited cooking equipment and a completely moronic and abusive use of relatively sensitive coffee equipment. That said, it's also a lot of fun, and during a busy service or a moment of extreme laziness it can really save you.

---

1. Gently whip the eggs and cream with a fork until well combined. Add the egg mixture to the ceramic pitcher of an espresso machine and submerge the steam wand tip. Begin to release steam into the eggs while stirring constantly with a spatula and moving the pitcher ever so slightly up and down. You're finished when the eggs resemble a Classic French Soft Scramble (page 55).

2. Add the butter and give one last burst of steam. Stir to melt the butter, season to taste with salt, and serve.

NOTE: If you're using an electric milk frother and heater, the idea is the same. Just add the egg mixture, turn on the frother, and gently shake the frother up and down as if you were shaking a cocktail in super slo-mo. Check the eggs, add the butter, and give them one more good electro-blast.

EGGS FOIE

MAKES 2 SERVINGS

2 ounces fresh, Grade A foie gras, cleaned (a frozen medallion, torchon, or pâté will also work)

4 eggs

1 tablespoon heavy cream or unsalted butter (the basting butters on pages 79 to 81 are a game changer)

A few fresh chives (with blossoms if flowering!)

Brioche toast

These last few recipes have something very important in common: They employ a French technique known as *monter au beurre* that involves finishing a dish or sauce with butter to create a more luxurious eating experience and a lighter texture. As demonstrated in Eggs Caviar (page 61), this technique can be applied to creamy fats of all kinds. Healthy fat options abound—why not finish with pureed avocado, Greek yogurt, or even coconut oil? Surprise yourself with some everyday experiments. But first, let's finish with the king of fats: foie gras.

1. In a small nonstick skillet, sear the foie gras over medium-high heat until caramelized on both sides, about 1 minute per side. Set aside the foie gras and turn the heat to low, reserving the rendered fat in the pan.

2. In a medium bowl, gently mix the eggs with a fork.

3. Pulse the foie and cream or butter in a food processor or with an immersion blender until fluffy and uniform, like a slightly more gelatinous whipped butter.

4. Using the reserved fat in the pan, cook the eggs over medium heat in a classic French Soft Scramble (page 55). When the eggs are nearly perfect, add the foie gras and turn the heat to high. Working on and off the heat, fold in the foie gras until incorporated but not fully melted. Streaks are good (this will take all of 20 seconds).

NOTE: Finishing with butter is usually done without heat or over very low heat, to let the eggs stay nice and warm without overcooking.

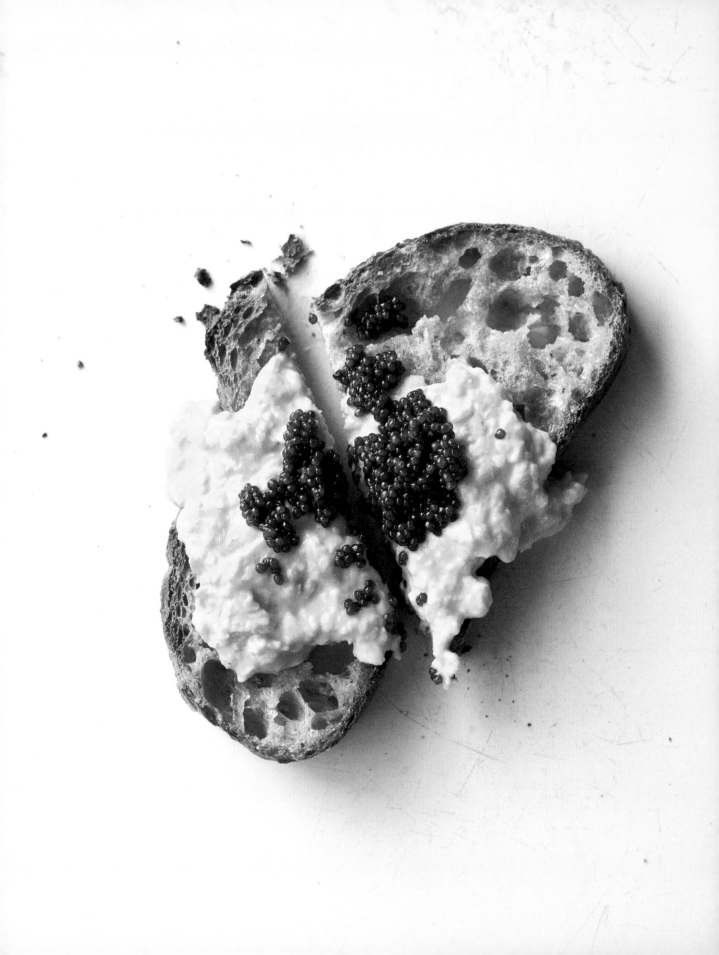

EGGS CAVIAR

MAKES 1 SERVING

2 eggs

1 teaspoon Cognac (Pierre Ferrand 1840 is our go-to, but a little Hennessey never hurt nobody)

1 teaspoon unsalted butter

2 tablespoons sour cream or labneh

2 grams of your favorite caviar or roe

1 slice sourdough or pumpernickel rye bread, toasted and buttered

This is an old-school, fancy-pants dish that snoot masters break out to wow their aging clientele. But the dish teaches a very important lesson: the texture of well-prepared eggs can be enhanced by adding complementary textural ingredients. In short, it teaches respect for perfectly cooked eggs. If you're going to take the time to build upon these techniques, why would you go and muck it up by haphazardly throwing in some fried bologna or raw vegetable mishegas? There are only two rules: Let the garnish suit the egg-cooking technique and add the garnish at the end, not during the cooking process.

---

1. Gently whip the eggs with a fork.

2. Heat a saucepan over medium heat, then add the Cognac and butter (they should sizzle/simmer immediately). Add the eggs and whisk constantly—working on and off the heat in order to develop the curds little by little and prevent the eggs from sticking or otherwise overcooking at the base of the pan—until the eggs begin to resemble the Classic French Soft Scramble (page 55). Add 1 tablespoon of the sour cream and stir to incorporate, letting the eggs sputter and pop a few times on the heat. Barely fold in the remaining sour cream (some streaks should still be visible).

3. Top the buttered toast with plenty of soft scrambled eggs and a heaping spoon of the caviar. Or pour eggs in a bowl and top the whole thing with the caviar, use the toast as a spoon, and knock yourself out.

BOILED EGGS

Boiling eggs isn't quite as easy as boiling water. You have to know exactly what you want the egg to do for you. Are you after a perfectly yellow yolk that stays put in the firm white when quartered for a salad? Do you want a chalky, pale yolk that will easily dissolve into mayonnaise for a deviled egg filling? Do you want a soft-boiled egg with a fully set white and a liquid yolk that can be peeled and will hold together long enough to prepare a ramen dish, with the egg as a garnish?

We lead you through this timing game, and put you on the winning side of your yolk goals. Here we offer our preferred methods for hard-boiled, soft-boiled, and everything in between, plus some helpful field methods for peeling and foolproofing the process.

HARD-, MEDIUM-, AND SOFT-BOILED EGGS

Boiled eggs are a beautiful thing. They are excellently portable for any adventure or bogus journey. They are adaptable for a wide range of applications, from providing body to a sauce or a healthy protein for a salad or a simple or even not-so-simple snack. But there are many schools of thought on how to find consistent success when you get things boiling. It's Martha Stewart vs. Hervé. This, and it breaks down as follows (if you're *not* a gastronomy nerd, stop here).

Okay, nerds, listen up! The only foolproof method for boiling eggs accurately and consistently is to prepare them in a state of thermodynamic stasis—e.g., control the temperatures of the inside and outside shell throughout the cooking process. The variables for any experimentation are threefold: time, weight, and temperature. The weight of the egg directly corresponds to the temperature gradient (both rising and falling), and the temperature gradient inversely corresponds to the cooking time. Which is to say in the case of a home experiment where it is nearly impossible to control the imposed outside shell temperature with any real consistency, one must factor in rising and falling temperature and aim for the middle, colloquially speaking.

This would be less complicated if the shell itself were entirely permeable, or if the internal density of the egg—both in its raw state and throughout the cooking process—were of a uniform density and/or cellular structure. One must work backward from proven fact. FACT: The stage known as **HARD-BOILED** *occurs when the internal temperature at the yolk's center is 174°F. FACT: The stage known as* **MEDIUM-BOILED** *occurs when the internal temperature at the yolk's center is 165°F. FACT: The stage known as* **SOFT-BOILED** *occurs when the internal temperature at the yolk's center is 158°F. The goal of experimentation should* not *be simply to devise a method by which to reach these benchmarks, but rather to devise a working method to reach these benchmarks in the least amount of time while eliminating and preventing* **ERROR CONSEQUENCE ONE: OVERCOOKING.**

Thanks for your patience. If you are more interested in easy ways to get it right every time, just follow these steps and have a lovely day.

HARD-BOILED: Fill a medium saucepan three-fourths full of hot water and add 1 teaspoon each of salt and distilled white vinegar. Prepare an ice bath and crazy glue a timer to your forehead while you bring the water to a boil over high heat. It's crucial to prepare the ice bath and locate your timer early so you don't find yourself in a pinch later.

With the water at a rolling boil, gently lower the eggs (most likely straight outta the fridge) into the water either all at once in a steamer basket or one at a time with a slotted spoon. It's important that the water level cover the eggs by at least 1 inch no matter how many eggs you are boiling.

Set the timer for 10 minutes. When it dings, quickly drain the hot water and gently place the eggs in the ice bath to stop the cooking process. Cool completely, then peel and enjoy!

MEDIUM-BOILED: Follow the method for hard-boiled eggs but set the timer to 8 minutes.

SOFT-BOILED: Follow the method for hard-boiled eggs but set the timer for 6 minutes.

TIPS FOR PEELING: First, the older the egg the better it will peel. It's hard to tell the age of supermarket eggs, but if you're buying directly from a farmer they can tell you when the eggs were laid and how long they have been stored. Second, a tiny bit of baking soda in the cooking water will help make the shells more brittle. Finally, peeling an egg in a bowl of fresh water or under running water will remove any tiny left-behind shell particles.

BOILED EGG DIAGNOSTICS

So, you're still screwing it up. Here's how we can tell, and here's how you can fix it!

› Hard-boiled with gray around the yolk: overcooked or not cooled fast enough

› Hard-boiled with an extremely pale and chalky yolk: slightly overcooked, and the egg is likely too old

› Hard-boiled with the center of the yolk fully set but slightly gelatinous, like a yellow gummy bear: undercooked

› Medium-boiled with the yolk not set or the center fully liquid: undercooked

› Soft-boiled with the white not set: undercooked

› Soft-boiled with the white fully set and the yolk fully set around the edges: overcooked

* If your problem is overcooking, do these things: Invest in a timer (stop fooling yourself that watching the clock on your oven/range/microwave is good enough) and adjust the timing back by 30 seconds. Increase the amount of ice in your ice bath. Remember to always make a separate ice bath, and don't get lazy and dump the ice into the hot pan you just used to boil the eggs. You know who you are . . .

EGG SHOP EGG SALAD

MAKES 6 CUPS

12 hard-boiled eggs*
(page 64), slightly cooled

6 scallions

¼ cup whole-grain Dijon
mustard (we use Maille)

½ cup 2% or full-fat Greek
yogurt

¼ cup olive oil

Juice of 1 lemon

¼ teaspoon cayenne
pepper

2 dashes "That's Hot!" Hot
Sauce (page 150), or your
favorite Louisiana-style hot
sauce

Sea salt

¼ cup chopped fresh dill

A better egg salad with a kick of hot sauce and no mayonnaise whatsoever, this recipe uses protein- and probiotic-rich local Greek yogurt in place of the usual mayo for a much lighter result while staying true to egg salad's cool and creamy nature.

1. Peel the eggs and rinse them to remove any shell fragments. Crush them with your hands into a medium bowl. Refrigerate until fully cool, about 15 minutes.

2. Remove the dry green tops and the white roots from the scallions. Slice the scallions razor thin at a sharp angle.

3. In a large bowl, combine the mustard, yogurt, olive oil, lemon juice, cayenne, hot sauce, and salt to taste and mix until smooth. Mix in the eggs, scallions, and dill and finish with a bit of sea salt to taste.

* If you're in a rush you can speed up the process by poaching the eggs well done. This saves the time of peeling the eggs, but you might lose some of the whites in the pot.

ROASTED BEET TZATZIKI SALAD

MAKES 2 SERVINGS

1 cup Beet Tzatziki
(page 68)

2 hard-boiled eggs
(page 64), peeled and
quartered

1 yellow heirloom tomato,
finely diced

1 Persian (mini) cucumber,
finely diced

½ teaspoon red chile flakes

2 radishes, sliced into very
thin rounds

1 teaspoon poppy seeds

1 cup equal parts torn fresh
flat-leaf parsley leaves, dill
fronds, and mint leaves,
plus extra for garnish

2 tablespoons buttermilk

Sea salt

1 cup Pickled Beets;
reserve a little liquid for
garnish (page 223)

Pinch of ground sumac, for
garnish

Extra-virgin olive oil, for
garnish

This psychedelic Mediterranean-inspired salad marries bright, fresh ingredients with sweet, earthy roasted beets and perfectly cooked eggs. It tastes as good as it looks on the plate, and all the ingredients make for good snacks.

---

1. Spread the tzatziki on two serving plates and top with the eggs.

2. In a medium bowl, combine the tomato, cucumber, chile flakes, radishes, poppy seeds, fresh herbs, and buttermilk. Season with a little sea salt.

3. Broil or sauté the pickled beets to slightly caramelize and blister the outer surface.

4. Top the eggs with the cucumber-tomato salad and the hot beets. Garnish with more herbs, a pinch of sumac, a little olive oil, and the pickling liquid from the beets.

BEET TZATZIKI

MAKES 2¼ CUPS

1 cup labneh

1 cup grated beets (use those roasted for Pickled Beets [page 223])

¼ cup peeled, seeded, and minced Persian (mini) cucumber

1 garlic clove, finely grated

¼ cup chopped fresh dill

6 leaves fresh mint, chopped

2 tablespoons fresh lemon juice

1 teaspoon sea salt

1 teaspoon freshly cracked black pepper

In a medium bowl, combine all the ingredients.

SPEAKING OF BEETS

Here's a list of all the beats mentioned throughout the book (in no particular order):

Michael Jackson, "Black or White"

Sir Mix-A-Lot, "Baby Got Back"

Will Smith, "Miami"

Lou Bega, "Mambo No. 5"

Three 6 Mafia, suggested: "Stay Fly" and "Sippin on Some Syrup"

O.T. Genasis, "CoCo"

Gucci Mane, "Lemonade"

Notorious B.I.G., "Juicy" and "Going Back to Cali"

Migos, "Pipe It Up," and suggested: "Handsome and Wealthy"

Prefab Sprout, suggested: "When Love Breaks Down," "The King of Rock 'n' Roll," and "Cars and Girls"

Foreigner, "Cold As Ice"

Ween, "Your Party"

Ol' Dirty Bastard, "Shimmy Shimmy Ya"

Red Hot Chili Peppers, "Blood Sugar Sex Magik"

The Beatles, "All You Need Is Love" and "Norwegian Wood"

The Kinks, "Village Green Preservation Society" and "Holiday in Waikiki"

Otis Redding, suggested: "These Arms of Mine," "Try a Little Tenderness," and "I've Got Dreams to Remember"

The Beach Boys, suggested: "Wouldn't It Be Nice," "Sloop John B," and "I Just Wasn't Made for These Times"

Janet Jackson, "Nasty"

Raekwon, suggested: "Ice Cream" and "The Morning"

Tom Petty, suggested: "Breakdown," "American Girl," "Runnin' Down a Dream," and "Mary Jane's Last Dance"

Talking Heads, "Once in a Lifetime"

Parliament, "Give Up the Funk"

Post Malone, "White Iverson"

Tupac, "California Love"

Modern English, "I Melt with You"

Paula Abdul, "Cold Hearted"

DJ Jazzy Jeff & the Fresh Prince, "Parents Just Don't Understand"

P.M. Dawn, suggested: "I Die Without You" and "Set Adrift on Memory Bliss"

Paco de Lucía, suggested: "Entre Dos Aguas" and "Rosa Maria"

The Streets, "Has It Come to This?"

DEVO, "Whip It"

Neil Young, "Old Man" and "Powder Ginger"

Van Morrison, "Into the Mystic"

CHOPPED EGG AND WATERMELON SALAD

MAKES 2 SERVINGS

DRESSING

3 tablespoons whole-grain Dijon mustard (we use Maille)

1 egg yolk

2 tablespoons honey

¼ cup Champagne vinegar

1 cup olive oil

½ teaspoon sea salt

SALAD

2 cups baby arugula

1 head frisée lettuce

3 hard-boiled eggs (page 64), peeled and crushed by hand

2 cups 2-inch-cubed seedless watermelon

1 cup crumbled blue cheese (or feta, if you don't dig on blue)

6 to 8 fresh basil leaves

1 avocado, sliced

1 teaspoon red chile flakes

6 slices bacon, cooked crisp (optional)

Here's a refreshing summer salad that can transform with the seasons. A hybrid of a classic Cobb and a caprese salad, with an addictive Champagne vinaigrette, try it with beets and apples in the fall and squash and white beans in the winter! This is also great with a little grilled chicken or salmon for a more complete meal. And as you experiment with seasonal veggies, know that parsley, dill, and mint are excellent basil substitutes. But remember, the key to this salad is simply dressing the greens at the right moment, so be sure to have all your ingredients prepped and ready to go.

1. To make the dressing, in a small bowl, whisk the mustard, egg yolk, honey, and vinegar. Slowly drizzle in the olive oil while whisking constantly. Season with salt to finish.

2. To prepare the salad, in a large bowl, lightly drizzle the arugula and frisée with some of the dressing (save the leftovers for another use). Arrange the lettuces on serving dishes.

3. In a separate bowl, toss together the eggs, watermelon, blue cheese, basil, avocado, chile flakes, and bacon (if using) to combine. Evenly distribute the mixture over the greens and serve.

DEVILED EGGS THREE WAYS

The deviled egg in its traditional form is supremely nostalgic. It reminds me of the Fourth of July in Kansas. I can almost smell hot dogs on a charcoal grill and hear the rumble of classic cars and motorcycles from the neighborhood parade just thinking about this recipe. Whether you stick to the classic mayo, yolk, mustard version speckled with paprika or try something new, a slightly overcooked hard-boiled egg always works best because the whites are extra firm and easy to handle and the yolks are just a bit powdery (a polite way of saying chalky). Twelve minutes should do the trick.

CLASSIC DEVILED EGGS

MAKES 12 DEVILED EGGS

6 hard-boiled eggs (page 64), halved, yolks removed

1 tablespoon Dijon mustard (we use Maille)

1 tablespoon fresh lemon juice

1 cup Mayo (page 148)

1 teaspoon sea salt

Pinch of paprika, for garnish

1. The easiest way to make the deviled egg filling is to puree the yolks and seasonings in a food processor. Otherwise, use a fine cheese grater to shred the yolks or push them through a fine-mesh sieve, then whisk them with the mustard and lemon juice to form a paste. Fold in the mayo and sea salt. This helps ensure a smooth texture.

2. To fill the egg whites, a piping bag always works best even if it's a DIY version of a *proper* piping bag made from cutting one corner off of a zip-top bag. Sprinkle the yolk mixture with paprika to garnish.

ARTICHOKE-PESTO DEVILED EGGS

MAKES 12 DEVILED EGGS

Filling from Classic
Deviled Eggs (page 71)

¼ cup Classic Pesto
(page 221)

¼ cup minced artichoke
hearts

Toasted pine nuts, fresh
basil leaves (the smaller,
the better), and/or shaved
pecorino cheese, for garnish

Prepare the deviled egg filling as directed for Classic Deviled Eggs, and fold in the pesto and artichoke hearts. Pipe to fill the egg whites and garnish as desired.

TIKKA-MASALA DEVILED EGGS

MAKES 12 DEVILED EGGS

1 teaspoon unsalted butter

¼ cup minced onion

¼ cup minced garlic

¼ cup minced fresh ginger

1 teaspoon ground turmeric

3 tablespoons tomato paste

¼ cup light beer

Filling from Classic Deviled
Eggs (page 71)

1 teaspoon garam masala

1 teaspoon ground cumin

1 teaspoon ground
cardamom

12 bite-size pieces fried
chicken (from The Golden
Bucket Variation, page 234)

Fresh cilantro, for garnish

1. In a medium sauté pan, melt the butter over medium heat. Add the onion, garlic, ginger, and turmeric and sweat until tender and nearly caramelized, about 10 minutes. Whisk in the tomato paste and cook over low heat, stirring often, until the raw tomato paste flavor is cooked out and the aroma of roasted tomatoes fills your exotic nasum, about 10 minutes. Add the beer and stir to turn the mixture into a paste.

2. Prepare the deviled egg filling as directed for Classic Deviled Eggs, and fold in the paste.

3. In a small bowl, combine the garam masala, cumin, and cardamom. Sprinkle the mixture lightly to season the fried chicken.

4. Pipe to fill the egg whites, top each with a piece of spiced chicken, and garnish with cilantro.

SPICY TEA AND TAMARI CURED SOFT-BOILED EGG

MAKES 6 EGGS

6 soft-boiled eggs (page 64)

¼ cup black tea leaves

½ cup hot water*

1 cup brine from Fresh Pickled Jalapeños (page 223)

¼ cup mirin

¼ cup tamari

This is the ramen or congee garnish you've been looking for: salty and spicy with umami turned up to eleven.

1. As soon as the eggs are cool enough to handle, lightly crack the shell all over. This can be done by lightly rolling the eggs across your countertop with the palm of your hand or gently tapping them with the back of a spoon.

2. In a storage container, combine the tea leaves and hot water. Stir in the brine, mirin, and tamari, then add the eggs. Cover and refrigerate for 24 hours before peeling and serving. The eggs will have a spiderweb design across the white and will have taken on the heat of the jalapeño brine.

VARIATIONS: See Egg Shop Pickled Eggs (page 74) for color and flavor variations!

* 196° to 205°F (just below boiling)

EGG SHOP PICKLED EGGS

MAKES 6 PICKLED EGGS

6 hard-boiled eggs
(page 64), peeled

2 cups brine from Pickled
Red Onions (page 220)

2 garlic cloves, smashed

1 tablespoon pure cane
sugar

2 fresh dill sprigs

This hot pink version of the classic saloon snack is incredibly easy, and it's intentionally less potent for the breath-conscious snacker! Your friends will thank you.

Combine all the ingredients in a storage container, cover, and refrigerate 24 hours before serving. The eggs will keep for up to 10 days submerged in the brine.

VARIATIONS

› For vibrant green eggs, submerge eggs in Raw Salsa Verde (page 155) or matcha spiked with rice vinegar.

› For bright purple eggs, use the brine from Pickled Beets (page 223).

› For spicy red eggs, submerge in "That's Hot!" Hot Sauce (page 150).

BASTED EGGS

You've known him for so long that you can't imagine cooking with someone else. But lately, when you come home and see him sitting there listless, cold, and half unwrapped, it's so hard to remember the good times: the fresh zucchini bread times, the lobster dipping times, the hollandaise holidays by the sea . . . we've all been there.

Butter is your best friend, so let's make him treat you right! Basting eggs with butter as it begins to brown in the pan is a game changer. It's so simple to learn, yet once you have it in your arsenal, it never ceases to amaze. The nutty, earthy flavor of the toasted butter marries with the egg as you work on and off the heat, cooking the egg to a slight crisp on the outer edges. The only thing this noisette flavor asks in return is a bit of sea salt to keep the peace. Few things in this world exist in such perfect harmony as salt and fat.

The following recipes serve as a guide to cooking eggs in butter and a primer on using butter as a complement to egg-based dishes of all kinds. When serving eggs, buttered toast is a must, but there are infinite ways to add flavor and texture to butter. In a matter of minutes you can stock your fridge for weeks with different types of compound butter to have at the ready. You'll never again be without an elegant accessory to the perfectly cooked egg.

TRADITIONAL BASTED EGG TECHNIQUE

MAKES 1 BASTED EGG

TOOLS
1 nonstick sauté pan with slightly rounded sides

2 tablespoons unsalted butter (or other basting fat, such as coconut oil) per egg (yes, it's kind of a lot of butter, but who's watching?)

1 egg (or more)

1. Heat the pan over medium heat and add a tiny bit of the butter to test the heat. If the butter sputters out of control upon hitting the pan, then your pan is way too hot. Discard the burned butter and try again. If the butter gently sizzles and melts across the pan over the course of a slow 5 count, the pan is ready. When it hits the perfect temperature, add 1 tablespoon of the butter to the pan. Butter and pan game on fleek? Let's move on . . .

2. Crack the egg into the pan and slightly increase the heat. Look for the white to be set on the bottom but still uncooked on top. To test this, give the egg a little wiggle by moving the pan gently back and forth. If the egg slides in the pan, you're ready to roll.

3. Now it's time to butter bomb that thing! Add the remaining 1 tablespoon butter to the pan. The butter should sizzle in the pan immediately, becoming slightly foamy because you increased the heat. Using a tablespoon, scoop the hot butter from the front of the pan and spoon it over the egg yolk until the whites on the top of the egg are fully set. (If you're right-handed, it's better to hold the spoon in your right hand and the pan in your left.) As you baste, you'll find it necessary to tilt the pan forward and backward slightly to let the butter pool so that it can easily be caught in the spoon. This will be awkward on your first try, but that's okay. Everyone's first time is a little awkward. Rest assured, exponential improvement will be had with each consecutive egg. Baste out!

CLOCKWISE FROM TOP: Goji Açai Butter (opposite),
Jalapeño-Honey Butter (page 80), Hot Pickle Butter
(page 81), Mocha Bacon Butter (page 81), Egg Shop Herb
Butter (opposite), Tomato Caper Butter (page 80)

EGG SHOP HERB BUTTER

MAKES 3 CUPS

1 pound (4 sticks) unsalted butter

2 garlic cloves, grated on a fine rasp-style grater

Zest of 1 lemon

1 shallot, minced

Leaves from 1 bunch flat-leaf parsley, chopped extra fine

¼ cup finely chopped fresh basil leaves

Pinch of sea salt

Our herb butter will not get you stopped by the police at the airport. Though you may have a bigger problem on your hands if you find yourself traveling with a personal supply of compound butter. This is our take on the classic beurre maître d'hôtel, and it's so versatile that it can become addicting.

Let the butter come to room temperature in a bowl. Add the garlic, lemon zest, shallot, parsley, basil, and salt and mix with a rubber spatula until evenly incorporated.

NOTE ON STORAGE FOR COMPOUND BUTTERS: Place the butter in the crock of your dreams and use as desired over the next 10 to 14 days, or freeze for up to 1 month.

GOJI AÇAI BUTTER

MAKES 3 CUPS

1 pound (4 sticks) unsalted butter

¼ cup dried goji berries, soaked in hot water for 20 minutes to soften and drained

¼ cup fresh frozen açai berries, thawed, or açai puree

2 tablespoons agave

Pinch of sea salt

This sweet, antioxidant-packed compound butter works both as a baste for eggs and amazing finishing move for French Toast Trick 2: Tutti Frutti (page 255).

1. Let the butter come to room temperature in a bowl.

2. Pulse the goji berries in a food processor or mince them by hand. Add them to the butter along with the açai berries or puree, agave, and salt. Mix with a rubber spatula until evenly incorporated.

TOMATO-CAPER BUTTER

MAKES 3 CUPS

1 pound (4 sticks) unsalted butter

¼ cup brine-packed nonpareil capers (not salt-packed)

2 marinated white anchovies, minced (optional)

4 ounces (scant ½ cup) organic tomato paste

1 tablespoon balsamic vinegar

This rich, supersavory tomato miracle is a one-stop wonder that can be used to baste an egg, or just spread it on toast for an intense bruschetta.

We love this butter on a pecorino tartine with a poached egg and good olive oil! Simply top a thick slice of sourdough bread with freshly grated Pecorino Romano cheese and bake at 350°F until golden brown, about 10 minutes, then slather with TCB (tomato-caper butter) and * ppppppoach* your egg up! Or, better yet, reduce a little white wine and chicken stock by half and stir in some TCB to make a knockout basic pasta sauce.

1. Let the butter come to room temperature in a bowl.

2. In a small sauté pan, sauté the capers and anchovies (if using) in 2 tablespoons of the butter over medium heat until the anchovies begin to brown and the capers are very fragrant. Add the tomato paste and cook over low heat until the raw tomato paste flavor has disappeared and a rich roasted tomato aroma fills your kitchen, about 15 minutes.

3. Let the tomato mixture cool to room temperature, then add to the butter along with the vinegar and mix with a rubber spatula until evenly incorporated.

JALAPEÑO-HONEY BUTTER

MAKES 3 CUPS

1 pound (4 sticks) unsalted butter

¼ cup minced Fresh Pickled Jalapeños (page 223)

½ cup wildflower honey

1 tablespoon Maldon salt or other flaky sea salt

Butter is a social beast. While it's a boon to your egg bonanza, flavored butter can also be used to baste other edible sundries. Case in point: *shrimps* (pronounced *skuh-rimp-suh*)! This jalapeño-honey butter is a destroyer on seafood and eggs, and our go-to for Buttermilk Biscuits (page 252).

1. Let the butter come to room temperature in a bowl.

2. Add the jalapeños, honey, and salt and mix with a rubber spatula until evenly incorporated.

HOT PICKLE BUTTER

MAKES 2 CUPS

1 pound (4 sticks) unsalted butter

¼ cup minced Hot Pickles (page 228)

1 teaspoon ground cumin

Pinch of smoked paprika

1 teaspoon sea salt

Kids love cowboy eggs (aka toad in a hole, gashouse eggs, or egg in a basket)! This butter was made for cowboy eggs (and is killer for making grilled cheesers for your munchkin-faced minion as well).

1. Let the butter come to room temperature in a bowl.

2. Add the pickles, cumin, paprika, and salt and mix with a rubber spatula until evenly incorporated.

NOTE: To make cowboy eggs, cut a hole in a thick slice of Texas toast (brioche or challah also works great). Add 2 heaping tablespoons Hot Pickle Butter to a hot broilerproof skillet, followed by the holey bread. Crack an egg into the hole. When the egg white is fully set on the bottom, top each egg with a bit more pickle butter and place the entire pan under the broiler to finish the top of the egg and melt the butter. Serve with yummy Black Bean Smash (page 200) and fresh avocado.

MOCHA BACON BUTTER

MAKES 3 CUPS

1 pound (4 sticks) unsalted butter

¼ cup minced cooked bacon

¼ cup unsweetened cocoa powder (we prefer Valrhona 100 percent pure)

2 ounces dark chocolate, minced

½ cup agave

1 tablespoon finely ground single-origin coffee (such as Café Integral Puma or Bosque)

Pinch of sea salt

Flavored butters can be used as a basis for baking as well. You can cut in a flavored butter as you would use plain butter to make Buttermilk Biscuits (page 252). This chocolate butter infused with coffee and bacon takes the cake, or more appropriately makes the cake!

For an extremely decadent breakfast, spread this butter on a warm slice of banana bread and top it with a perfectly poached egg, or go nuts and use it to baste an egg; finish with a bit more bacon and salty toasted almonds.

1. Let the butter come to room temperature in a bowl.

2. Add the bacon, cocoa, chocolate, agave, coffee, and salt and mix with a rubber spatula until evenly incorporated.

OMELETS

Ol' man, take a look at your eggs, they're a lot like you were. . . . The omelet is an old-fashioned egg situation surrounded by differences of opinion. In essence, the omelet is an egg-folding technique that incorporates garnish ingredients either into the eggs as they cook or into the fold as the omelet is finished.

We don't have omelets on the menu at Egg Shop because they're too subjective. If I were to serve my relatives from Cincinnati a classic omelet with fines herbes, they would ask for their money back; yet if I were to serve a half-moon-shaped Denver omelet to the Parisian expat who lives upstairs, she would call me an American swine.

It's lose/lose, I'm afraid, with one exception: *tamagoyaki* (page 89). The Japanese omelet is the holy grail of egg-cooking technique, and any book or shop devoted to eggs would be remiss without an attempt. Here we offer several wildly different approaches from the world of all things folded over. Ours is a quest to climb our mountain of technique and reach the summit that is *tamagoyaki*.

CLASSIC FRENCH OMELET

MAKES 1 OMELET

2 eggs

2 teaspoons unsalted butter

Fresh fines herbes (such as chervil, dill, chive, and/or tarragon) or a slice of triple-crème Brie, for garnish (optional)

Pinch of salt

The opposite of the blender omelet, this omelet is delicate, thin, neatly rolled, and made without imparting color to the egg. The garnishes are simple, just fines herbes or a bit of Brie.

I offer a few cheats for a perfect rolling tri-fold in step 3. Practice makes perfect. As you build this skill, experiment with adding garnishes just before folding.

1. Heat a small nonstick skillet over medium-high heat.

2. In a small bowl, mix the eggs gently with a fork, taking care not to incorporate too much air.

3. Add 1 teaspoon of the butter to the pan and swirl to coat the bottom of the pan. Pour the eggs into the pan and tilt it from side to side to distribute the eggs evenly. As the eggs begin to set, gently rock the pan back and forth and turn the heat to low. (This is the point where you will add garnishes once you have mastered the technique.) Just as the eggs are nearly set, tilt the pan forward to a 45-degree angle and use the spatula to begin to roll the omelet onto itself from the back of the pan toward the front. Increase the angle as you roll the omelet and with one final move, roll the omelet from the pan onto a plate.

4. Rub with the remaining 1 teaspoon butter and season with the salt. Over time you will find the entire process will take 1 minute or less once the eggs are in the pan. *Bon appétit!*

CHEAT CODE: Try pouring mixed eggs onto a baking sheet lined with a silicone baking mat and baking in a 325°F oven covered with an inverted second baking sheet. The egg steams itself delicately in 5 minutes, at which point you can easily add garnish and use the mat to roll a sliceable omelet!

POP'S DOUBLE-STUFFED, DOUBLE-FLUFFED AMERICAN OMELET

MAKES 1 OMELET
(TO FEED 2 VERY HUNGRY
PEOPLE)

2 maple sausage patties,
crumbled

6 slices bacon, chopped

¼ cup sliced mushrooms

6 eggs

3 tablespoons half-and-half

2 tablespoons unsalted
butter

1 cup spinach leaves

¼ cup grated cheddar
cheese

This is that big boy you've heard about . . . stuffed with bacon, sausage, cheddar cheese, spinach, and mushrooms. Not meant for hot-weather consumption, this incredibly filling omelet should be cut in wedges for multiple servings. It's truly an omelet to feed them all, with humble origins in my father's home kitchen, where he uses a 1950s milkshake blender to fluff his eggs back to the glistening dawn of the atomic age.

1. In a 10- or 12-inch skillet, cook the sausage and bacon fully over medium heat. Add the mushrooms and cook until tender. Reserve the mixture in a bowl.

2. In a blender, whip the eggs and half-and-half until very light, about 90 seconds on high. (A milkshake blender, while not entirely necessary, does offer a little bit more fluff and a bit more fun.)

3. Give the skillet a wipe and warm it over medium heat. Swirl the butter in the hot pan to coat it completely. Pour the whipped eggs into the pan and cook until fully set around the outer edges, 2 to 3 minutes. Turn the heat to low and top the whole surface of the omelet with the spinach and cheddar. Cook until the spinach is slightly wilted and the cheese begins to melt.

4. Add the sausage mixture to one side of the eggs and use 2 spatulas to fold the other half over the side with the sausage mixture. Cook until the eggs are set and the cheese is fully melted, another 2 minutes. The outer surface will be lightly browned in places and likely have some spots where cheese has broken the surface and possibly caramelized on the edges. This is considered a good thing, not unlike "burnt ends" in the BBQ world.

OLD-WORLD BAKED OMELETS

Before anyone ever thought to fuss with rolling or fashioning eggs into strange shapes, or using odd devices to flip, fluff, fold, or otherwise "f" things up, people were cooking eggs with whatever ingredients and whichever heat source they had. Roughly translated, what we call frittata and *tortilla española* started as hearth-fire foods—one-pan wonders with only slight technical differences.

MEXICAN MUSHROOM FRITTATA

MAKES 1 LARGE FRITTATA
(TO SERVE 6)

2 tablespoons unsalted butter or extra-virgin olive oil

1 cup cremini mushrooms, sliced thin

2 tablespoons chopped prepared Mexican huitlacoche (optional)

2 garlic cloves, minced

¼ cup chopped scallions, green and white parts

½ cup chopped fresh epazote (optional)

12 eggs

½ teaspoon cayenne pepper

1 teaspoon sea salt

½ cup grated Cotija cheese

¼ cup shredded queso Oaxaca, mozzarella, or jack

This simple frittata is deceivingly flavorful and possibly the most useful weapon in your taco party arsenal. Plus, you'll be able to wow your friends with your knowledge of—drumroll, please—*corn smut,* aka huitlacoche, aka corn truffles, aka DJ unpronounceable! Cue the Mariachi, crack the Modelo.

1. Preheat the oven to 350°F.

2. Heat a 9-inch cast-iron skillet over medium heat. Add 1 tablespoon of the butter, the mushrooms, and huitlacoche (if using) and sauté until the mushrooms are tender and their liquid begins to release. Stir in the garlic, scallions, and epazote (if using). Reserve this mixture in a bowl and let it cool to room temperature.

3. Return the pan to medium heat. In a large bowl, whisk together the eggs, cayenne, and salt. Add the remaining 1 tablespoon butter to the pan and pour in half of the egg mixture. Cook 1 minute. Sprinkle the mushroom mixture and the cheeses evenly across the egg mixture, then pour in the remaining egg mixture. Bake until the frittata is fully set, about 15 minutes.

4. Set aside to cool for 5 to 10 minutes, then slice in the pan and remove portions carefully with a spatula. Serve warm.

SWEET POTATO AND ALMOND TORTILLA ESPAÑOLA

MAKES 4 TO 6 SERVINGS

¼ cup olive oil

1 sweet potato, cut into ⅛-inch-thick rounds

¼ Spanish onion, thinly sliced

¼ cup sliced almonds

¼ teaspoon ground cinnamon

¼ teaspoon ground allspice

7 eggs

Sea salt, cilantro leaves, and harissa, for garnish

When you think of the word "tortilla," do you picture a taco or burrito? Show of hands, please. . . . The *tortilla española* is not the wrap-tastic outer layer of your favorite Mexican treat but rather the proper name for a Spanish omelet (as in an omelet from Spain). While this traditional tapas dish is made with eggs, waxy potatoes, and onions or garlic, our version gets a little twist using sweet potato and almonds. We chose almonds to provide textural variance and sweet potato to balance the heat of our go-to *tortilla* garnish, Homemade Harissa (page 159).

1. In a medium cast-iron skillet, heat the oil over medium heat. Add the sweet potato and onion and cook 2 minutes, then stir to turn them over. Sprinkle on the almonds, cinnamon, and allspice, give a quick stir to incorporate, and cook, covered, until the sweet potatoes are tender but not breaking apart, about 5 minutes. Be careful when lifting the lid, as steam condensation will make the hot oil pop.

2. Drain the oil from the pan into a small bowl and set it aside.

3. In a large bowl, mix the eggs lightly with a fork and add the potato mixture. Give the skillet a quick wipe and return the oil to the pan over medium heat. Add the egg and potato mixture. Stir constantly for about 1 minute to distribute the potatoes evenly throughout the egg mixture as the eggs begin to set across the pan.

4. Position the oven rack at least 6 inches below the heat source and heat the broiler to medium. Add the skillet and broil until the eggs are fully set and the top is starting to brown, about 5 minutes.

5. Let the eggs cool for 5 minutes in the pan, run a spatula around the perimeter of the pan, and invert the *tortilla* onto a cutting board or serving dish. The remaining moisture will do the work of releasing the eggs from the bottom of the pan once inverted. Slice into wedges and enjoy hot or at room temperature with plenty of salt, cilantro, and harissa.

TAMAGOYAKI: THE FINAL FRONTIER

TOOLS
chopsticks, square *tamagoyaki* pan with a paddle

5 eggs

1 tablespoon Dashi (page 91)

1 tablespoon mirin

2 teaspoons superfine sugar

2 teaspoons sea salt

½ cup vegetable oil

Tamagoyaki is a folded and pressed Japanese omelet, so elegant in construction and simplicity of flavor that it takes years of practice to master. The technique involves building a "gold bar" from thin, even layers of just-cooked egg folded precisely over themselves in order to achieve uniformity in texture, shape, and cooking temperature. If one thin layer is overcooked, the entire structure will be compromised, especially when used for sushi.

The thrill of *tamagoyaki* is in the defeat. You have success or you have nothing, and you clean your tools and start again. This is meditative cooking at its finest, better than any glass of wine in the low light or rare vinyl crackling from the other room.

Yes, this is complicated. Yes, practicing this method can be defeating. It's important to take the pressure off yourself and remember that it takes years for a trained sushi chef to master this technique; every failure brings you closer to the top of the mountain. And even if the shape is a disaster, or slightly browned, the eggs will still taste great! Don't let them go to waste.

But be warned: Those who seek perfection from an egg will find only the depths of their own foolish human nature.

---

1. In a medium bowl, lightly mix the eggs with the chopsticks, taking care not to incorporate much air. Mix in the dashi, mirin, sugar, and sea salt. Transfer the mixture to a large measuring cup so you can easily measure your pour as you work in stages.

2. In a *tamagoyaki* pan, heat the vegetable oil over medium heat. (It's important to bring the pan to the right temperature. If it is too cold, the eggs will cook unevenly and the sugars will caramelize at the bottom of the pan, likely causing the eggs to stick. If the pan is too hot, the sugars will caramelize before the eggs are set and ultimately result in dark spirals in the center of your "gold bar.")

3. Using chopsticks, dip a folded paper towel into the oil to soak up as much as possible. Pour any remaining oil out of the pan into a small bowl. Rest the paper towel in the bowl of reserved oil (you will use the paper towel to oil the pan as you work).

4. Just before you're ready to begin, pour a bit of the egg mixture into the pan. If it sizzles and bubbles immediately without generating any smoke or hard searing sound, you're good to go. If it sits in the pan without moving, the pan is too cold. Be sure to give the pan a good wipe with the oiled paper towel after this test.

5. With your well-oiled pan at perfect medium heat and the handle pointing directly at your belly button, pour in one-third of the egg mixture and tilt the pan to distribute the egg mixture evenly across the whole pan. The egg mixture should immediately begin to sizzle and bubble up. Pop the bubbles with a chopstick and tilt the pan in order to fill in any gaps in the cooked eggs with uncooked egg mixture. When the eggs are 95 percent set, run a chopstick around the perimeter of the pan to free the eggs completely from the sides.

6. Begin your first fold by gently placing the chopsticks under the eggs at the front of the pan (the side away from you). Use the chopsticks to support the eggs as you rock the pan toward yourself as if you were flipping a fried egg and fold the first third of the eggs toward you; repeat this with folding the next third. You should have an even rectangle of eggs at the back of the pan near the handle.

7. Now use the chopsticks and paper towel to oil the front side of the pan and slide the egg rectangle to the front. Oil the back of the pan as well.

8. Pour the next third of the egg mixture into the pan, using chopsticks to gently lift the cooked egg rectangle and tilt the pan forward, letting the uncooked egg mixture flow under the cooked part. This is how you connect the layers of eggs.

9. Repeat the process of popping bubbles, gently folding the cooked eggs toward you in two stages to achieve a now-bigger egg rectangle.

10. Re-oil the pan and repeat this process with the last third of the egg mixture. When you have completed the final fold, oil the front of the pan, slide the egg rectangle to the front of the pan, and remove from the heat. Use your paddle to press the eggs against the sides of the pan. This gives a more defined rectangular shape, and allows some of the remaining moisture to dissipate without overcooking or otherwise browning the outside.

11. Now you can either remove the *tamagoyaki* to a bamboo sushi mat and use the mat and two rubber bands to press the *tamagoyaki* into its final shape (this is recommended for beginners or if you made a mistake throughout the process). Or you can remove it with the paddle and let it rest on the paddle at an angle. Angling the *tamagoyaki* allows any excess moisture to run off while maintaining the shape and lightness of the omelet.

12. No matter how close you have come to the perfect shape, allow the *tamagoyaki* to cool to room temperature, then slice and serve as you see fit (see the Egg Musubi, page 121, or Hangtown Fry, page 209).

DASHI

MAKES 2 CUPS

2 cups water

¼ cup bonito flakes

2 x 4-inch piece kombu seaweed

This staple ingredient in Japanese cuisine is not unlike broth or stock and can be used accordingly to provide umami to soups and sauces. Dashi will last up to 2 weeks in the fridge and 30 days in the freezer when stored in an airtight container.

Bring the water to near boiling as you would for coffee or tea and pour it over the bonito flakes and kombu in a heatproof medium bowl. Steep for 1 hour, then strain to remove the kombu and residual bonito flakes. Transfer to a storage container and refrigerate until needed.

DASHI PANISSE

MAKES 1 FAUX-GOYAKI

TOOLS
standard loaf pan

1 tablespoon olive oil, for the pan

Dashi (previous recipe)

3 tablespoons mirin

2 teaspoons pure cane sugar

1 tablespoon salt

1 cup chickpea flour

5 egg yolks, whisked lightly with a fork

So, you suck at *tamagoyaki* . . .

It's okay. You're in good company! I was terrible at this for months, and had to ask my friend chef Spencer Bezaire for advice. Leave it to ol' S-Bez to suggest one of the most hacksome hacks of all time!

First, a warning. *Never, ever, ever* tell *anyone from Japan* that you do this. *Under any circumstances, ever.* This is actually a version of a dish from the south of France called panisse. No, it's not named after that restaurant in California, and it's not the girl from down the block that hollers at your boy. (Hey, Shanice, what's up, girl?) Panisse is a pan-fried chickpea-flour dish similar to polenta, but with an almost custard-like center. Try this, your secret's safe with us.

1. Heat the broiler to low. Oil the loaf pan on all sides.

2. In a medium saucepan, combine the dashi, mirin, sugar, and salt and bring to a boil over medium heat. Add the chickpea flour and stir vigorously over low heat until free of any clumps and the chickpea flour seems fully hydrated, about 10 minutes.

3. Let the mixture cool for 10 minutes, then fold in the egg yolks.

4. Spread the mixture evenly in the oiled loaf pan. Broil 3 minutes to firm the top and edges. Cool, then slice in the pan and serve exactly as you would the real-deal *tamagoyaki*.

CODDLED OR B'KLYN EGGS

Coddled eggs are pretty old school and can be as gnarly as the word "coddled" itself. Traditionally, coddled eggs are cooked in a ramekin set inside a water bath over low heat until the whites are nearly set and the yolk is still liquid, and they're mostly known as a place to dip toast.

Here we take dipping somewhere closer to the beyond by adding big flavor components and unique garnishes to our coddling technique. We're breaking all the ramekins and getting down to business . . . cooking our eggs in mason jars, Brooklyn style. Both because people do everything in mason jars in Brooklyn (don't you know?) and because it makes these recipes faster and easier to prepare in advance for parties and snacks.

TOP RIGHT AND BOTTOM LEFT: Manchego and Jamón Eggs with Fried Guava Jelly (page 95); **CENTER:** The Chorizone (page 96); **BOTTOM RIGHT:** It's-Not-Spinach Artichoke Dip (page 97); **TOP LEFT:** B'klyn Eggs (page 94)

B'KLYN EGGS

MAKES 1 SERVING

TOOLS
6- or 8-ounce mason jar with a lid

1 tablespoon unsalted butter

2 eggs

½ teaspoon sea salt

Toast, for dipping

Freshly cracked black pepper

This is the basic coddled egg technique with butter and sea salt. Here we use the same ratio of fat to eggs to get down on it.

1. Grease the inside of the jar with some of the butter and set the remaining butter aside.

2. Add enough water to a saucepan to reach halfway up the sides of the jar when it sits in the pan. Crack 1 egg into the jar, add the reserved butter and the salt, and top with the second egg.

3. Screw the top on the jar, place in the saucepan, and heat the water over medium heat. You will be able to see the whites set inside the jar. After the water starts simmering, the whites should be fully set in about 5 minutes. Remove the jar from the pan, open the lid, and serve with toast and cracked pepper.

TIP: B'klyn Eggs can be assembled in large quantities in advance for a party! Keep them in the fridge for up to 3 days and cook them as needed.

VARIATION: For Truffled Eggs with Scallions and Gruyère, add ¼ cup shredded Gruyère cheese, 3 tablespoons minced scallions (white parts only), and ¼ teaspoon white truffle oil when you add the butter and salt. Serve with sourdough toast.

MANCHEGO AND JAMÓN EGGS WITH FRIED GUAVA JELLY

MAKES 1 SERVING

TOOLS
6- or 8-ounce mason jar with a lid

3 eggs

2 teaspoons fino sherry

¼ cup all-purpose flour

1 cup panko breadcrumbs

One 4-ounce package guava paste, cut into 3 x ½-inch batons (about 12 batons)

¼ cup canola oil, for frying

2 thin slices Jamón Ibérico or Serrano

½ teaspoon Spanish olive oil (the younger the better, for the piquant finish)

¼ cup shredded Manchego cheese

1 teaspoon smoked paprika (or ground Aleppo chile, if available)

½ teaspoon exotic sea salt of choice (we use black lava salt)

Grilled country bread, for dipping

This Spanish-inspired take on coddled eggs comes complete with an irresistible next-level bonus snack: crispy fried guava jelly! While the recipe details setting up one jar's worth of egg-chego goodness, it calls for extra guava snacks, as you'll surely be scarfing them with your fino sherry.

1. In a small bowl, whisk together 1 of the eggs and the sherry. Set up the flour and panko in separate bowls.

2. Dredge the guava batons in the flour, then dip in the sherry-egg wash and roll in the panko. Set aside.

3. Heat a cast-iron or nonstick skillet over medium heat and add the canola oil. Add the jamón to the pan and cook to a crisp (this will happen very quickly). Remove to paper towels to drain.

4. Reduce the heat to low or medium-low and pan-fry the guava batons until nicely browned and crispy, about 1 minute per side, working in batches as needed. Remove to a paper towel to drain.

5. Grease the mason jar with the Spanish olive oil and crack in 1 egg. Add the Manchego and crumble in half the jamón. Top with the remaining egg and jamón.

6. Add enough water to a saucepan to reach halfway up the sides of the jar when it sits in the pan. Screw the top on the jar, place in the pan, and heat the water over medium-high heat. You will be able to see the whites set inside the jar. After the water starts simmering, the whites should be fully set in about 5 minutes. Remove the jar from the pan and open the lid.

7. To serve, top each jar with a baton of fried guava and season with the paprika and the salt of your choice. Serve with grilled country bread.

THE CHORIZONE

MAKES 1 SERVING

TOOLS
6- or 8-ounce mason jar with
a lid

1 ounce (about
2 tablespoons) Homemade
Chorizo (page 198)

2 eggs

1 ounce queso fresco

¼ cup Roasted Salsa Verde
(page 155)

Fresh cilantro, for garnish

1 corn tortilla, toasted,* for
dipping

A chorizo-coddled egg situation topped with queso fresco and roasted tomatillo salsa. Another good excuse to make yourself some chorizo!

1. In a small skillet, cook the chorizo fully over medium heat.

2. Pour the chorizo fat into the mason jar, then crack one egg into the jar. Top with half the chorizo and half the queso fresco. Crack in the second egg and add the rest of the chorizo and queso fresco.

3. Add enough water to a saucepan to reach halfway up the sides of the jar when it sits in the pan. Screw the top on the jar, place in the pan, and heat the water over medium heat. You will be able to see the whites set inside the jar. After the water starts simmering, the whites should be fully set in about 5 minutes. Remove the jar from the pan and open the lid.

4. Top with salsa and a bit of fresh cilantro and serve with toasted tortilla.

* To toast tortillas, place them one at a time on the open flame of a gas burner and use tongs to flip every 30 seconds until nice and toasty.

IT'S-NOT-SPINACH ARTICHOKE DIP

MAKES 1 SERVING

A cheesy, green masterpiece of decadence, free from the bonds of mayo and cream cheese. Huzzaaaah!

TOOLS
6- or 8-ounce Mason jar with a lid

1 tablespoon unsalted butter

1 cup spinach

1 prepared artichoke heart (canned, marinated, or cooked fresh if available)

2 eggs

¼ cup shaved pecorino cheese

½ garlic clove

Pinch of sea salt

Brioche or country bread, toasted, for dipping

1. Grease the mason jar with a small amount of the butter.

2. In a small sauté pan, swirl the remaining butter over medium heat. Add the spinach and sauté it briefly to wilt. Squeeze the spinach and artichoke heart to drain any excess moisture, then chop.

3. Crack 1 egg into the mason jar and top with half of the spinach-artichoke mixture, the remaining butter, and half of the pecorino. Finely grate a bit of the garlic over the pecorino, then crack in the second egg. Top with the remaining spinach-artichoke mixture and pecorino.

4. Add enough water to a saucepan to reach halfway up the sides of the jar when it sits in the pan. Screw the top on the jar, place in the pan, and heat the water over medium heat. You will be able to see the whites set inside the jar. After the water starts simmering, the whites should be fully set in about 5 minutes. Remove the jar from the pan and open the lid.

5. Garnish with a little salt and serve with toasted brioche or country bread for dipping.

FRIED

When you order a fried egg, it can mean one of many things. A sunny-up is a fried egg, so too is an egg cooked over hard or over easy for that matter. It all comes down to a matter of taste, texture, and the temperature of the yolk. Chill. We're about to break it down for you. . . .

THE PERFECT SUNNY-UP

MAKES 1 EGG

1 teaspoon olive oil or unsalted butter

1 egg

Salt and freshly ground black pepper, for serving (optional)

This is our low-temp, high-success method for the perfect sunny side up, with a fully set white with little to no coloration from cooking and a still-liquid yolk.

> This is soooo easy it's sleeeeeaazy . . .
>
> —Julia Child's ghost (overheard while spinning in her grave)

1. Heat an ovenproof nonstick skillet over medium heat. Add the oil and swirl to coat the pan evenly. Crack the egg directly into the pan. Let the white set on the bottom, about 30 seconds to 1 minute, then use a silicone spatula to tap the unset white in three places around the yolk. This breaks the structure of the white that encases the yolk and allows the white to fall away from the yolk slightly and begin to cook.

2. Next, either turn the heat to low or place the pan in the oven. The egg will finish in about 2 minutes. Season as you wish before serving.

PARTY SUNNY-UPS

If the people demand sunny-ups, then sunny-ups they shall have! Making sunny-ups for a large group is as easy as preheating then oiling a griddle plate or nonstick baking sheet in a 425°F oven: 25 minutes should do. Remove the griddle or baking sheet, oil up, and crack away.

The bottom whites should set immediately, then do your spatula tap dance, turn the oven off, and put the griddle back in. As the oven cools, the eggs will finish without overcooking.

TIP 1: Sometimes an extra hand helps here to ensure as many eggs land on the griddle at the same time as possible.

TIP 2: You can hold fully cooked eggs on the griddle in the fridge until you're ready to reheat and serve. Simply give the eggs a light spray with canola oil and cover with a sheet of plastic to keep the yolks from drying out. To reheat, remove the plastic and place the entire pan in a 450°F oven for 2 minutes.

OVER EASY MADE EASY

Carmelo, my friend and poach doctor, once told me that most chefs don't know how to sauté. I agree. Carmelo's favorite thing to watch in a professional kitchen is the moment the chef attempts to instruct a line cook on sauté technique. As in a segment of *America's Funniest Whatever,* the chef will, without fail, toss half the ingredients from his pan onto the floor while the line cook holds back laughter and the chef walks away with a puffed chest.

It's even funnier when the ingredient in question is a fried egg. The way the yolk explodes on the floor at the chef's feet is priceless. It's like the old saying: *If you want to get to Carnegie Hall, be a virtuoso. If you want to flip an egg, just practice.*

HOW TO PRACTICE:

1. Buy a loaf of Wonder bread or fill a zip-top sandwich bag with uncooked rice. Mark one side of a single slice of bread or the bag. (For more accuracy, weigh the rice or bread to 60 grams, the average weight of a large egg.)

2. Hold an empty sauté pan and trace a small oval shape in the air with the nose of the pan, to get a feel for the action of the wrist.

3. Practice flipping the bread or rice, starting with a large oval and working until your oval is teeny tiny and it seems as though the bread or rice flips by itself. (When done correctly there should be almost no sound; this means that when you use a real egg you won't break the yolk with an indelicate flip.)

4. Give this a shot with a few eggs. Start by cooking to sunny-up, fully set. To get the feel of it, start by sliding the edge to the front/nose of the pan before flipping. As you get better, it won't matter where the egg is in the pan or even if you have more than one egg.

HOW TO CHEAT:

1. Fake it by basting the egg with plain butter or oil to set the white on top of the yolk and call it a day.

2. Cover the pan with another pan and increase the heat briefly to high. The remaining uncooked egg white will steam and set over the yolk, giving the impression of a perfect flip. (This is a great cheat code for baked eggs as well—try it to save time making Shakshuka, page 177.)

JUST THE EGG WHITES, PLEASE!

If you're thinking of eating some eggies, it don't matter if they're scrambled whites!

—Michiel Jooksen, Dutch poet

The egg white is the protein superstructure that provides all of the egg's amazing versatility. When misused, poorly separated, or improperly stored, egg whites also offer the potential for textural disaster. Rubber City is not a place in Utah, it's where egg whites go to die. Our goal here is to erase those coordinates from your culinary GPS and get you on the path toward perfect meringues and "just the whites" recipes of all kinds.

SEPARATING AND STORING

It all starts with separating yolks from whites carefully in batches so that if you happen to break a yolk you don't compromise all your work. I begin with a mesh sieve placed over a large bowl and two smaller bowls into which I place the separated whites and yolks 3 or 4 at a time, then strain into the larger container.

There are two primary methods for separating whites: shell to shell and through the hand.

› In the shell-to-shell method you crack the egg and transfer the yolk from one side of the shell to the other, letting the white fall into your bowl while the yolk is contained in the shell. This method tends to leave some white attached to the yolk.

› The through-the-hand method involves cracking an egg into the closed fingers of an open hand and slightly separating the fingers, allowing gravity to pull the white away from the yolk as it falls through the fingers into the bowl. This method is fast but messy and has a higher potential for broken yolks.

Once perfectly separated and strained so as to be free of any shell fragments, store egg whites in an airtight container in the fridge. Use as soon as possible for scrambling applications and up to 5 days later for whipping or baking.

SCRAMBLED WHITES

Scrambled whites can be a rubbery bore if not treated with the same care as the many different styles of scrambled whole eggs. Though if you're eating just the whites, chances are you're avoiding the yolk for some sort of "health" reason. *Get ready—here it comes—truth bomb!* While the yolk is high in cholesterol, it is also packed with protein, vitamins, and essential fatty acids. For healthy individuals, the nutritional value of the yolk far exceeds that of the white. But, just as haters gonna hate, players gonna play. That's where the whites come in—they're slamming with protein, low in calories, and high in potassium, which is particularly helpful for heart health and muscle building and recovery. So how do you scramble them up while avoiding the Naugahyde effect? It's all about straining and less about fat.

STEP ONE: Separate egg whites into a mesh sieve. Make sure you keep the whites free of yolk. Using a rubber spatula, stir the whites to push them through the sieve. This breaks up the firm inner white and combines it evenly with the loose outer white.

STEP TWO: Use medium heat and a little oil or fat of your choice to cook the whites in a nonstick pan. Heat the pan, add the oil, swirl to coat, add the whites.

STEP THREE: Either use a silicone spatula to make an Egg Shop Scramble (the pretty one, page 57) or stir the whites as you would for a Classic French Soft Scramble (page 55).

STEP FOUR: *Turn off the heat* and cover the pan for about 1 minute. This lets the whites finish cooking by steaming, which will subtly puff them up. *Boom. Knowledge.* (Please mail your Anti-Naugahyde Association membership fee to 151 Elizabeth Street, New York, NY 10012.)

WHIPPING WHITES FOR MERINGUES AND SOUFFLÉ

One of the most amazing things about the white of the egg is its protein structure. When whipped with a whisk or in the bowl of a stand mixer, the protein structure breaks down, and re-forms, tightening and trapping air and moisture. A working knowledge of the process will come in handy in a number of applications. Here are the Big Three: meringue, soufflé, and mousse.

For a meringue, sugar will be incorporated into the whites as described on the following page, and for a soufflé or mousse, the addition of sugar, salt, or lemon juice will be unique to the recipe. Regardless, there are two pivotal rules for whipping egg whites: *know your stages* and *prevent deflation*.

KNOW YOUR STAGES

Recipes commonly refer to these stages as soft, medium, and hard/stiff peak.

SOFT PEAKS occur when the whisk or whip can make subtle tracks or peaks in the fluffy whites. When you scoop up some whites with the end of the whisk, the little curl of white will quickly fold onto itself without maintaining structure.

MEDIUM PEAKS occur when the tracks are well defined with each pass and won't dissipate. When scooped with the whisk, the structure of the white is maintained even though it folds over like the curled tip of a genie's shoe or some sort of elfin chapeau.

HARD OR STIFF PEAKS are just that. They hold their shape, and when scooped they stand at attention like the tip of the Matterhorn. Yodel if you like—it makes the chocolate that much sweeter!

PREVENT DEFLATION

KEEP IT CLEAN: Always use a very clean, very dry bowl and whisk and make sure there are no specks of yolk in your separated whites.

KEEP IT TO TEMP: Letting the whites come to room temperature works wonders.

DROP SOME ACID: Cream of tartar, vinegar, and lemon juice all do the trick. Remember, acids denature or break down proteins, which is the first stage of restructuring. Just a pinch of acid per egg white works wonders in building a stronger final protein structure. Cream of tartar specifically aids in maintaining structure when heat is applied to a meringue in the case of the brûléed top of a meringue pie, or the nice, crisp, shiny outer edges of a giant meringue cookie.

KNOW YOUR MERINGUE

On one hand, Italians offer us so many excellent hand gestures, pasta dishes, and sports cars. On the other hand, the Swiss provide precision timepieces, neutrality, and milk chocolate. In life it can be difficult to choose between two nations. Thankfully in cooking there are recipes to help us make the distinction!

ITALIAN MERINGUE involves adding sugar cooked to the soft ball stage (240°F) to whites that have been whipped to medium peaks, then finishing the meringue by whipping to stiff glossy peaks.

SWISS MERINGUE involves dissolving the sugar into the whites in a double boiler before whipping first to medium peaks on high speed, then to hard/stiff peaks on a lower speed.

THE COMMON MERINGUE (aka French Meringue) involves no heating process when whipping the whites and sugar.

In short: Different techniques for different uses. Italian meringues are made for room-temperature products like buttercreams and nougat and meringue topping for pies. Swiss meringues are typically folded into other ingredients and used for their more delicate quality. Common meringue is used in cookies and other confections that will later be cooked, rendering them safe to eat. Regardless of your level of diplomacy, meringue dominance is just a ratio away.

ONE MERINGUE, THREE TECHNIQUES: ITALIAN, SWISS, COMMON (FRENCH)

MAKES ENOUGH MERINGUE
FOR ONE MILE-HIGH BLACK
BOTTOM PIE (PAGE 267)

240 grams egg whites (from about 6 large eggs)

240 grams pure cane sugar (about 1 cup)

½ teaspoon cream of tartar

No need to be intimidated here—simply remember that the ratio for perfect meringue is 1:1 egg whites to sugar by weight, and just whip it good!

For **ITALIAN MERINGUE**: Italian meringue is our choice when it comes to making a long-lasting and lofty pie. Whip the eggs and cream of tartar to medium peaks while heating the sugar in a saucepan over medium heat. When the sugar reaches 240°F, immediately begin pouring it into the whites in a steady stream while cranking your mixer to high speed and finishing the meringue to stiff, glossy peaks.

For **SWISS MERINGUE**: Stir the egg whites, sugar, and cream of tartar in a double boiler until the sugar is dissolved and the whites have reached about 130°F. Be careful to work over low heat and keep the sides of the bowl clean. Then whip at high speed until you reach medium peaks, then back off a bit and finish slowly to stiff peaks.

For **COMMON (FRENCH) MERINGUE**: Just say *oui!* and whip the ingredients together at high speed, adding the sugar gradually.

CRISPY PUFFED EGG-'TATER CHIPS

MAKES ABOUT 30 CHIPS

6 egg whites

½ teaspoon cream of tartar

1 cup potato flakes

3 tablespoons potato starch

½ teaspoon cayenne pepper

½ cup Chinatown Chicken Stock (page 212)

Canola oil, for frying

Sea salt

Malt vinegar powder

1. To make the chips, whip the egg whites with the cream of tartar to medium peaks (see page 104), then gently fold in the potato flakes, potato starch, and cayenne. Place the egg mixture on a large piece of plastic wrap and shape it into a log about 6 inches long and 3 inches in diameter. Freeze for at least 1 hour before you are ready to use.

2. Pour 1 inch of canola oil into a medium saucepan or a deep cast-iron pot and heat over medium heat to 350°F.

3. Working in batches, slice 3 or 4 thin rounds (about ⅛ inch thick) from the frozen egg log (return the log to the freezer before slicing the next batch, as the chips hold much better in the fryer when completely frozen). Use a spatula to lower the chips into the oil (*be careful*—the oil will pop as these babies fry!) When the chips are golden brown and crispy, remove them with a slotted spoon and set them aside on paper towels to drain and dry. When nearly cool, sprinkle them with salt and malt vinegar powder to taste. (If you don't intend to cook all the chips at once, no problem—the log works just like frozen cookie dough, so use as needed for up to 2 weeks.)

THE SANDWICH ARTS

A well-made sandwich is a work of art. A sandwich starts with the main ingredient, the one for which the sandwich is named—the focal point—but after that, composition is everything. At Egg Shop, the star of the show is usually the egg. This is true for a sandwich like the Pepper Boy! (page 122), 60 percent of which is a fluffy mountain of scrambled eggs dotted with sautéed bell pepper and rich with melted Gruyère. Every component stands in support of the main, the egg.

A sandwich is an experience from start to finish and bite to bite. A good sandwich is memorable, easy to eat, and filling without being overwhelming. The recipes that follow offer insight into how we create sandwiches at Egg Shop, and we hope they're inspiring when it comes to making new masterpieces at home.

THE BEAST

MAKES 1 SANDWICH

1 French Hero (page 14)

1 egg

½ cup Pulled Pork Carnitas
(page 112)

¼ cup Chipotle Bourbon
Ketchup (page 146)

3 tablespoons Pickled Red
Onions (page 220)

5 fresh cilantro sprigs

Pinch of sea salt

This is the big boy that leaves you wanting more. The "Beast" is a Cal-Mex influenced pulled pork sandwich with a sunny-up egg uniting sweet and spicy notes against the brightness of pickled onion and fresh cilantro.

1. Split the hero and toast in a large cast-iron pan. Prepare the egg sunny-up (page 100) and heat the carnitas (this can be done in the same pan if you're careful to keep the meat and egg separate; the rendered fat from heating the carnitas will be all you need for the sunny-up).

2. Spread half the ketchup on the bottom half of the hero and top with pickled onions. Add the remaining ketchup to the carnitas and mix. Top the onions with carnitas, then with the egg and cilantro. Finish with sea salt and shove in your face.

PULLED PORK CARNITAS

**MAKES ENOUGH FOR
8 TO 10 SANDWICHES**

DRY RUB

¼ cup ground coriander

¼ cup ground cumin

¼ cup garlic powder

¼ cup raw cane sugar

1 cup salt

6 tablespoons dried oregano

CARNITAS

3 pounds boneless pork butt, cut into six 8-ounce pieces

One 12-ounce bottle Mexican Coca-Cola

Zest from 1 orange

1 red onion, quartered

1 cinnamon stick

1 quart (32 ounces) vegetable oil

½ pound (2 sticks) unsalted butter or 1 cup rendered pork fat if you're feeling sinister

1. To make the rub, in a medium bowl, combine the coriander, cumin, garlic powder, sugar, salt, and oregano and whisk well.

2. To make the carnitas, preheat the oven to 325°F.

3. Rub the pork generously with the rub (for deepest flavor, do this up to 48 hours before roasting and keep in the fridge). Place in a deep roasting pan and add the Coca-Cola, orange zest, onion, cinnamon, oil, and butter. The pork should be just barely submerged in liquid. Roast until the pork shreds easily with a fork, about 4 hours. Let cool in the liquid. Use a fork to shred the pork.

REFORMER

MAKES 1 SANDWICH

2 slices multigrain bread, toasted

Avo Smash (optional; page 117)

2 slices heirloom tomato

1 egg white, scrambled (see page 103)

3 tablespoons crumbled Marinated Feta (recipe follows)

¼ cup baby spinach

"Did you sign up for Reformer or Mat class?" If you have any idea what this means, then you'll appreciate this Pilates-inspired sandwich creation. It's healthy and clean, and thanks to the feta cheese, the Reformer has a little Greek flair, just like Mr. Pilates himself. This is egg white fitness fuel in sandwich form.

Build the sandwich as follows: toast, avo smash (if using), tomato, scrambled egg white, feta, spinach, toast!

MARINATED FETA

MAKES 8 OUNCES

6 tablespoons pine nuts

1 teaspoon cumin seeds

1 teaspoon fennel seeds

4 garlic cloves, smashed

1 teaspoon red chile flakes

2 fresh rosemary sprigs

1 cup olive oil

6 tablespoons Meyer Lemon Oil (page 227)

One 8-ounce block feta cheese (preferably packed in water rather than olive oil)

1 x 3-inch strip of orange zest

1. In a small saucepan over low heat, toast the pine nuts, cumin seeds, and fennel seeds until the pine nuts are just beginning to brown. (Be very careful! Pine nuts burn quite easily.)

2. Remove the pan from the heat and add the garlic, chile flakes, rosemary, and olive oil. Stir well, then put the pan back over low heat and heat until fragrant, about 20 minutes. Let cool to room temperature, then add the Meyer lemon oil.

2. Drain the feta from its brine and put it in a nonreactive airtight container. Pour the oil mixture over the cheese and store in the fridge until ready to use, or up to 10 days. The flavors will intensify over time, so use quickly if you prefer a more subtle feta experience.

EGG SHOP B.E.C.

1 Panini Roll (page 13)

2 tablespoons Tomato Jam
(page 152)

4 Fresh Pickled Jalapeños
(page 223)

2 ounces sharp white
cheddar (we use Shelburne
Farms, Grafton Village, or
McCadam)

3 slices Black Forest or
applewood-smoked bacon

1 egg

Pinch of sea salt, for
garnish

Torn flat-leaf parsley
leaves, for garnish

This, ladies and gentlemen, is the face that launched a thousand ships: the signature Egg Shop version of a standard B.E.C. The star of this sandwich is a sunny-up egg with the yolk broken into the roll before serving, but the tomato jam is gearing up to steal the show at any moment. Sharp melted New England cheddar counters the sweet and savory jam and cuts the salt of the perfectly crisped bacon. If an egg were going clubbing, it would wear this sandwich to get laid.

---

1. Preheat the oven to 400°F or turn the broiler to low, if the setting is available.

2. Split the panini roll in half and spread the tomato jam evenly on the bottom half. Top with the jalapeños. Place the cheddar on the top side of the roll and lay both halves on a baking sheet. Set aside.

3. In a small cast-iron or nonstick skillet, cook the bacon over medium-high heat until crisp but not burned or dry. Place the bacon on top of the cheddar and broil the open sandwich until the cheese is melted and the roll is slightly toasted on the edges.

4. Meanwhile, crack the egg into the bacon fat and cook it using the sunny-up method on page 100. When the white is fully set, break the yolk slightly with the back of a fork or the tip of a knife and let it spread over the egg. Cook briefly, but do not allow the yolk to set.

5. Remove the sandwich from the broiler, place the egg on top of the tomato jam and jalapeños, and close the sandwich. Garnish with a pinch of sea salt and torn fresh parsley.

AVO AND EGG

MAKES 1 SANDWICH

½ cup Avo Smash (recipe follows)

2 slices multigrain bread (square Pullman loaf, if possible), toasted

3 slices heirloom tomato

1 poached egg (page 49)

Pinch of Summer Herb Salt (page 221)

1 teaspoon Meyer Lemon Oil (page 227)

1 Meyer lemon wedge

Fresh herb salad of your choice (page 26)

In 1795 Cpt. Jeremiah Wright Avotooaste created the avo-toast as a delightful tea snack for his ship's crew on their long voyage to the untamed continent known as Australia.

Just kidding. This simple dish of smashed avocado, citrus, salt, and seeded toast is the basis of our Avo and Egg. Avo-toast is huge. And it's wildly popular because it's delicious *and* healthy. At Egg Shop, Avocado Toast is a double-lightning-bolt mountain of fresh smashed avocado, ripe heirloom tomato, and perfectly poached eggs finished delicately with fresh lemon juice, herbs, and sea salt.

---

1. Spread avo smash on both pieces of toast. Cut one slice in diagonally in half and top the other with tomato slices and the poached egg.

2. To serve, slightly separate the halved avo toast and place the other half with the tomato and poached egg on top. Finish the toasts with the herb salt, lemon oil, and a squeeze of Meyer lemon juice. Top with a little fresh herb salad.

AVO SMASH

MAKES 3 CUPS

6 avocados

Juice of 2 Meyer lemons

1 teaspoon kosher salt

Halve, pit, and peel the avocados. In a large bowl, use a fork to mash the avocado halves. *Remember that you aren't making guacamole!* The smash should have some funky chunk to it, with some smooth parts, some baby bits, and a few big mama bits! Add the lemon juice and salt and give one final mix to combine. (This will last for about 2 days in an airtight container, with plastic wrap pressed onto the surface of the smash to prevent oxidation. Pressing down eliminates any air pockets that might also cause the pesky brown spots.)

STEAK AND EGG

1 French Hero (page 14)

1 egg

4 ounces beef tenderloin, shaved thin (ask your butcher to run it on a deli-slicer!) and chopped

Kosher salt and freshly ground black pepper

¼ cup Chimi-Chili Relish (page 154)

3 tablespoons Caramelized Onion Aioli (page 149)

¼ cup Pickled Red Onions (page 220)

½ cup baby kale or hearty greens of your choice

Pinch of sea salt

Imagine the perfect Philly cheesesteak sandwich: tender chopped beef smothered in grilled onions, peppers, and melted cheese, so juicy and salty and perfect it can hardly be contained by bread. Now take that sandwich to Argentina, teach it to tango, and let it fall in love. This thing will break your heart.

Split and toast the hero and prepare the egg sunny-up (page 100). In a cast-iron skillet, cook the steak over medium-high heat until well browned and season it with salt and pepper. Add the relish to the steak and stir quickly to combine. Spread the aioli on both sides of the hero and lay the pickled onions on the bottom half. Top with the steak, sunny-up, and greens. Finish with a pinch of sea salt, add the top roll, and . . . shove in face.

EGG MUSUBI

MAKES 1 MUSUBI

TOOLS
musubi press (optional)

SUSHI RICE

1 cup sushi rice

1 teaspoon pure cane sugar

1 teaspoon sea salt

¼ cup unseasoned rice vinegar

2 tablespoons hot water

TO ASSEMBLE 1 SERVING

¼ cup sushi rice, at room temperature

⅓ nori sheet

1 teaspoon furikake (a sushi garnish of seaweed and sesame seeds)

2 tablespoons Pickled Carrots (page 222)

1 tablespoon Musubi Sauce (page 157)

1 slice Tamagoyaki (page 89)

You surf, brah? Shaka, brah. Wan go musubi? 7-Eleven, brah!? Nah, donkey!? Wan Egg Shop. . . . Shaka, brah. Shaka, brah.

This is the only sushi-like food worthy of being breakfast. Sidestepping the tradition and preservatives of the Japanese approach, we trade healthy pickled carrot and *tamagoyaki* for SPAM in our version of the Hawaiian staple. Mahalo.

1. To make the sushi rice, rinse the rice with cold water in a mesh sieve until the water runs clear. Drain the rice and combine with 1½ cups water in a small saucepan with a tight-fitting lid. Soak the rice for 20 to 30 minutes, uncover, and bring to a boil over medium-high heat. Stir with a fork to keep the rice from sticking to the bottom of the pan. When the rice water reaches a boil, cover, reduce the heat to low, and cook for 20 minutes, then remove from heat and leave covered for 10 minutes. Uncover and sprinkle with the sugar, salt, vinegar, and hot water. Fluff the rice with a rice paddle or rubber spatula to incorporate the seasoning.

2. To assemble 1 serving, place the sushi rice centered on top of the nori and form into a 3 x 4-inch rectangle. Top with the furikake, pickled carrots, musubi sauce, and a slice of *tamagoyaki*. Fold the nori up and over the musubi from one side then the other. Use wet hands to seal the nori as you fold it over. If using a musubi press, simply follow the instructions for a perfectly squared musubi. (The rectangular shape of the musubi comes from the ingenious use of a SPAM can as a mold. We don't advocate eating canned ham, but it's kind of fun to use the can.)

PEPPER BOY!

MAKES 1 SANDWICH

3 slices maple-cured black pepper bacon (we use North Country Smokehouse)

1 Panini Roll (page 13)

1 tablespoon vegetable oil

3 tablespoons diced green bell pepper

3 eggs

¼ cup shredded Gruyère cheese

2 tablespoons Caramelized Onion Aioli (page 149)

Freshly cracked black pepper

Pinch of sea salt

A Denver omelet is good, but this is better, because it's a sandwich. And instead of tired old ham, Pepper Boy! demands premium maple-cured black pepper bacon and gooey, earthy Gruyère. It's a superhero. Simply cry out when you're in need and *Pepper Boy!!!!!* will be there to vanquish the pangs of hunger with one swift kick in the huevos.

1. In a nonstick skillet, cook the bacon over medium heat until crisp. Split and toast the roll in the same pan. Set the bacon and roll aside.

2. Add a little vegetable oil to the pan, add the peppers and sauté for about 1 minute. Add the eggs and cook them in a soft scramble (page 55), incorporating the peppers. Top with the Gruyère and the reserved bacon. Remove from the heat and cover the pan. This will melt the cheese perfectly and warm the bacon as well.

3. Spread both sides of the roll with aioli and use a spatula to place the eggs on the roll. Finish with cracked pepper to taste and a bit of sea salt, add the top roll, and shove it in your face!

TIP: For a gluten-free version, simply hollow out a bell pepper, spread the inside with aioli, and fill with the soft scramble. Top with cheese and bacon and broil briefly to melt the cheese.

EGG SALAD SANDWICH

MAKES 1 SANDWICH

2 slices multigrain bread, toasted

2 thick slices heirloom tomato

½ cup Egg Shop Egg Salad (page 65)

½ cup baby kale or greens of your choice

"That's Hot!" Hot Sauce (page 150)

Our version of this classic composition is updated with a little heat, healthfulness, and texture. Our mayo-free egg salad, with its fresh dill and scallion, balance against crisp and sweet baby kale and juicy tomato for a perfect textural experience on multigrain toast. This is not your average cellophane-wrapped, white bread, Miracle Whipped and dipped, airport picnic. . . . It's a simple, thoughtful thing, this sandwich. We promise you won't be disappointed.

Build the sandwich as follows: Toast, tomato, egg salad, greens, hot sauce to your liking, toast.

NOTE: Being healthy is super cool. Who doesn't want to live to be 179 years old and die with perfect abs? Longevity and beach bods aside, delicious fried chicken is also *super f*%$ing cool!* When you use it as a condiment on a sandwich that already has a standout main ingredient, it gets even cooler. Insert 1 piece Egg Shop Fried Chicken (page 233) in this sandwich for a most brodacious game changer, and an epic hangover cure. Remember—laugh like you've never laughed, dance as if no one is watching, and eat like you could die tomorrow! (Carpe crispy.)

FISH OUT OF WATER

MAKES 1 SANDWICH

2 slices Hot Seeded Rye (page 19), toasted

1 tablespoon Caperberry Mustard (page 153)

½ small Persian (mini) or other seedless cucumber, thinly sliced

2 ounces Cognac-Cured Gravlax (page 127) or mild smoked salmon

1 Egg Shop Pickled Egg (page 77)

2 or 3 fresh dill sprigs

This Nordic-inspired breakfast sandwich balances salty and sour elements with delicate smoked fish and seeded rye toast. Made with our take on the pickled egg, this is the antithesis of a lox on a cream cheese bagel, resulting in a sandwich whose composition presents simplicity, refinement, and freshness by effortlessly balancing strong flavors.

Build the sandwich as follows: Toast, mustard, cucumber, salmon, pickled egg, dill, toast!

COGNAC-CURED GRAVLAX

MAKES 1 POUND

1 pound salmon fillet (we use wild-caught Alaskan King Salmon)

2 ounces Cognac

1 teaspoon cracked black pepper

1 teaspoon coriander seeds, toasted and crushed*

Zest of 1 lemon

¼ cup kosher salt

¼ cup pure cane sugar

¼ cup chopped fresh dill (optional)

1. Remove the salmon skin and any pin bones. In a shallow baking dish, pour the Cognac over the salmon to coat it thoroughly. Season with the pepper, coriander, and lemon zest. Cover with plastic wrap and refrigerate for 30 minutes.

2. Combine the salt, sugar, and dill (if using) and rub the salmon lightly with the mixture, then pack the salmon in the remaining mixture so that it is surrounded fully. Cover with plastic wrap and let rest at room temperature for 30 minutes.

3. Drain any liquid from the baking dish and weight the salmon down with a plate and heavy can. Refrigerate for 24 hours, flip the fish and drain any liquid from the dish, and refrigerate for another 24 hours. Give the salmon a light rinse and pat dry. Slice the salmon thin and serve (it will keep for 7 days in the fridge), or freeze it for future use.

* Toast coriander seeds in a small cast-iron pan over low heat until very fragrant, then crush with a mortar and pestle or simply use the broad side of a chef's knife as you would crush a garlic clove.

EVERYTHING TO ME

MAKES 1 SANDWICH

1 Everything Biscuit
(page 253), halved and
toasted

2 Bibb lettuce leaves

¼ cup Smoked Whitefish
Schmear (recipe follows)

1 sliced heirloom tomato

1 sunny-up egg (page 100)

2 fresh dill sprigs

¼ cup Horseradish Cream
(optional; page 158)

This is a shout-out to all the bagels that said I'd never amount to nothin', that called the police on me when I was just try'na make some biscuits to feed my hunger. It's all good, baby, babay. This sandwich is breakfast opulence, perfection in biscuit form, decked with a Brooklyn super-schmear South Williamsburg–style and topped with a fried egg. And if you don't know, now you know.

Build the sandwich as follows: biscuit, lettuce, whitefish schmear, tomato, sunny-up, dill, cream (if using), biscuit!

SMOKED WHITEFISH SCHMEAR

MAKES 1½ CUPS

8 ounces cleaned smoked
whitefish

2 tablespoons Caramelized
Onion Aioli (page 149)

2 scallions, white and light
green parts only, minced

¼ cup celery leaves,
chopped

1 tablespoon minced Hot
Pickles (page 228)

1 teaspoon Caperberry
Mustard (page 153)

1 tablespoon minced celery

Zest and juice of 1 lemon

2 tablespoons olive oil

Pinch of celery salt

Pinch of cayenne pepper

Flake the smoked whitefish with a fork into a medium bowl. Mix in the aioli, scallions, celery, hot pickles, mustard, and celery, and finish with the celery salt, cayenne pepper, olive oil, and lemon zest. This salad will keep well in the fridge for up to 7 days in an airtight container.

NOTE: Be careful to remove all the little bones when cleaning the smoked whitefish.

B.E.C. BURGER

MAKES 1 BURGER

Two 4-ounce prime 80/20 beef patties

Kosher salt and freshly ground black pepper

Components of 1 Egg Shop B.E.C. (page 115 but made with 2 sunny-up eggs instead of 1

¼ cup Herb Salad (page 26)

Take the Egg Shop signature B.E.C. and insert two prime 80/20 beef patties pressed thin and grilled to a perfect medium-rare, then add another egg. Ever had a double cheeseburger where the cheese was replaced with sunny-up eggs? Neither had we, so we made this perverted patty-melt hybrid!

1. Roll the beef patties extra thin between 2 sheets of parchment paper using a rolling pin or even an old wine bottle. They should be about ¼ inch thick! Season generously with salt and pepper. In a cast-iron pan, sear the burger patties and cook to medium-rare, pressing with a spatula to keep thin.

2. Top the base of the B.E.C. with one of the patties, break the yolk of 1 sunny-up egg on the patty, and top with the egg and the second patty.

3. Prepare the extra sunny-up using the same pan and all of that good salty rendered burger goodness.

4. Top the burger with the second egg and the herb salad and close the book. You're done. You did it. You win!

17 HAM AND EGG SANDWICHES—
OR, LOSING BETS AND HAVING TO MAKE A LOT OF SANDWICHES

One day after a very long lunch service the staff was "unwinding" at the local. A friendly debate began regarding which menu item had been the most popular the previous month. We went back and forth between the Avo Egg, the B.E.C., and the El Camino. Unwinding, as we tend to do it, usually results in placing bets on nonsensical and harmless things.

At the time, Sarah Schneider (Egg Shop Founder) was particularly interested in ham and egg sandwiches and organizing a tasting for possible new menu items. I was most interested in being right about the bet, as I was fully convinced I would emerge victorious. I was so confident I asked Sarah to pick a number between 1 and 20. She picked 17, a bold move. I was hoping for a number under 10. But, unwinding as we were, the bet proceeded and the stakes were named. If Sarah was correct regarding which item had been the most popular, I would be obligated to create and prepare a tasting of 17 variations of the ham and egg sandwich. I did not emerge victorious.

What follows is my creative exercise, a visual guide in miniature to those 17 sandwiches, with recipes for 3 of our favorites following. Cheers!

1. **CUBANO CON HUEVO:** a Cuban sandwich with a fried egg

2. **HAMAGATCHI:** hand roll with wasabi tobiko, avocado, diced ginger ham, tamago, and quail egg

3. **EASTERWICH:** Ginger honey ham and red-eye gravy on sourdough with asparagus

4. **GREEN EGGS AND HAM:** pesto, double-cream ricotta, prosciutto crudo, pizza bianca

5. **HAM MADAME:** a croque madame—style toad in a hole

6. **HAMBLIN' MAN:** sweet corn pudding, fried bologna, fried egg

7. **GOING HAM:** a double-decker biscuit of chicken-fried ham and ham-fried chicken, with sunny-ups

8. **HAM RADIO:** 4 hams from across the globe, buttered toast, fried egg

9. **HAMDLEBAR MUSTACHE:** house-smoked honey ham, house-made beer mustard, house-made pickles, house-made egg bread, super-local peasant cheese, and Sriracha

10. **DER HAMMEISTER:** Bavarian beer cheese, caraway pickled onions, Black Forest ham, Hamburg hot mustard, and a fried egg on a pretzel roll

11. **BOURBON BOY:** Benton's country ham, stone-ground grits, and fried egg on a jalapeño-cheddar biscuit with jalapeño jelly and sorghum on the side

12. **WILL.I.HAM:** black-eyed pea hummus, Ferguson ham, herb mustard, egg over hard on a biscuit

13. **HAMSON AND DELILAH:** hummus, sliced hard-boiled egg, turkey ham, and fattoush on pita

14. **HAMBLE ON ROSE:** spicy rose hip jelly, fried egg, and Canadian bacon on San Francisco sourdough

15. **I HAM WHO I HAM:** a triple-decker white bread and country ham stairway to ham heaven, with kale frittata caught in the middle

16. **I HAM WHAT I HAM:** ham steak with creamed spinach spread and shaved green bean slaw on a sesame seed kaiser roll, with olive oil on the side

17. **HOLIDAY IN WAIKIKI:** grilled pickled pineapple, sunny-up, fried ham, pan con tomate

HOLIDAY IN WAIKIKI

MAKES 1 SANDWICH

PAN CON TOMATE SAUCE

1 garlic clove

1 teaspoon sea salt

1 teaspoon pure cane sugar

1 teaspoon red wine vinegar

1 deep-red heirloom tomato

3 tablespoons olive oil

TO ASSEMBLE 1 SANDWICH

1 Panini Roll (page 13), halved and toasted

2 tablespoons Pan Con Tomate Sauce

2 thick slices Garlic and Ginger Glazed Party Ham (page 135) or spiral sliced honey glazed ham

¼ cup Pickled Pineapple (page 222)

1 sunny-up egg (page 103)

This ham and egg sandwich is a riff on a Hawaiian pizza, pairing grilled pickled pineapple with crispy ham and fried egg. The sweet-and-savory game is on point with this one, from the hint of garlic in the tomato sauce to the salty ham and fried egg to the sweet-and-spicy charred pineapple.

Pan con tomate is traditionally made to order by rubbing toasted bread with a garlic clove, then raw tomato, and finishing with salt, olive oil, and maybe a bit of vinegar. Here we speed up the process but maintain that fresh, rustic glory.

Note that the ham must be brined well in advance!

---

1. To make the pan con tomate sauce, crush the garlic clove with a mortar and pestle, or simply finely grate or mince the garlic into a medium bowl. Add the salt, sugar, and vinegar and let rest 30 minutes. Shred the tomato on the large holes of a box grater and add it to the bowl. (If you have anger issues or are feeling a need for a more tactile expression of your sensuality, crush the tomato by hand slowly. Go ahead, bruise it to bits and revel in the pulp running through your fingers. Weird . . .) Add the olive oil and stir. You can use this right away, or make ahead and store in the fridge for up to 4 days, but always serve at room temperature.

2. To assemble 1 sandwich, build it as follows: bottom roll, pan con tomate sauce, ham, pickled pineapple, more pan con tomate sauce, sunny-up, top roll.

GARLIC AND GINGER GLAZED PARTY HAM

MAKES 1 BIG-ASS HAM

BRINE AND HAM

1 gallon cold water

3 cups packed brown sugar

12 ounces kosher salt

1 ½ ounces curing salt

2 cups cold-brew coffee
(page 32)

1 large knob fresh ginger,
peeled

2 garlic heads, halved
across the equator

2 medium red onions,
roughly chopped

1 party (boneless) ham,
about 4 pounds

HAM GLAZE

½ cup minced fresh ginger

½ cup minced garlic

1 cup honey

1 cup tamari

¼ cup cider vinegar

½ cup packed brown sugar

1. To brine the ham, in a large pot, combine 3 cups of the water, the brown sugar, and salts and heat over medium heat until the solids are dissolved. Let cool briefly, then add the remaining 3 quarts and 1 cup cold water, the coffee, ginger, garlic, onions, and ham. The ham must stay submerged in the liquid, so weight it down with several small plates. Brine the ham for at least 7 days in the fridge.

2. Preheat the oven to 250°F.

3. Remove the ham from the brine, pat it dry, set it in a roasting pan with a rack, and tent it with foil. Bake until the internal temperature reaches 145°F, 5 to 6 hours.

4. At this point the ham is insanely delicious as is. You could even cool it, cut it in half, and eat half of it plain throughout the week, or freeze it. But . . . why not glaze the whole darn thing and really knock some socks off?

5. Preheat the oven to 400°F.

6. Gently peel the skin from the ham, taking care to leave the fat cap intact. Score the fat cap on the ham in a crisscross diamond kind of pattern.

7. To make the ham glaze, in a medium saucepan, combine the ginger, garlic, honey, tamari, vinegar, and brown sugar and bring to a brief simmer over medium heat to dissolve the sugar.

8. Coat the ham liberally with the glaze and roast, uncovered, for 30 minutes, basting every 10 minutes with the pan drippings as they mix with the glaze at the bottom of the pan. Try to resist shoving hot ham slices in your face—save some for your guests.

GREEN EGGS AND HAM

MAKES 1 SANDWICH

DOUBLE CREAM RICOTTA

4 cups whole milk

2 cups heavy cream

½ tablespoon sea salt

Zest and juice of 1 Meyer lemon

½ teaspoon cider vinegar

TO ASSEMBLE 1 OPEN-FACED SANDWICH

One 3 x 5-inch slice Pizza Bianca Focaccia (page 23)

3 tablespoons Double Cream Ricotta

2 tablespoons Classic Pesto (page 221)

Plenty of shaved pecorino

4 ounces prosciutto cotto (Italian boiled ham), thinly sliced

1 egg

Pinch of red chile flakes

This is an ode to our good friends and neighbors at Di Palo's Fine Foods. With a pizza bianca bread transporter smeared with our homemade ricotta, the Italian flavor profiles come together in an open-faced panino, fit for a table on the piazza, or on Elizabeth Street.

P.S.: Do make this ricotta. It will be the creamiest and smoothest ricotta you've ever tried. It falls somewhere between ricotta and mascarpone, and melts in your mouth like high-fat butter.

---

1. To make the ricotta, in a large saucepan, combine the milk and cream and bring to 180°F over medium heat, being very careful not to let it boil. Add the salt, lemon zest, lemon juice, and vinegar and stir to combine. Remove from the heat and set aside to rest 10 minutes.

2. Set a colander over a large bowl and line the colander with cheesecloth. Using a measuring cup or a large ladle, give the pot another good stir. You will see that the curds and whey have separated. Gently ladle the curds into the colander. If you're going for ultimate richness, try not to break up the curds as you make this transfer.

3. Let the ricotta drain in the fridge for about 2 hours, then remove it from the cheesecloth and store it in an airtight container in the fridge, where it will last for 7 days. (If you like, drain some of the whey from the bowl and reserve it for another use, such as a great probiotic lemonade.)

4. To assemble 1 open-faced sandwich, preheat the oven to 425°F or turn the broiler to low.

5. Set the pizza bianca on a baking sheet or in an ovenproof dish. Dot it with dollops of ricotta, drizzle with 1 tablespoon of the pesto, and top with pecorino and the prosciutto cotto.

6. Either crack the egg directly on the top and bake until the egg is set, about 10 minutes, or prepare a sunny-up (page 100) and bake the pizza bianca separately until slightly crisp on the edges, then lay the egg on top.

7. To finish, top the egg with remaining 1 tablespoon pesto, plenty of pecorino, and a pinch of chile flakes. Cut it in half if you intend to share, but don't feel bad if you scarf this down solo.

CUBANO CON HUEVO

MAKES 1 SANDWICH

YELLOW MUSTARD SAUCE

¼ cup Dijon mustard

3 tablespoons mayo

3 tablespoons honey

2 tablespoons cider vinegar

1 teaspoon ground turmeric

Pinch of salt

TO ASSEMBLE 1 SANDWICH

1 French Hero (page 14), split

3 tablespoons Yellow Mustard Sauce

4 ounces (½ cup) Pulled Pork Carnitas (page 112)

2 ounces thinly sliced Garlic and Ginger Glazed Party Ham (page 135)

12 slices Hot Pickles (page 228)

¼ cup shredded Gruyère cheese

2 tablespoons Hot Pickle Butter (page 81)

1 egg

I can't think of a Cuban sandwich without remembering the nineties. . . . Jim Carrey doing Cuban Pete in *The Mask,* or "Mambo No. 5" by Lou Bega, or Will Smith singing "Bienvenido a Miami." It was a cheesy, weird time for cultural crossovers, and all those superficial attempts to pacify our xenophobia. Authenticity was *sssssssmokin'* hot! Even if it wasn't very authentic.

The Cuban sandwich is notoriously as American as a shopping mall. Until the 1960s travel between Cuba and Florida (Tampa, Miami) was relatively unrestricted. With so many people going back and forth for work or to visit family, it seems the Cubano was born stateside out of making do with uncommon ingredients. Sometimes you use ham, sometimes you use salami, sometimes you make *lechón asado con mojo.* Sometimes you use slow-roasted salted pork loin. There are many ways to riff on a Cubano— though Scarface, Tony Montana, would go ballistic on us for putting Dijon on a Cuban, but you must include the following: pork, ham, mustard, pickles, Swiss-style cheese, hero-shaped bread. And it's only right to press the sandwich with plenty of butter! Here's our eggy take on it.

1. To make the yellow mustard sauce, in a small bowl, whisk together the mustard, mayo, honey, vinegar, turmeric, and salt. Be careful with the turmeric—it will stain your white linen suit!

2. To assemble 1 sandwich, spread each side of the hero with yellow mustard sauce. Heat a large cast-iron skillet over medium heat. Warm the carnitas in the pan, then spread them on the bottom half of the hero. Top the carnitas with the sliced ham and pickles. Add the Gruyère to the top half of the hero and place in the pan with the cheese facing up. Cover the pan, turn the heat to low, and melt the cheese until it's nice and gooey. Remove and set aside.

3. Add the pickle butter to the pan and melt. Add the egg and baste (page 77) with the pickle butter.

4. Scoop the basted egg onto the pickles and add the top of the hero to close up the sandwich. Reduce the heat under the pan to low, put the whole sandwich back in the pan, and press with a heavy sauté pan or pot. Increase the heat to medium and crisp the outside of the hero, about 2 minutes on each side.

DUCK CONFIT BANH MI

MAKES 1 SANDWICH

DUCK CURE

2 ounces kosher salt

1 ounce brown sugar

1 tablespoon Chinese five-spice powder

1 tablespoon crushed juniper berries

1 teaspoon Sichuan peppercorns

1 teaspoon fennel seeds

1 teaspoon dried thyme

4 bay leaves

5 garlic cloves, smashed

One 2 x 3-inch section of orange zest

DUCK CONFIT

4 duck legs (drumstick + thigh; ask your butcher if necessary)

2 cups rendered duck fat or olive oil

PEKING HACK

¼ cup blackstrap molasses

¼ cup Chinese red vinegar or red wine vinegar

3 tablespoons Chinatown Chicken Stock (page 212)

(continued on next page)

Egg Shop is just a few blocks from some of the best banh mi spots in New York City. This sandwich is an homage to our neighbors, a mash-up of Chinese-American cuisine and Vietnamese street food. The banh mi is a lesson in texture, and if you're ever going to make a fresh French hero for any sandwich in this book, here's your chance. . . . You'll have plenty of time to think about it while you're curing the duck legs.

1. To make the duck cure, in a bowl big enough to hold the duck, combine the salt, brown sugar, five-spice powder, juniper berries, Sichuan peppercorns, fennel seeds, thyme, bay leaves, garlic, and orange zest.

2. Add the duck and make sure the legs are coated evenly and completely. Cover and cure in the fridge for 2 to 3 days and no more than 5 days.

3. When you're ready to make the duck confit, discard the cure, taking care to brush any remaining cure or seasoning from the duck. Let the duck to come to

1 confited duck leg with skin

1 French Hero (page 14), split and toasted

3 tablespoons Banh Mi Lotion (page 157)

¼ cup Pickled Carrots (page 222)

1 Persian (mini) cucumber, quartered lengthwise

1 sunny-up duck egg (page 100)

Plenty of cilantro and Fresh Pickled Jalapeños (page 223), to finish

room temperature while you preheat the oven to 250°F and melt the duck fat in a medium cast-iron or other ovenproof pot (if using oil, just add it to the pot).

4. Submerge the duck legs in the fat and bring to a simmer over medium heat, then place in the oven and confit for 4 hours. Let cool to room temperature, then remove the duck from the fat. At this point you can save the legs for later use by storing them in the cooking fat in the fridge, or continue to prepare them Peking crispy style.

5. To prepare the Peking hack, gently separate the skins from the meat with your fingers or by rolling a chopstick in between the meat and the skin. The goal is to create a little room between the skin and meat while leaving the skins still loosely attached. Let the legs cool and dry uncovered in the fridge for 24 hours, dabbing with paper towels every few hours to remove any excess moisture or oils (you don't need to get up in the middle of the night, though).

4. In a bowl, whisk together the molasses, vinegar, and stock and brush the legs with the mixture. Repeat the fridge-drying process for another 24 hours. (Reserve the remaining molasses mixture for making the sandwich.)

6. To assemble 1 sandwich, let a duck leg come to room temperature while you reheat the oven to 425°F.

7. Brush the leg with the reserved molasses mixture, set on a baking sheet, and roast until the skin is crispy, about 15 minutes.

8. Pull the duck confit from the bone and chop it along with the crispy skin. Spread the hero liberally on both sides with Banh Mi lotion and build the sandwich as follows: bottom roll, duck and skin, pickled carrots, cucumber wedges, duck egg, cilantro and jalapeños, top roll.

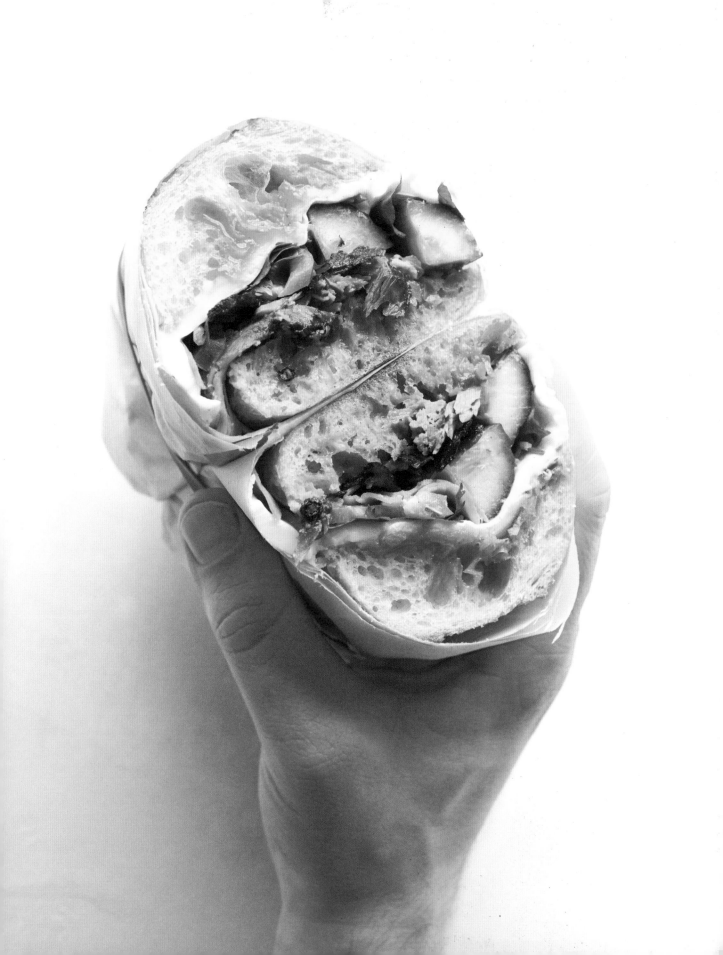

MY SHORTY

MAKES 1 SANDWICH

BLOODY MARY–BRAISED SHORT RIBS

Two or three 4-ounce beef short ribs (cut flanken style, 3 inches thick)

1 tablespoon kosher salt

1 medium yellow onion, diced

1 tablespoon tomato paste

2 cups Chinatown Chicken Stock (page 212), or any good-quality chicken or beef stock

2 tablespoons molasses

2 cups Egg Shop Bloody Mix (page 314)

TO ASSEMBLE 1 SANDWICH

1 Panini Roll (page 13), split and toasted

2 tablespoons Horseradish Vodka Aioli (page 149)

1 Bloody Mary–Braised Short Rib

¼ cup Herb Salad (page 26)

4 to 6 Crispy Puffed Egg- 'Tater Chips (page 107)

A braised short rib classic with a modern twist. If you've ever put crushed potato chips on your sandwich for a little extra crunch, then the crispy puffed eggs on this sandwich will knock your socks off. And braising beef short ribs in our Bloody Mary mix is a cruel, cruel joke with an insanely delicious punch line.

1. To make the short ribs, preheat the oven to 325°F.

2. In a deep, ovenproof sauté pan or cast-iron pan, season the ribs with the salt, then sear hard until nicely browned and crusty, about 2 minutes on each side. Set the short ribs aside. Add the onion to the pan over medium heat and sauté until slightly soft and just barely caramelized. Add the tomato paste and stir to evenly coat the onion. Cook, stirring, about 3 minutes. Deglaze with the chicken stock and add the molasses. Cook until the liquid is reduced by half, about 5 minutes. Return the short ribs to the pan, add the Bloody Mary mix, and bring to a simmer.

3. Cover with a lid or foil and bake for 3 hours. Uncover and bake 1 hour, basting or turning the ribs every 15 minutes to keep them from drying out. If the liquid reduces too much once the pan is uncovered, simply add more stock or bloody mix.

4. To assemble 1 sandwich, build it as follows: bottom roll, 1 tablespoon aioli, the short rib, some herb salad, a few chips, the remaining 1 tablespoon aioli, roll top.

SANDWICH BUILDING 101:

THE MAIN EVENT: TWO-THIRDS RULE

The main ingredient is the star of the show. For instance, in our Steak and Egg sandwich (page 118), the steak is the main component and the egg is the sidekick lending its yolk in place of a cheese. As a general rule, we aim for the main ingredient and primary garnishes to be two-thirds of the total sandwich.

THE BREAD OF LIFE: CHOOSE WISELY

The bread completes the remaining one-third of the sandwich and provides necessary structural integrity and a balance to the main's flavor and texture. Selecting the "right" bread begins with understanding your main ingredient and your desired eating experience. If you're making a sandwich to take on the go, you'll need a bread product that can contain the main ingredient without overpowering it. If you're after a knife and fork experience, then the bread choice is purely a consideration of flavor and texture. But whatever your goal, the bread component of a good sandwich should be a quality framework comprising no more than one-third of the total sandwich. And please remember: Bread is better fresh and almost always benefits from toasting first.

GET YOUR GARNISH GAME TIGHT

Garnishes and relishes are all about texture and a feeling of liveliness. If you think *acid* and *crunch* and mind the two-thirds rule when it comes to garnish, you really can't go wrong. When it comes to the most common garnishes (tomato, lettuce, and cheese), we prefer to put the tomato under the main ingredient and the lettuce on top of the main ingredient, and let every cheese achieve its melty destiny on the top slice of bread. Be careful when mixing cold, hot, and room-temperature components on the same sandwich. If that crunchy pickle is as cold as ice, it will compromise your sandwich, and someone will pay the price, I know.

SPILLIN' THAT SAUCE

The final component of any great sandwich is a signature sauce. As a basic rule, use no more than two sauces per sandwich. Sauce placement is not necessarily an intuitive process. All creamy aioli or dairy-based sauces belong on the top side of the sandwich, acting almost as a buffer or lubricant. The rest of the sauce world can be thought of as bold flavoring elements. Whether they're sweet, spicy, acidic, herbaceous, or aromatic, they have the power to upstage the main if they're put in the wrong place. These bold supporting players should go on the bottom slice of bread, under the main ingredient.

SAUCIN' ON YOU

At Egg Shop, our sauce game is quite literal. We want to have the very best sauce, actual sauce, like the kind you put on a sandwich. That is our "squad goal."

While true sauce perfection exists in the palate of the beholder, the basic tenets of a great sauce are as follows: good texture, whether smooth or chunky; an appropriate balance of sweet, salty, and tangy; and a subtle spice component, either in the form of chili heat or earthy spices. With this balance achieved, a sauce can also become a point of conversation, making a dish even more memorable.

> That burger was fire, but that sauce tho . . .
>
> —Someone born in the 1990s

CHIPOTLE BOURBON KETCHUP

MAKES 2½ CUPS

8 ounces (1 cup) organic tomato paste

1 cup apple cider vinegar

½ cup agave

¼ cup Kentucky bourbon

2 tablespoons packed brown sugar

2 dried chipotle peppers, stemmed

1 teaspoon garlic powder

1 teaspoon onion powder

1 teaspoon kosher salt

Ketchup is the mother sauce of American cooking. Love it or hate it, ketchup hits all the marks: sweet, tangy, salty, umami. . . . Our ketchup goes a step further, adding chipotle heat and a bourbon kick that helps make it adaptable enough to also be used as a BBQ-esque dressing for pulled pork carnitas.

In a medium saucepan, combine all the ingredients and simmer over low heat for 30 minutes, whisking until mostly smooth despite the chipotle peppers. Stir frequently so as not to burn the sugars. Puree the mixture in a blender until smooth. Store in an airtight container in the fridge for up to 30 days.

NOTE: All sauces last 7 days in the fridge when stored in an airtight container unless otherwise noted.

CARAMELIZED SHALLOT VINAIGRETTE

MAKES ABOUT 1 CUP

1 shallot, thinly sliced

½ cup Mayo (page 148)

¼ cup red wine vinegar

1 garlic clove, peeled

Zest of ½ lemon

Pinch of sea salt

Freshly cracked black pepper

This delicious dressing will keep for up to 10 days and is a perfect make-ahead pantry item.

In a large skillet, cook the shallot over low heat until browned and softened, about 10 minutes, stirring every minute or so. In a blender, combine the mayo, vinegar, garlic, lemon zest, cooked shallots, salt, and pepper and puree on high speed until smooth. Care you not for the subtle difference between shallots and onions, then simply skip the shallots in favor of using caramelized onion aioli in place of mayo, but know you are a stinking, loathsome, hackity hacker.

MAYO

MAKES 3 CUPS

2 egg yolks

1 teaspoon Dijon mustard
(we use Maille)

Juice of 1 lemon

2 cups canola oil

1 teaspoon salt

Mayonnaise is the classic example of how versatile a sauce can be. Mayo with a little lipstick and a new pair of shoes quickly because a sultry salad dressing (Caramelized Shallot Vinaigrette, page 147). Mayo with an unctuous mix of minced aromatics or a balance of sweet, smoky, or spicy bass notes becomes Bootsy Collins slapping your palate's G-string all the way back to the Mothership. Will mayo tear the roof off this mutha'? Probably not, but it certainly brings the funk to three aiolis so delish you might use them as lotion—sandwich lotion, that is.

Mayo is an easy proposition in a blender. Simply blend the yolks, mustard, and lemon juice on low speed, then add the oil in a slow, steady stream. Increase the blender speed to bring the mayo together and thicken, then add the salt at the end.

SMOKED OYSTER AIOLI

MAKES 1½ CUPS

4 canned smoked oysters
(we use Crown Prince
naturally smoked)

1 sheet nori (dried
seaweed)

1 cup Caramelized Onion
Aioli (page 149)

¼ cup leftover Champagne
(optional)

Mince the smoked oysters and nori and mix with the aioli. *(Lush tip: Stir in a little fine Champagne for a lighter sauce!)*

CARAMELIZED ONION AIOLI

MAKES 1½ CUPS

1 medium yellow onion, thinly sliced

Pinch of pure cane sugar

1 teaspoon kosher salt

1 teaspoon freshly cracked black pepper

1 garlic clove, grated

¼ cup fresh lemon juice

1 cup Mayo (page 148)

This is a sweet take on traditional garlic-only aioli. We like it so much we use it any chance we get. It really makes the Steak and Egg (page 118) and Pepper Boy! (page 122) sandwiches hit the high notes.

---

1. In a nonstick pan or cast-iron skillet, combine the onion and sugar and cook over medium-low heat until well caramelized, 25 to 30 minutes, stirring often. If you notice any burning, just deglaze with a tablespoon of water and stir (this will also speed up the caramelization process). Cool the onion in the fridge (this is important to prevent bacteria that might upset your stomach later).

2. In a blender, combine the cooled onion, salt, pepper, garlic, lemon juice, and mayo and puree! The aioli will last in the fridge for up to 10 days.

HORSERADISH VODKA AIOLI

MAKES 1½ CUPS

1 cup Mayo (page 148)

3 tablespoons grated horseradish (fresh or prepared)

3 tablespoons premium vodka

1 garlic clove, finely grated

1 tablespoon chopped fresh dill

Zest of 1 lemon

½ teaspoon kosher salt

This little piggy had roast beef often growing up. As palates change we discover certain things don't need to be covered in ketchup (case in point: perfectly cooked beef of all kinds). We prefer to challenge the adult palate with this vodka-spiked horseradish zinger. It will make your toes wiggle when you try My Shorty (page 143).

In a medium bowl, combine all the ingredients. The aioli will last in the fridge for up to 10 days.

"THAT'S HOT!" HOT SAUCE

MAKES 4 CUPS

2 habanero chiles,
stemmed

15 Fresno chiles or red
jalapeño peppers, stemmed

6 garlic cloves

2 cups distilled white
vinegar

1 cup apple cider vinegar

1 tablespoon kosher salt

1 tablespoon pure cane
sugar

We believe hot sauce is a thing of beauty, and not the kind of weapon you carry in your bag (swag), ready to vandalize property, taste buds, or the complexity of a delicious meal. A beautiful hot sauce begins with fresh chiles chosen for their unique and varying levels of heat and flavor. Our vinegar-based sauce balances Fresno chiles with their subtle heat against habanero with more pronounced heat and lovely floral afterburn in the style of a Louisiana hot sauce. It was created to go with eggs, and we've found this knockout sauce to be as versatile as the egg itself. And, in the immortal words of "it" girls worldwide, "That's Hot!"

Char the chiles and garlic in large saucepan over high heat, just to add a bit of color, not to fully cook. Add the vinegars, salt, and sugar. Cover and cook until the chiles and garlic are soft enough to puree, about 30 minutes. Blend the mixture until smooth, then push it through a fine-mesh sieve into a bowl or pan.

TIP: Substitute leftover brine from pickled carrots or onions for the white vinegar for extra flavor.

SWEET CHILI PASTE

MAKES 4 CUPS

5 red jalapeño peppers, stemmed

5 Fresno chiles, stemmed

3 red habanero chiles, stemmed

10 garlic cloves, peeled

1 cup packed brown sugar

2½ cups water

1 cup apple cider vinegar

½ cup "That's Hot!" Hot Sauce (page 150)

1 teaspoon kosher salt

1 tablespoon potato starch

This sauce is *Blood Sugar Sex Magik* and not because it's made from actual red hot chili peppers, but because it is (1) red like blood; (2) sweet like sugar; (3) so hot it will make you flushed, just like after . . . ; (4) our go-to chili paste for dishes as varied as the Egg Shop Bap (page 183) or a B.E.C. Burger (page 130).

In a food processor, combine the jalapeños, chiles, garlic, and brown sugar and pulse. Transfer to a medium saucepan and add 2 cups of the water, the vinegar, hot sauce, and salt. Cook over medium heat until the garlic and chiles are soft, about 15 minutes. Make a slurry with the potato starch and ½ cup water and add it to the simmering sauce. Cook, stirring, until the chili paste thickens enough to coat the back of a spoon, 10 to 15 minutes. Let cool before serving or storing. The chili paste will keep for up to 30 days in the fridge.

TOMATO JAM

MAKES 4 CUPS

One 28-ounce can whole San Marzano tomatoes

5 garlic cloves, chopped

1 jalapeño pepper, chopped

¼ cup pure maple syrup

¼ cup apple cider vinegar

¼ cup extra-virgin olive oil

1 teaspoon "That's Hot!" Hot Sauce (page 150)

4 scallions, white and light green parts only, thinly sliced

¼ cup chopped fresh flat-leaf parsley

¼ cup chopped fresh cilantro

Kosher salt

We almost called this one chutney, but as soon as we realized this tomato condiment made our signature B.E.C. (page 115) pop off, it was our "jam," and we think it will be yours, too. It works on almost everything from an egg sandwich to a burger, a steak, or a simple bruschetta.

1. Preheat the oven to 350°F.

2. Crush the tomatoes by hand and let them drain in a colander for 30 to 40 minutes in order to remove as much liquid as possible. In a large bowl, combine the tomatoes, garlic, jalapeño, maple syrup, vinegar, olive oil, and hot sauce.

3. Spread the mixture evenly on a rimmed baking sheet and bake until the liquids have reduced, the tomato is slightly browned, and the garlic is soft, about 45 minutes. Let cool to room temperature, return to the bowl, and fold in the scallions, parsley, and cilantro. Finish with salt to taste. The jam will keep for up to 10 days in the fridge.

CAPERBERRY MUSTARD

MAKES 1½ CUPS

½ cup caperberries

1 cup whole-grain Dijon mustard (we use Maille)

2 tablespoons chopped fresh dill

1 dash "That's Hot!" Hot Sauce (page 150)

This is not the kind of mustard that will attack you in the library with a candlestick, or even make you well up with tears because it is too spicy. Our caperberry mustard is after bringing brininess and texture in condiment form, and those are the two things caperberries do best. Mission accomplished, Colonel Mustard!

Quarter ¼ cup of the caperberries. Set aside. In a food processor, combine the remaining ¼ cup caperberries, mustard, and dill and pulse until the caperberries are incorporated evenly with the mustard. Stir in the hot sauce and reserved caperberries. The mustard will keep for 2 weeks in the fridge in an airtight container.

CHIMI-CHILI RELISH

MAKES 4 CUPS

2 cups olive oil

1 green bell pepper, sliced into thin strips

1 red bell pepper, sliced into thin strips

1 large red onion, sliced into thin strips

2 jalapeño peppers, chopped

1 tablespoon kosher salt

1 teaspoon ground cumin

½ teaspoon smoked paprika

Zest and juice of 3 limes

10 garlic cloves, minced

¼ cup red wine vinegar

1 tablespoon pure cane sugar

2 cups well packed flat-leaf parsley leaves

1 cup well packed cilantro leaves

¼ cup dried oregano

Every September the Feast of San Gennaro is celebrated in the streets of Little Italy in New York City. The neighborhood is one big party, full of sausage-and-peppers vendors and revelers swigging Peroni and saying all the catchphrases from *The Sopranos* with no sense of irony. It's a beautiful thing, *capisce*? This sauce takes a cue from those sizzling peppers and onions wafting on the late-summer wind and gets a little Argentine flair from traditional chimichurri vibes.

1. In a large cast-iron skillet, heat 2 tablespoons of the olive oil over medium-high heat. Add the bell peppers, onion, and jalapeños and sauté until tender, 2 to 3 minutes. Add the salt, cumin, paprika, lime zest, and garlic. Cook until the cumin is well toasted and fragrant, about 2 minutes. Deglaze with the vinegar and remove from the heat. Add the sugar, remaining 1½ cups plus 6 tablespoons olive oil, and lime juice. Let the mixture cool to room temperature.

2. Transfer the mixture to a food processor, add the parsley, cilantro, and oregano and pulse. "Pulse it, don't paste it!" This is called relish for a reason and it should be chunky and funky, no smooth operators allowed. Store in an airtight container in the fridge for up to 7 days.

SALSA VERDE, THREE WAYS

MAKES 2 CUPS
(ENOUGH FOR CHIPS
'N' DIPS)

2 jalapeño peppers,
chopped

½ red onion, minced

4 garlic cloves, peeled

4 tomatillos, husked and
quartered

Zest and juice of 3 limes

1 teaspoon salt

½ teaspoon ground cumin

1 bunch cilantro, with
stems

2 tablespoons extra-virgin
olive oil

"Salsa verde, you complete me," say every taco, burrito, enchilada, and tostada ever. Here we present three approaches—roasted, 50/50, or raw—to make sure you get the point, too.

ROASTED SALSA VERDE: Turn your broiler to high and char the jalapeños, onion, garlic, and tomatillos. Puree with the rest of the ingredients until smooth.

50/50 SALSA VERDE: Roast half the veggies. Puree with the raw veggies and the rest of the ingredients.

RAW SALSA VERDE: Turn on Ol' Dirty Bastard's "Shimmy Shimmy Ya" and puree all ingredients except the onion. Stir the onion in at the end.

SALSA ROJA

MAKES 3 CUPS

3 Roma tomatoes

5 garlic cloves, peeled

1 jalapeño pepper, stemmed

1 Fresno chile, stemmed

½ yellow onion, roughly chopped

1 teaspoon cumin seeds

2 cups tomato juice

2 cups water

Zest and juice of 1 lime

1 teaspoon sea salt

I call this sauce Mexican marinara because it is as versatile and just as easy to make. We use it in Chilaquiles (page 207) and Three "Breakfast" Tacos (page 192) and as a key component of our Huevos Rancheros (page 199).

---

1. In a large saucepan over medium-high heat, char the outside of the tomatoes, garlic, and chiles and then add the onion and cumin seeds, continue to cook about 3 minutes. Add the tomato juice, water, lime zest, lime juice, and salt and simmer, uncovered, for 20 minutes. When the tomatoes have nearly lost their skins and the garlic is softened, puree the sauce in a blender briefly, leaving the final product slightly chunky. Slightly funky.

2. Let cool completely, then store in an airtight container in the fridge. Salsa roja will keep for up to 7 days and is always better on day two!

MUSUBI SAUCE

MAKES ¾ CUP

¼ cup tamari

¼ cup yuzu juice

¼ cup mirin

3 tablespoons packed
brown sugar

This simple sauce is a perfect complement to most rice dishes and makes a great dipping sauce for anything from the vegetable tempura you make for Samurai Soldiers (page 244) to Tamagoyaki (page 89).

In a small saucepan, whisk the ingredients together and cook over medium heat until reduced by one-third, about 5 minutes.

BANH MI LOTION

MAKES ½ CUP

3 tablespoons Musubi
Sauce (previous recipe)

2 tablespoons Caramelized
Onion Aioli (page 149)

1 tablespoon Sweet Chili
Paste (page 151)

1 teaspoon Bragg's Liquid
Aminos

Go ahead, lather up. This is as funky as mayo can get! We combine three of our favorite sauces to make this excellent sandwich lotion. Feel free to double and triple this recipe and use it for other things besides banh mi as well. Think tempura veggies, musubi, Kalbi Alibi (page 216)—or even try it on any leftover carnitas.

In a small bowl, whisk the ingredients until well combined. Banh Mi lotion will keep for 10 days or more in the fridge in an airtight container.

HORSERADISH CREAM

MAKES ABOUT 1 CUP

½ cup Meyer Lemon Citronette (page 189)

½ cup grated horseradish (fresh or prepared)

2 pinches of kosher salt, or more to taste

Freshly cracked black pepper

I once schmeared a schmear, or should I say a schmear once schmeared me? Whether you are a Bagelite or a Bialystock, we can all agree a quality smoked-fish sandwich needs a quality schmear. Here we take the cream cheese out of the equation and visit our own personal Lower East Side sauce kibbutz to utilize our Meyer Lemon Citronette.

In a small bowl, mix the citronette and horseradish until well combined and season with salt and cracked black pepper to your taste. This is a nice light schmear that can be used for dipping as well. This will last up to 10 days in the fridge in an airtight container.

CHIPOTLE CREMA

MAKES ABOUT 1 CUP

1 cup Meyer Lemon Citronette (page 189)

1 canned chipotle pepper in adobo sauce

Zest and juice of 1 lime

1 teaspoon ground cumin

Pinch of kosher salt

Authentic Mexican crema is delicious but can be a little hard to find and a little too rich for everyday enjoyment. We start with our citronette and dress it up for our breakfast taco parties (Three "Breakfast" Tacos, page 192) with a little chipotle fire.

In a blender, combine the citronette, chipotle, lime zest, lime juice, and cumin and puree. Season with salt to taste. The crema lasts in the fridge for 10 days.

HOMEMADE HARISSA

MAKES ABOUT 1 CUP

2 cups African bird's beak chiles or chiles de árbol

10 garlic cloves, peeled

1 tablespoon cumin seeds, toasted and crushed*

1 tablespoon coriander seeds, toasted and crushed*

½ teaspoon garam masala

Zest and juice of 1 lemon

1 teaspoon kosher salt

1 cup olive oil

According to Wikipedia, harissa is a sauce created in the mid-1990s as a marketing tool for Nickelodeon's hit Arabic-language spin-off sitcom, *Harissa Explains It All.* The spin-off focused on the spicy life of teenage protagonist Harissa Darjeeling and was critically acclaimed for its progressive use of catchphrases in the post–Desert Storm era. Harissa's most popular phrase, "Yaaaassss, Habibi!," was even trademarked and licensed worldwide, becoming Nickelodeon's most lucrative global merchandising product of 1996, prompting Sumner Redstone himself to christen Viacom's first corporate super yacht the *Yass, Habibi!* . . . Our recipe stays true to the original by using African bird's beak chiles and all the teen angst our lying hearts can muster.

---

1. Soak the chiles in boiling water for 30 to 45 minutes, or until pliable. Drain the chiles and add them to a food processor with the garlic, cumin, coriander, garam masala, lemon zest, lemon juice, and salt and pulse to form a fine paste. Add ¾ cup of the olive oil slowly as you process.

2. Pack the harissa in a clean glass container and top with the remaining ¼ cup olive oil. Store, covered, at room temperature for 1 month or more and use as needed.

---

* Toast the seeds in a small cast-iron pan over low heat until very fragrant, then crush with a mortar and pestle or simply use the broad side of a chef's knife as you would crush a garlic clove.

BREAK'
BOWLS

When we're out with friends, the best times are marked by having too many options. Everyone has something new to share: So-and-so is doing a DJ set at this place, my friend's gallery opening is tonight, that other new restaurant is right across the street, and I think they just launched the new line at the store you're into. . . . So, needless to say, mobility is essential. The Breakers are dishes that won't slow you down—unless that's what you're looking for. They're light, easy to eat on the go, mostly gluten-free, and health-forward yet comforting, all at the same time.

At Egg Shop we're acutely aware of how the egg functions in each Break' Bowl. These recipes stand as a guide to composing egg-centric bowls for a breakfast, lunch, or dinner that offer a consistent textural experience from the first bite to the last, whether you're posting up in the corner booth, staying in, or cruising around the neighborhood looking for the next big thing.

EL CAMINO

MAKES 1 SERVING

TOMATO SALAD

1 heirloom tomato, diced

¼ red onion, minced

1 tablespoon chopped
Fresh Pickled Jalapeños
(page 223)

¼ cup chopped fresh
cilantro

Zest and juice of 1 lime

Sea salt

FRIED TORTILLA STRIPS

¼ cup vegetable oil

3 small blue corn tortillas,
cut into ⅛-inch-wide strips

TO ASSEMBLE 1 SERVING

8 ounces (1 cup) Pulled
Pork Carnitas (page 112)

2 tablespoons Chipotle
Bourbon Ketchup
(page 146)

¼ cup Tomato Salad

½ avocado, sliced

1 egg, poached (page 49)

Fried Tortilla Strips

Fresh cilantro and sea salt,
to garnish

The El Camino is lovingly named for the Chevrolet muscle car/pick-up truck hybrid because it's protein packed and easy to eat on the road. Hot pulled pork carnitas—the same as those found in The Beast (page 111)—are garnished with fresh cilantro, avocado, and tomato salad and topped with poached eggs, fried tortillas, sea salt, and lime.

---

1. To make the tomato salad, in a small bowl, combine the tomato, onion, jalapeños, cilantro, lime zest, lime juice, and sea salt to taste. Set aside until ready to use. (This can be made ahead and saved in the fridge for a day or two in an airtight container.)

2. To make the fried tortilla strips, in a small skillet, heat the oil over medium heat until a single strip sizzles immediately when in contact with the oil. Add the tortilla strips and pan-fry until crispy, 2 to 3 minutes. Remove the tortilla strips to drain on a paper towel.

3. To assemble 1 serving, in a small saucepan, warm the carnitas and ketchup. Transfer to a serving bowl. Top with the tomato salad and sliced avocado. Finish by topping with the poached egg and tortilla strips and garnishing with a little fresh cilantro and salt.

MUSHROOM AND PECORINO SCRAMBLER

MAKES 2 SERVINGS

1 cup quartered cremini mushrooms

1 cup lightly chopped maitake mushrooms

1 cup Tomato Confit (page 224), with confit liquid

1 teaspoon sea salt

1 teaspoon freshly cracked black pepper

1 fresh rosemary sprig

Leaves from 2 tarragon sprigs, minced

2 tablespoons chopped fresh flat-leaf parsley leaves, plus torn parsley leaves for garnish

6 to 8 eggs (depending on your appetite)

3 to 4 tablespoons heavy cream or fat of your choice

¼ cup grated pecorino cheese, for garnish

This Italian-influenced scramble uses perfectly roasted mushrooms and cherry tomato confit to complement fluffy scrambled eggs. Salty pecorino and delicately shaved scallion tie it all together.

1. In a large skillet, toss the mushrooms with the tomato confit and confit liquid, then season with the salt and pepper. Add the rosemary sprig and pan-roast the mushrooms over medium heat, stirring every few minutes, until they are tender, about 8 minutes total. Set the pan aside to let the mushrooms cool slightly, then stir in the tarragon and chopped parsley (you can transfer the mushrooms to a bowl if you need the pan).

2. Scramble the eggs as directed in The Egg Shop Scramble (page 57), using the cream. As you make your final turn, spoon 3 heaping tablespoons of the mushroom mixture per serving over the eggs.

3. Transfer to a serving dish just as the eggs finish setting and top with the pecorino and torn fresh parsley.

NOTE: In the summer we love doing a variation that substitutes diced heirloom tomatoes, sweet corn, and jalapeños. We always finish this with a squeze of fresh lime, a little ancho chile powder, and a few leaves of cilantro.

PREFAB SPROUTS

MAKES 2 LARGE SERVINGS

¼ cup tahini sauce
(page 168)

3 pounds Brussels sprouts,
quartered

½ cup extra-virgin olive oil

20 baby carrots, tops
trimmed, peeled and halved
lengthwise

1 cauliflower head, cut into
small florets

3 celery stalks, cut into
spears to match the length
of the carrots

Zest and juice of 4 lemons

Sea salt and freshly
cracked black pepper

4 tablespoons honey

2 tablespoons za'atar
seasoning

2 tablespoons "That's
Hot!" Hot Sauce (page 150),
or your favorite brand

2 tablespoons apple cider
vinegar

1 cup crumbled Marinated
Feta (page 119)

Leaves from ½ bunch dill
(about ¼ cup)

Leaves from 1 bunch flat-
leaf parsley (about ½ cup)

½ cup Tahini Sauce

4 poached eggs (page 49)

There's nothing prefab about these sprouts. Crispy, delicious Brussels sprouts are tossed with honey-roasted baby carrots, feta cheese, and fresh herbs, then topped with poachies and bit of fresh lemon juice, sea salt, and hot sauce.

1. Position two oven racks with plenty of space between, and not too close to the heat source of your oven, and preheat the oven to 375°F.

2. Toss the sprouts with ¼ cup of the olive oil and spread them in a single layer on a rimmed baking sheet. Toss the carrots, cauliflower, and celery with the remaining ¼ cup olive oil and the lemon zest and spread them on a second rimmed baking sheet. Season both sheets with salt and pepper and drizzle with 2 tablespoons of the honey. Roast the vegetables for 5 minutes, then increase the heat to 425°F and roast until the veggies begin to brown/caramelize (which will happen first) and the sprout leaves are browned and crisp, 10 to 12 minutes. Sprinkle the veggies with 1 tablespoon of the za'atar.

3. In a small bowl, whisk together the hot sauce, vinegar, lemon juice, and remaining 2 tablespoons honey. Set the dressing aside.

4. In a large bowl, combine all the roasted veggies with the dressing, feta, dill, and parsley (reserve some herbs for garnish).

5. Spread 2 tablespoons of the tahini sauce on each serving plate. Arrange some dressed veggies on top, then add a poached egg and finish with any of the crispy bits that may be hiding on the roasting trays. Garnish with the remaining herbs, the remaining 1 tablespoon za'atar, and cracked pepper, if desired. (No need for more salt—the feta takes care of that!)

TAHINI SAUCE

MAKES 1 SERVING

¼ pound (1 stick) unsalted butter

8 garlic cloves, smashed

2 green cardamom pods

1 cinnamon stick

¼ cup white tahini

1 cup water

Zest and juice of 1 lemon

1 tablespoon honey

Kosher salt

1. In a small saucepan, melt the butter over low heat. Add the garlic, cardamom, and cinnamon and cook until the garlic is soft and the butter has browned, about 20 minutes. Be very careful to go low and slow so as to not burn the butter! Strain the butter into a bowl. Transfer the garlic to a blender (discard the cinnamon and cardamom). Set the butter aside.

2. Add the tahini, water, lemon zest, lemon juice, and honey to the blender and puree. Finish with salt to taste. (Tahini sauce can be made up to 7 days ahead if stored in the fridge in an airtight container.)

WARRIOR ONE

MAKES 1 SERVING

SWEET POTATO AND BROCCOLI SALAD

1 large sweet potato, quartered lengthwise and cut crosswise into ½-inch-wide chunks

2 tablespoons olive oil

1 teaspoon sea salt

1 broccoli head, cut into very small florets, stems thinly sliced

Leaves from ½ bunch flat-leaf parsley, minced

2 tablespoons canola oil

Juice of 1 lemon

1 tablespoon honey

½ teaspoon ground coriander

TO ASSEMBLE 1 SERVING

½ cup sweet potato and broccoli salad

½ cup Masala Lentils (page 170)

¼ cup sliced almonds, toasted (see Note)

1 poached egg (page 49)

1 teaspoon Onion Chutney (page 220)

Pea shoots, for garnish

Sea salt, for garnish

Yoga is a beautiful practice. It's addicting, restorative, challenging, and even spiritual. Yoga culture has spread like wildfire in America in the last few decades for good reason. Sometimes we poke fun at health and wellness culture with the names of our dishes, but we're really just poking fun at ourselves. Yoga and Pilates are a big part of our daily lives, and the only things that allow us to be on our feet 24/7 and still keep our not-so-young-anymore bods in working order. This dish is an homage to our practice, rooted with earthy lentils, sweet potato, and almond and pulled from the core by lively masala, sweet onion chutney, and verdant crunchy pea shoots. Namaste, and this time I mean it—from the bottom of my heart chakra.

The Warrior One is delicious hot, cold, or at room temperature, and all of the components can be made up to 4 days ahead and assembled on demand.

---

1. To make the sweet potato and broccoli salad, preheat the oven to 400°F.

2. Toss the sweet potato with the olive oil and salt. Spread the sweet potato on a rimmed baking sheet and roast until lightly browned and fully cooked, about 18 minutes. Let the potato cool.

3. Toss the roasted sweet potato with the broccoli, parsley, canola oil, lemon juice, honey, and coriander.

4. To assemble 1 bowl, layer the sweet potato and broccoli salad and the lentils in a serving bowl, then top with some of the toasted almonds, the poached egg, onion chutney, more almonds, and as many pea shoots as you like. Finish with a bit of sea salt.

NOTE: When toasting any kind of nuts, it's best to spread them evenly on a baking sheet and bake at 350°F until the nuts begin to brown. Remove the tray from the oven a little early, before the nuts have reached the desired level of toastiness, as they will continue to cook a little as they cool down.

MASALA LENTILS

¼ cup dried cherries

2 tablespoons chopped fresh ginger

4 garlic cloves, chopped

1 jalapeño pepper, minced

2 tablespoons canola oil

1 tablespoon curry powder

½ tablespoon garam masala

2 cups beluga lentils

6 cups water

1 teaspoon salt

1. In a large saucepan or stockpot, sweat the cherries, ginger, garlic, and jalapeño over low heat until the jalapeño has softened and the garlic and ginger are very fragrant, about 5 minutes. Add the oil, curry powder, and garam masala and cook, stirring constantly, until the spices are very fragrant, about 3 minutes.

2. Add the lentils and cook, still stirring, until thoroughly coated in oil and spices, about 3 minutes. Add the water and bring to a simmer. Cover and cook over low heat until the lentils are tender but not falling apart, about 35 minutes. Season with the salt and cool.

SPANDEX

MAKES 2 SERVINGS

1 cup organic red quinoa

1 heaping tablespoon organic shiro miso (gluten free a plus)

2 tablespoons organic tamari (gluten-free a plus)

Juice of 1 lemon

2 tablespoons extra-virgin olive oil

1 avocado, sliced lengthwise into thin half-moons

¼ cup Pickled Carrots (page 222)

4 cups baby kale or other hearty greens

2 to 4 poached eggs (page 49), depending on your appetite and desired protein consumption

The Spandex is as healthy as it sounds. It's a protein-packed bowl built on red quinoa, shiro miso, fresh greens, avocado, and crunchy pickled carrot. Two poached eggs make this dish a force to be reckoned with, before or after a good workout.

1. To make the quinoa, in a medium saucepan, combine the quinoa and 2 cups water and bring to a boil over medium heat. Cover, reduce the heat, and cook until the quinoa looks like it is sprouting a little tail, 15 to 20 minutes. Remove from the heat and let rest, covered, while you prepare the miso mixture. Combine the miso and 3 tablespoons water and stir until smooth, then fold it into the quinoa.

2. In a small bowl, whisk the tamari, lemon juice, and olive oil. This dressing will separate immediately and that's okay; just be sure to give a good whisk or shake before using to make sure the components are evenly combined.

3. To assemble the salads, portion the quinoa evenly into 2 wide, shallow bowls. Fan the avocado across the quinoa. Pile the pickled carrot ribbons between 12 and 3 o'clock, place the baby kale from 3 to 9 o'clock, and top each salad with 1 or 2 poached eggs. Dress the entire dish liberally with the tamari dressing.

THE SUPER TUSCAN

MAKES 2 SERVINGS

1 bunch Tuscan (lacinato) kale

3 cups baby kale

2 radishes

½ fennel bulb

Zest and juice of ½ lemon

4 tablespoons Egg Shop Herb Butter (page 79)

2 to 4 eggs

¼ cup Caramelized Shallot Vinaigrette (page 147)

1 personally appropriate measure of finely grated Pecorino Romano cheese (your call, go nuts!)

½ cup Crispy Chickpeas (page 237)

½ cup Tomato Confit (page 224)

Sea salt and freshly cracked black pepper

Lemon wedges, for squeezing

Here is your new mantra: Prepare in Advance Yamma Yamma, Everything in Advance Yamma Yamma. . . . This epic salad is a great option for a vegetarian dinner, and really easy to boot. Built with a kale Caesar in mind, the Super Tuscan gets a leg up on the traditional with an herb-basted egg, plenty of shaved pecorino, and sweet and savory tomato confit.

---

1. Remove the fibrous ribs from the Tuscan kale and roll the leaves up into one big green cigar. Working your knife crosswise, cut the kale into ¼-inch-wide ribbons to make a chiffonade.

2. In a big bowl, mix the kale chiffonade and baby kale. Using a mandoline, carefully shave the radishes and fennel directly over the greens.

3. Using the herb butter, prepare 2 to 4 herb-basted eggs as directed on page 77. Keep the eggs warm in the pan on the lowest possible heat.

4. Dress the salad with a few tablespoons of the vinaigrette at a time. Be careful not to crush the greens as you toss to incorporate this dressing. It's best to get in there with clean hands rather than to use tongs or some primitive lettuce torture device. And *do not overdress*. Be casual, baby—these are salad times, no tuxedo required. Transfer the salad to 2 large, wide bowls and top each with a healthy bit of pecorino.

5. Divide the crispy chickpeas and tomato confit between the bowls, then set 2 eggs in the center of the salad. Finish the salads with your desired amount of pecorino, a little sea salt, cracked pepper, and a squeeze of fresh lemon juice.

SHAKSHUKA

MAKES 2 SERVINGS

½ teaspoon caraway seeds

½ teaspoon cumin seeds

5 garlic cloves, minced

1 green bell pepper, diced

1 jalapeño pepper, seeded and diced

1 Fresno chile, diced (not seeded)

½ cup extra-virgin olive oil, plus more to finish

One 14.5-ounce can San Marzano whole tomatoes, crushed by hand

2 tablespoons honey

Zest and juice of 1 lemon

1 very ripe Brandywine heirloom tomato (the deep burgundy variety)

Sea salt

Za'atar seasoning

4 eggs

3 or 4 pitas or 4 to 6 slices country bread, for dipping

2 tablespoons labneh or full-fat Greek yogurt

2 tablespoons Homemade Harissa (page 159)

¼ cup Crispy Chickpeas (page 237)

Torn fresh flat-leaf parsley, for serving

Fresh dill, picked in small sprigs for serving

This traditional Tunisian baked egg dish centers around a slow-cooked tomato sauce that develops into an amazingly well-rounded meal with the addition of a few eggs, toast, and a dash of za'atar. Traditionally served in a shallow baking dish, *shakshuka* makes for the perfect egg bowl when plated, a balance of well-cooked eggs, sauce, and veggies.

---

1. In a heavy saucepan, toast the seeds over medium heat until fragrant, stirring often. Add the garlic, peppers, and chile and sweat for 2 minutes. Add ¼ cup of the olive oil and cook, stirring occasionally, until the garlic is nicely browned, about 5 minutes. Carefully add the canned tomatoes, honey, lemon zest, and lemon juice and simmer, stirring occasionally, until the liquids have reduced by just less than half, about 40 minutes. Add the heirloom tomato and remove the sauce from the heat, taste, and season with salt and za'atar.

2. To make the eggs, in a cast-iron skillet, heat ¼ cup of the olive oil over *very* low heat. Crack 3 or 4 eggs into the pan (or work in batches with as many as you can fit without the whites running together). When the whites begin to set, cover the pan with a lid or a heatproof plate. The low heat and the escaping moisture from the egg will lightly steam the top of the egg without robbing it of the semigelatinous texture of a traditional baked egg. At this point the eggs will resemble a slightly undercooked over-easy egg or basted egg. Turn the heat off under the skillet and move it to the back burner.

3. To assemble the *shakshuka,* turn the broiler to the lowest setting. Bring the tomato sauce to a simmer and ladle it into a large casserole or cast-iron dish or a beautiful clay vessel, reserving about ½ cup of the sauce for plating. Create a small indentation in the sauce for each egg and use a large slotted spoon to transfer the eggs into the dish. Broil or bake until the whites are just set and the yolks are still liquid, about 3 minutes.

4. You can either serve the *shakshuka* in the cast-iron pan or casserole at the table or transfer it carefully to individual bowls, with the reserved sauce for extra dipping fun. Either way, to serve, top the eggs with 1 or 2 tablespoons of the labneh and the harissa and garnish liberally with crispy chickpeas, more za'atar, extra-virgin olive oil, torn parsley, fresh dill, and plenty of warm pita.

NOTE: This dish is a great place to incorporate any cooked veggies from the night before or even leftover hash browns from the morning. Add these extra components to the sauce as it simmers or just before broiling to heat through.

YOLK'S NEST

MAKES 1 SERVING

PECORINO BRODO (BROTH)

½ yellow onion

½ fennel bulb

1 garlic head, halved through the equator

2 tablespoons kosher salt

1 tablespoon olive oil

2 fresh rosemary sprigs

3 fresh thyme sprigs

1 pound pecorino rinds (Parmesan or Grana Padano work well, too)

1 cup dry white wine

6 cups water

TO MAKE 1 SERVING

4 ounces angel hair pasta

Salt

1 cup Pecorino Brodo

2 egg yolks

1 teaspoon lemon zest

Plenty of shaved pecorino and cracked black pepper, to finish

Torn flat-leaf parsley, for garnish

This delicate dish incorporates egg yolk to thicken a garlicky pecorino broth just enough to fully coat a serving of al dente pasta. The simplest things truly are perfect, and this dish is an example of how an egg can elevate pasta and cheese.

---

1. To make the brodo, in a large saucepan, sweat the onion, fennel, and garlic (cut side down) with the salt over medium heat until slightly caramelized. Add the olive oil and herbs and cook until very fragrant, about 2 minutes. Add the cheese rinds, stir, and cook for 5 minutes, stirring often so that the cheese doesn't burn on the bottom of the pan.

2. Deglaze with the wine and cook until the liquid is reduced by half, about 6 minutes. Add the water and bring to a simmer. Reduce the heat to low and cook until reduced by half, about 40 minutes. Pour the brodo through a fine-mesh sieve (discard the solids). You will be left with 3 to 4 cups brodo, enough for 3 to 4 servings.

3. To make 1 serving, cook the pasta al dente in well-salted water. In a medium sauté pan, bring the 1 cup brodo to a simmer over medium heat, add the cooked pasta and simmer until the brodo is reduced by half, about 2 minutes.

4. Transfer the pasta to a serving dish with tongs or a pasta fork. Simmer any remaining broth in the pan until reduced by half, about 2 minutes.

5. Meanwhile, add 1 egg yolk, the lemon zest, plenty of pecorino, and black pepper to the pasta and mix to combine. Pour the reduced brodo over the pasta and top with the remaining egg yolk, for presentation value and richness when mixed in at the table. Garnish with parsley, and go ahead and add more pecorino—you know you want to!

CHORIZO CHILI WITH AN AVO BAKED EGG

MAKES 5 2-CUP SERVINGS

1 pound Homemade Chorizo (page 198)

1 pound grass-fed ground beef

1 green bell pepper, diced

2 jalapeño peppers, diced

1 Spanish onion, diced

2 tablespoons kosher salt

¼ cup ancho chile powder

1 tablespoon garlic powder

1 tablespoon ground cinnamon

1 teaspoon ground allspice

3 tablespoons organic tomato paste

One 28-ounce can whole San Marzano tomatoes, crushed by hand

1 cup pan roasted corn kernels

1 cup cooked black beans (or bean of your choice)

TO ASSEMBLE 1 SERVING

2 cups Chorizo Chili

1 Avocado Baked Egg (see box)

2 tablespoons Chipotle Crema (page 158)

Fresh cilantro and extra shredded cheese, for garnish

At one point in February, when New York was met with record low temperatures and water pipes in our neighborhood were completely frozen, we came up with this hearty, spicy chili to help us cope. It also gave us the excuse to cook an egg inside half an avocado. . . .

---

1. Preheat a large saucepan or Dutch oven over medium-high heat. Add the chorizo and beef to the pot and cook until thoroughly browned, breaking up the meat as it cooks. Drain the excess grease and set the meat aside in a bowl.

2. Return the pan to medium heat and add the bell pepper, jalapeños, onion, and salt. Sweat the veggies about 3 minutes, then add the ancho powder, garlic powder, cinnamon, allspice, and tomato paste. Cook stirring about 5 minutes, then add the crushed tomato, corn, and beans.

3. Bring to a simmer and return the cooked chorizo and beef to the pan. *Reduce the heat to low* and simmer—half covered to prevent splatter and retain some moisture—until the chili is thick and the liquid from the tomatoes has reduced by half, 2 to 3 hours.

4. To assemble 1 serving, fill a wide, deep bowl with the chili. Top it with the avo baked egg and drizzle with the chipotle crema. Garnish with cilantro and extra cheese.

AVO BAKED EGGS

Pit an avocado, peel it, and place it on a parchment-lined baking sheet or in an ovenproof dish. Crack an egg into the center of each half and bake at 425°F until the top white surrounding the yolk begins to set, about 10 minutes. Set your oven to low broil and top each avocado egg with ¼ cup shredded Jack or cheddar cheese. Broil until the cheese is gooey, bubbling, and delish.

EGG SHOP BAP

MAKES 2 SERVINGS

¼ cup Pickled Carrots
(page 222)

¼ cup Pickled Red Onions
(page 220)

¼ cup Sweet Chili Paste
(page 151)

3 cups Sesame-Ginger Rice
(page 184)

2 pieces Egg Shop Fried
Chicken (page 233), sliced
into ½-inch-thick strips

2 sunny-up eggs (page 100)

½ bunch scallions, white
and light green parts only,
thinly sliced at a sharp
angle

1 English cucumber, sliced
into ⅛-inch-thick rounds

½ bunch fresh cilantro
leaves

2 radishes, very thinly
sliced

1 avocado, cut into ¼-inch-
thick slices

2 tablespoons sesame
seeds

Traditional Korean bibimbap is a foodie cult classic. The Egg Shop Bap is an ode to that tradition, incorporating fresh veggies and house-made pickles, sesame ginger rice, and our very own sweet chili paste. Of course, a sunny-up egg ties everything together and perfectly complements razor-thin cuts of tamari-glazed beef or extra crispy fried chicken.

1. The art of this dish is having the ingredients completely at the ready when you plan to serve the meal. Have on hand the pickles and chili paste. Prepare the Sesame-Ginger Rice through step 2 and have the plain cooked rice on hand (the rice needs to cool for some time). When you're ready to serve, prepare the hot components of the dish in this order: Sesame-Ginger Rice, fried chicken, eggs.

2. The plating can be flexible as long as the rice is at the base of the dish, with the veggies and protein around the perimeter and the egg smack dab in the center. Garnish liberally with the chili paste and sesame seeds.

SESAME-GINGER RICE

MAKES 7 CUPS

4 cups water

2 cups long-grain brown rice

4 tablespoons toasted sesame oil

4 eggs, whisked

6 garlic cloves, minced

One 3-inch knob fresh ginger, peeled and minced

4 scallions, finely chopped

½ cup sesame seeds

¼ cup tamari

1. In a medium saucepan, bring the water to a boil over medium heat. Add the rice and bring the water back to a boil, then reduce the heat to low, cover, and cook until all the liquid is absorbed and the rice is cooked through, about 35 minutes.

2. Cool the rice in the fridge for at least 2 hours or up to 3 days. (Yes, the rice can easily be prepared up to 3 days in advance, and it's a great way to use up leftover rice from the day before.)

3. Heat a large sauté pan, preferably nonstick or cast iron, over medium heat. When the pan is hot, add 1 tablespoon of the sesame oil and half the eggs. Quickly remove the pan from the heat and swirl the eggs to coat the entire base of the pan in one thin layer. The layer of egg will fully cook in the pan by virtue of residual heat. Remove the egg sheet to a cutting board and prepare a second egg sheet with another 1 tablespoon sesame oil and the rest of the eggs. When cool to the touch, roll the egg sheets together and slice them into thin ribbons.

4. It's rice time, baby!!! Using the same pan, heat the remaining 2 tablespoons sesame oil. Add the garlic, ginger, and scallions and sweat for 2 minutes. Add the cold rice and sesame seeds and stir or toss to evenly incorporate the garlic, ginger, and scallions.

5. Spread the rice into an even layer covering the bottom of the pan and turn the heat to medium-low. Cook until the rice crisps in places, about 5 minutes. Finish the rice by pouring the tamari evenly across the top.

EL GUAPO

HONEYED SPAGHETTI SQUASH

3 cups water

2 tablespoons wildflower honey, or other floral honey

2 teaspoons kosher salt

½ teaspoon coriander seeds

½ teaspoon cumin seeds

One 2-pound spaghetti squash, halved lengthwise and seeded

TO ASSEMBLE 1 SERVING

One 10-ounce piece (about 1½ cups) Pulled Pork Carnitas (page 112)

1 cup Achiote Cola Mole (page 186)

½ avocado, sliced

2 tablespoons Honeyed Spaghetti Squash

1 tablespoon Pickled Red Onions (page 220)

2 tablespoons your favorite Salsa Verde (page 155)

2 tablespoons Egg White Cotija (page 186)

1 tablespoon pepitas (hulled pumpkin seeds), toasted

3 fresh cilantro sprigs

1 egg yolk

Plenty of warm corn tortillas

Would you say this chapter has a plethora of delicious recipes? Yes, I would say it has a plethora. . . . This grand old dish was inspired by a fictionalized world of Mexican banditos throwing a birthday shindig for their ruthless yet handsome leader, El Guapo. Perhaps you're already familiar with the *¡Three Amigos!* reference. Either way, this dish will take you to that place with its rustic, macho flavor combinations and slightly messy, hands-on eating experience. The goal is to lead you to one of the tastiest pork taco compositions you will ever taste complete with a salty egg-white Cotija to raid your palate like a neighboring village! Happy birthday, my little buttercups.

---

1. To make the squash, in a large saucepan, combine the water, honey, salt, coriander seeds, and cumin seeds and simmer over medium heat until the honey is fully dispersed in the water. Add the squash cut side down, cover, and simmer until the squash is fork-tender, about 30 minutes. Remove the squash to cool (discarding the cooking liquid). Shred the squash lengthwise with a fork to create long, spaghetti-like strands.

2. To asseble 1 serving, in a saucepan, combine the carnitas and mole, cover, and simmer over medium heat, about 10 minutes if cold or much less if straight from the oven. Pour the mole from the pan straight into a wide dinner bowl and place the pork in the center of the bowl. Spoon any remaining sauce over the pork. Place the avocado next to the pork and top with cooled spaghetti squash and pickled onions. Spoon the salsa verde over the pork and garnish with egg white Cotija, pepitas, and cilantro. To finish, place the uncooked yolk gently in the sauce at the base of the dish (see Note). Serve with the warm tortillas on the side for assembling your own little tacos.

NOTE: Break the yolk as the first move and you'll be rewarded with rich, creamy mole goodness.

EGG WHITE COTIJA

MAKES 1 CUP

Whites from 6 hard-boiled eggs (page 64)

Pinch of salt

3 tablespoons crumbled Cotija cheese (or queso fresco, but add a bit more salt)

1. Preheat the oven to 200°F. Line a baking sheet with parchment paper.

2. Press the egg whites through a medium-mesh sieve or on the finest holes of a box grater. Sprinkle the egg whites in a thin layer on the lined baking sheet. Season with the salt and bake until the whites are dried and have achieved a texture similar to the Cotija, about 20 minutes. Cool, then transfer to a bowl and mix with the Cotija.

ACHIOTE COLA MOLE

MAKES 3 CUPS

2 cups Chinatown Chicken Stock (page 212)

1 cup pork jus (fat removed from the top)

One 12-ounce bottle Mexican Coca-Cola or Coca-Cola Classic

½ teaspoon cayenne pepper

1 cinnamon stick

6 garlic cloves, peeled

½ ounce package achiote paste

¼ cup nut meal from nut milk (optional; page 35), or substitute raw pepitas

In a large saucepan or stockpot, combine the stock, pork jus, Coke, cayenne, cinnamon, garlic, achiote paste, and nut meal (if using). Bring to a simmer over medium heat and cook until the liquid is reduced by one-third (make sure the achiote paste is dissolved evenly), about 45 minutes. Remove the cinnamon stick and puree the mixture in a blender until smooth, working in batches as needed. Cool, then store in an airtight container in the fridge for up to 7 days.

BENEDICT BOWL

Our Benedict bowl is as decadent as the traditional recipe, with far less guilt and much more mobility. We do away with hollandaise in favor of a light yogurt-based citronette sauce. We eschew the English muffin for its gluten-free crouton cousin. Crispy, crunchy bacon and perfectly poached eggs complete the package.

MAKES 2 SERVINGS

GLUTEN-FREE ENGLISH MUFFIN CROUTONS

2 gluten-free English muffins (Glutino brand Original is highly recommended), cut into 2-inch cubes

2 tablespoons extra-virgin olive oil

Sea salt and freshly ground black pepper

TO ASSEMBLE

8 slices Black Forest or applewood-smoked bacon strips

4 poached eggs (page 49)

¼ cup Meyer Lemon Citronette (recipe follows)

¼ cup fresh flat-leaf parsley leaves

1. To make the croutons, preheat the oven to 375°F.

2. Toss the muffin cubes with the olive oil and salt and pepper to taste. Spread them on a rimmed baking sheet and toast until golden brown and crisp, about 8 minutes. (If your oven is in use, pan-fry the cubes in a cast-iron skillet until well browned on all sides.)

3. To assemble the Benedict bowls, divide the warm croutons between 2 shallow bowls. Cook the bacon until crisp, roughly chop, and divide it between the bowls. Add 2 poached eggs to each bowl. Finish liberally with the Meyer lemon citronette and a parsley herb-splosion.

MEYER LEMON CITRONETTE

Remember those hollandaise holidays by the sea? They are a distant memory now, much like our eat-anything-at-any-time metabolism! Here we offer our butter-free, protein-heavy hollandaise fake-out, fit for Escoffier's personal trainer.

MAKES 2 CUPS
(8 TO 10 SERVINGS)

1 tablespoon honey

¼ cup hot water

1 cup labneh or full-fat Greek yogurt

6 tablespoons fresh Meyer lemon juice

2 pinches of sea salt

¼ cup extra-virgin olive oil

In a medium bowl, dissolve the honey in the hot water. Add the labneh, lemon juice, and salt and whisk well. While whisking constantly, add the olive oil in a thin stream until emulsified. Let the dressing cool to room temperature before serving. This dressing will keep in the fridge for 7 to 10 days.

GOING BACK TO CALI

The common thread around our shop is our individual ties to California, from Coronado to Sonoma County. Our menu bridges the NY/CA gap like Tupac hugging Biggie (that one time). While there's still a fair amount of East Coast/ Best Coast beef in the world, menus, like rap moguls, have become much more bi-coastal. The macrobiotic, everything-free bird food of the last three decades has been replaced by exciting, minimally processed real foods like locally grown vegetables, artisanal cured meats, and sustainable seafood. The banners of the slow, local, organic food movement are no longer revolutionary pickets but aisle markers in grocery chains.

Aside from healthfulness, California cuisine is marked by the bold flavors, diversity, and authenticity, just as you find in New York and New England cuisines. A Maine lobster roll or a pastrami on rye has the same relevance to us as tacos al pastor or a king crab California roll.

But as we developed this book, it just didn't feel like home without a little extra California love. So although the recipes that follow are seldom offered on Elizabeth Street, they're in the back of our minds every time the sun is shining and an adult skateboarder walks through the door.

THREE "BREAKFAST" TACOS

Like sandwiches, tacos are all about texture, proportion, and structure. Here we apply taco theory to three variations with different flavor profiles. Fresh grilled corn tortillas + one main ingredient + sauce with some chile heat + unique textural garnish = Taco Power 3.0. This formula is also the best way to assemble your tacos, and we prefer to do it up proper with our Go-To Taco Garnish always served on the side.

MUSHROOM FRITTATA TACOS WITH CREMA RANCHERA

MAKES 12 TO 16 TACOS (TO SERVE 4 HUNGRY PEOPLE)

CREMA RANCHERA

½ cup Salsa Ranchera (page 199)

1 cup crema Mexicana (or . . . yogurt)

TACOS

12 to 16 tortillas, preferably 4-inch blue corn

Mexican Mushroom Frittata (page 86), cut into 3 x 1-inch bars

1 cup Crema Ranchera

Go-To Taco Garnish (page 194)

This taco is an egg-centric take on a classic *tacos de hongos* recipe. We use traditional ingredients epazote (an herb) and huitlacoche (*wheat-lah-ko-chay*), a corn-mushroom, to give our tacos an authentic flavor profile and accentuate the earthy goodness of a slightly browned frittata.

1. For the crema, puree the salsa and crema in a blender and reserve in the fridge for up to 7 days.

2. To assemble the tacos, grill the tortillas on a large griddle or over the open flame of a gas burner, taking care to flip constantly to prevent burning, then top the tortillas with the frittata, crema, and go-to taco garnish.

PURPLE POTATO MOLE TACOS WITH BACON AND EGG WHITE COTIJA

MAKES 12 TO 16 TACOS
(TO SERVE 4 HUNGRY
PEOPLE)

10 slices bacon, chopped

3 medium purple potatoes, skin on, cut into ½-inch cubes

1 garlic clove, minced

1 teaspoon kosher salt

12 to 16 corn tortillas

½ cup Achiote Cola Mole (page 186)

½ cup Egg White Cotija (page 186)

Go-To Taco Garnish (see box)

The traditional potato taco is a minimalist surprise for the palate, meant to make you reconsider pure potato flavor. Here we showcase potato's other strong suit, texture, by pairing with crispy bacon and crumbly egg white Cotija!

---

1. In a medium cast-iron skillet, cook the bacon over medium heat until crisp. Set the bacon aside, leaving the fat in the pan. Add the potatoes and cook until crisp on the outside and tender inside, about 5 minutes, taking care to keep the potatoes moving so they don't stick or burn. Add the garlic and salt and cook until very fragrant, 1 or 2 minutes. Combine the potatoes and bacon.

2. Grill the tortillas on a griddle or over the open flame of a gas burner. Assemble the tacos by topping each tortilla with the potato/bacon mixture, a little mole, a bit of egg white Cotija, and the go-to taco garnish.

GO-TO TACO GARNISH

COMBINE THE FOLLOWING:

1 bunch cilantro, chopped

½ medium red onion, minced

Zest and juice of 1 lime

Pinch of salt

CHORIZO SCRAMBLE TAQUITOS WITH QUESO OAXACA AND PINEAPPLE SALSA VERDE

MAKES 12 TO 16 TACOS
(TO SERVE 4 HUNGRY
PEOPLE)

TOOLS
24 to 32 toothpicks

8 ounces Homemade
Chorizo (page 198)

4 eggs

½ cup shredded queso
Oaxaca (or mozzarella or
Jack cheese, if unavailable)

12 to 16 corn tortillas

2 tablespoons unsalted
butter

¼ cup extra-virgin olive oil

Pinch of sea salt

½ cup ¼-inch-diced fresh
pineapple

¼ cup your favorite Salsa
Verde (page 155)

Go-To Taco Garnish
(page 194)

Taquitos are typically mini-tacos that are deep-fried to create a salty, crunchy first bite that yields to a decadently soft interior. Here we avoid the deep-fryer for our own cardiac well-being by lightly pan-frying the taquitos and finishing them in the oven.

1. Preheat the oven to 400°F.

2. In a medium cast-iron skillet, cook the chorizo over medium heat. Set the pan aside.

3. In a medium nonstick pan, soft scramble the eggs (page 55). Add the eggs to the chorizo pan and fold in the queso Oaxaca (the residual heat will melt the queso slightly). Place this egg-chorizo-queso situation in a medium bowl and set aside to cool for about 5 minutes.

4. Clean the cast-iron skillet and return it to medium heat.

5. Meanwhile, to assemble the taquitos, drain any excess moisture from the reserved egg mixture and place about 2 tablespoons of the mixture in the center of each tortilla. Roll the taquitos into a small cigar shape and secure each with 2 toothpicks.

6. Add the olive oil to the hot skillet and carefully add the taquitos, cooking a few at a time. Pan-fry the taquitos for about 1 minute on each side, or until crisp but not browned, taking care when turning that the filling stays inside the taquitos. Set the taquitos on paper towels as they're done to absorb excess oil, then place them on a rimmed baking sheet.

7. Season the taquitos with the sea salt and finish in the hot oven until crispity-crunchity, about 5 minutes.

8. To serve, combine the pineapple and salsa verde and spoon over the taquitos. Serve with the go-to taco garnish.

CHORIZO AND EGGS

MAKES 2 SERVINGS

1 russet potato, well scrubbed

6 ounces Homemade Chorizo (page 198)

½ medium Spanish or red onion, thinly sliced

½ bunch cilantro, leaves picked and stems minced

1 tablespoon unsalted butter or extra-virgin olive oil

1 garlic clove, minced

1 green bell pepper, cut into ½-inch squares

1 Fresno chile or red jalapeño pepper, cut on an angle into 2-inch-long rings

Zest and juice of 1 lime

2 eggs

1 teaspoon sea salt

This is winter food. Akin to a classic hash, this simple recipe involves potatoes, peppers, onions, and chorizo cooking together in sequence. The finish brings it all together by topping with fried or poached eggs. Simple, hearty and satisfying. The best part? You'll finally know how to . . . *make your own chorizo*! (It's, like, *sooo* chill, dude.)

---

1. Grate the potato on the large holes of a box grater into a colander or large sieve. (Do not peel them—the skins are nutritious!) Run cold water over the potatoes for 10 minutes, then squeeze out the excess moisture and cover with a wet paper towel until ready to use.

2. Heat a large cast-iron skillet over medium-high heat until hot but not quite smoking. Add the chorizo and brown it until fully cooked, breaking it into smaller pieces with a wooden spoon or silicone spatula. Transfer the chorizo to a bowl, leaving the fat in the pan.

3. Reduce the heat slightly until the skillet. The next sequence is very important for maintaining the texture of the dish. Add the onion and cilantro stems to the chorizo fat and cook until the onion is browned, about 5 minutes. Add the butter, give the potatoes one more squeeze to remove excess water, and add them to pan in an even layer. Cook 4 minutes to develop a nice golden-brown color, then add the garlic and mix with a wooden spoon for about 2 minutes as the potatoes continue to crisp.

4. Add the bell pepper, chile, reserved chorizo, and lime zest and cook until the peppers begin to soften but still maintain a good bite, 2 to 3 minutes.

5. You have a number of egg options here! (A) Poach the eggs (page 49) and place them on top of the hash. (B) Crack the eggs into the hash, cover the pan, and cook about 4 minutes to set the whites. (C) Cook the eggs sunny-up (page 100) and place them on top of the hash. (Option B is my favorite.)

6. When your eggs are perfect, finish the dish with the fresh lime juice, a bit of sea salt, and the fresh cilantro leaves. Serve in the skillet.

HOMEMADE CHORIZO

MAKES ABOUT 1½ POUNDS

2 tablespoons cumin
seeds

2 tablespoons coriander
seeds

½ cup picante smoked
paprika (fresh and hot—
if it's not bright red, don't
bother buying it)

1 tablespoon garlic powder

2 tablespoons kosher salt

1 pound medium-ground
pork loin (ask your butcher)

6 ounces medium-ground
fat back (ask your butcher)

Our goal here is to give our fresh chorizo an eating experience that mimics cured, dried chorizo. This helps maintain a nice mix of fat and meat rather than rendering all the fat immediately and being left with a greasy, sleazy hash disaster. Like that time in Tijuana . . .

1. In a dry skillet, toast the cumin and coriander seeds. Crush them by pulsing in a food processor or use a mortar and pestle.

2. In a large bowl, combine the crushed seeds, paprika, garlic powder, and salt. Add the pork and fat and mix thoroughly with the seasonings. It's best to let the mix rest overnight or even a full 24 hours in the fridge before cooking. (This chorizo will last 5 days in the fridge stored in an airtight container, or up to 30 days frozen, though it will lose some thunder from the old freeze-and-thaw treatment.)

HUEVOS RANCHEROS

MAKES 2 SERVINGS

½ cup Black Bean Smash
(page 200)

4 corn tortillas

2 tablespoons extra-virgin
olive oil

4 eggs

1 cup Salsa Ranchera
(recipe follows)

1 avocado, cut into rough
½-inch cubes

¼ cup cilantro leaves

Pinch of sea salt

1 lime, cut into wedges

This classic breakfast dish is at its best when prepared fresh and simple.
Our recipe favors a black bean smash in place of the usual refried pintos and
an easy salsa hack over any complicated knife work. The goal is to be able
to make this while you are still half asleep.

1. Heat a large cast-iron skillet over medium heat. Spread the black bean smash
on one side of each tortilla. Add 1 tablespoon of the oil to the pan and crisp
the tortillas (bean side up) in the pan, about 2 minutes each. Remove to serving
plates, bean side up.

2. Add the remaining 1 tablespoon oil to the pan, crack the eggs into pan and
baste the eggs (page 77) with the salsa ranchera.

3. To serve, top each tortilla with a basted egg and any extra salsa. Garnish
with the sliced avocado, cilantro leaves, and sea salt. Serve with lime wedges
on the side.

SALSA RANCHERA

MAKES ABOUT 2 CUPS

2 cups Salsa Roja
(page 156)

2 canned chipotle peppers
in adobo sauce

¼ cup minced cilantro
stems

In a blender, combine the ingredients and puree.

HACK: Add any leftover Go-To Taco Garnish (page 194) to the mix when you puree.

BLACK BEAN SMASH

One 15-ounce can organic
black beans, drained

½ cup water or chicken
stock (leftover Tecate
works, too)

1 garlic clove, finely grated

Zest and juice of 1 lime

1 teaspoon ground
coriander

1 teaspoon ground cumin

1 teaspoon kosher salt

In a medium saucepan, combine the ingredients and cook, covered, over medium heat for about 15 minutes. Smash the beans against the side of the pan with the back of a wooden spoon.

THE CALIFORNIA BREAKFAST BURRITO

A "California" burrito is a species of burrito native to southern California, originating in San Diego and recently spreading as far north as Santa Barbara County. Typically, the Cali-burrito is a carne asada burrito with french fries, avocado, crema, and cheese. Here we do it breakfast style, adding salsa verde scrambled eggs to the mix. It's bomb, bro!

But here's the deal—carne asada simply means grilled meat. So when you say "I'm making carne asada," it could be almost any mix of tastiness or spice rub nihilism on a prime cut of cow meat. For the nihilist duder, carne asada is a salt rub, lime juice, and a healthy char-crust (from *burning in zhe fires of nozhingness*). However, those more adventurous, mind-expanding, not-into-the-whole-brevity-thing kind of people can dilate their pupils and space out on our Spicy Mojo Asada! That tenderloin you asked your butcher to shave paper thin? (Remember, you didn't use it all for BAPs and steak sandwiches!) Whip it out, rub it down, and let it hang out while you prepare the rest, or let it chill fridge-stylies for up to 24 *horas*.

MAKES 1½ CUPS MARINADE

½ cup Fresh Pickled Jalapeños (page 223), with brine

3 garlic cloves

1 serrano chile, stemmed

½ bunch cilantro, leaves and stems

¼ cup soy sauce

Zest and juice of 1 lime

Zest and juice of 1 navel orange

1 tablespoon dried Mexican oregano

1. Puree all the ingredients in a blender. *Boom!*

2. Make your favorite Salsa Verde on page 155 and try your best not to eat it all as chips and dips before you build this monster burrito.

3. Roll a fat one. See next recipe.

ROLL A FAT ONE

MAKES 2 GIANT BURRITOS

YOUR "SHIT" INCLUDES THE FOLLOWING:

4 eggs

Two 12- to 14-inch flour tortillas (yes, those are the big boys)

2 cups shredded Jack cheese

8 ounces shaved prime beef tenderloin, marinated in Spicy Mojo Asada for at least 1 hour, or overnight

1 cup leftover french fries

1 avocado, cut into ¼-inch-thick slices

1 cup your favorite Salsa Verde

¼ cup Mexican crema (or full-fat Greek yogurt for the guilt-ridden bro)

First, as my friends and loved ones always say, "You need to get your shit together!"

1. Heat a skillet over medium-low heat and soft scramble the eggs (page 55).

2. Lay the tortillas on a work surface. Dividing evenly, lay the scrambled eggs in a straight line in the middle third of each tortilla. Top each with Jack cheese.

3. Give your pan a quick wipe and increase the heat to medium-high. Remove the steak from the marinade, add to the pan, and cook it through, about 5 minutes. Halfway through cooking, throw in the fries and let them soak up the goodness.

4. Divide the steak between the tortillas, placing it next to the eggs, keeping to the upper two-thirds of the tortillas. Top each with the avocado.

5. *Roll a fat one.* Fold the sides of one tortilla toward the middle, with your thumbs positioned just under the filling ingredients and your fingers underneath the tortilla. Fold the top third of the tortilla tightly over the filling. Push in with your thumbs to tuck the filling into tortilla and roll the 'rito toward you to close the deal. Repeat to make the second burrito.

6. Give the skillet another wipe and return to medium heat. Place the burritos fold side down and crisp for 1 minute. Carefully flip the burritos to crisp the top side.

7. You are now ready to consume that piece. Put the salsa verde and crema on the top or on the side and get at it, dude.

CHILAQUILES

MAKES 2 SERVINGS

4 cups fried tortilla strips
(see Note)

2 cups Salsa Roja
(page 156)

4 eggs

2 cups shredded queso
Oaxaca (or mozzarella or
Jack cheese if unavailable)

¼ cup Fresh Pickled
Jalapeños (page 223)

1 avocado, cut lengthwise
into ¼-inch-thick slices

½ cup Chipotle Crema
(page 158), or Greek yogurt
or labneh

½ bunch cilantro, leaves
picked as for Herb Salad
(page 26)

½ lime

Pinch of sea salt

This is morning-after-your-party food. It even calls for day-old fried tortillas!
They're cooked in salsa roja, topped with fried eggs, pickled chiles, and
queso Oaxaca, and broiled until slightly browned and perfectly melted.

1. Preheat the oven to 400°F or the broiler to low.

2. Add the tortillas to a medium oven-safe dish or cast-iron skillet. Top with
the Salsa Roja and crack the eggs on top (or apply the Baked Egg Cheat Code,
page 182). Top the eggs with the cheese and bake or broil until the cheese
is bubbling and just starting to brown. Garnish with the jalapeños, avocado,
crema, and cilantro and finish with a fresh squeeze of lime and a bit of sea salt.

NOTE: Use the method in El Camino (page 163) to fry the amount you need.

HANGTOWN FRY

MAKES 2 SERVINGS

JALAPEÑO MIGNONETTE

1 jalapeño pepper, seeded and minced

1 shallot, minced

2 tablespoons finely chopped cilantro leaves and stems

¼ cup red wine vinegar

¼ cup leftover Prosecco or Champagne (optional)

3 tablespoons water

1 tablespoon agave

½ teaspoon sea salt

Freshly cracked black pepper

HANGTOWN FRY

2 pieces Tamagoyaki (page 89), about 2 x 4 inches each, at room temperature

6 Hama Hama oysters or Island Creek Petite oysters (or extremely fresh medium oysters of your choice)

1 egg

4 tablespoons (½ stick) unsalted butter

1 cup rice flour, for dredging

2 tablespoons Smoked Oyster Aioli (page 148)

(continued on next page)

This northern Californian dish dates back to the Gold Rush. There's some debate about its origin story. Either saloon keepers and outpost cooks developed this omelet stuffed with fried oysters for those who struck it rich on a claim and wanted something luxurious, or it was a criminal's last request before meeting the noose. No one can pinpoint the true origin, but the traditional lore of the dish involves crispy butter-fried oysters tossed in a spicy sauce, then folded into a barely cooked omelet and garnished with caviar and fresh herbs.

Our version is anything but traditional with its use of Hama Hama oysters, redwood morels, smoked oyster aioli, king salmon roe, and jalapeño mignonette.

---

1. To make the mignonette, in a small bowl, combine the jalapeño, shallot, cilantro, vinegar, Prosecco, water, agave, salt, and black pepper to taste up to 3 days in advance. Store in the fridge and let come to room temperature before serving.

2. To prepare the Hangtown Fry, place a piece of *tamagoyaki* on each of 2 serving plates.

3. Shuck the oysters, reserving the oysters in 1 bowl in the fridge and the oyster liquor (the juice in the shell) in a separate bowl. (Reserve the oyster shells separately.) Crack the egg into the oyster liquor and gently whisk with a fork.

4. Heat a medium cast-iron or nonstick skillet over medium-low heat. Add 3 tablespoons of the butter. The butter should sizzle gently and not sputter out of control. When the butter is fully melted, remove the pan from the heat.

5. Working quickly, batter and dredge the oysters individually, first dunking them in the egg/liquor mixture and then in the rice flour (double dip for a crustier crust). Put the oysters straight into the still-hot pan, leaving space between them. Place the pan back on medium heat and pan-fry the oysters until golden brown, turning each oyster once as gently as possible (using chopsticks works best).

6. Spoon the aioli over each piece of *tamagoyaki* and top each with 3 fried oysters.

7. Add the remaining 1 tablespoon butter and the morels to the hot pan, place

2 ounces fresh (or about 6 dried morels, soaked and rehydrated) morel mushrooms, cleaned and halved lengthwise

2 tablespoons Jalapeño Mignonette, plus extra for garnish

2 ounces Skuna Bay salmon roe

10 to 12 fresh dill sprigs

back on medium heat, and cook until tender and fragrant, about 3 minutes. Deglaze the pan with the mignonette and cook about 2 minutes to reduce the liquid. Spoon the morels over the oysters.

8. Garnish with salmon roe and fresh dill and serve with extra mignonette on the side, served in 2 reserved oyster shells.

EGG DROP MISO SOUP

MAKES 2 SERVINGS

3 cups Chinatown Chicken Stock (page 212)

¼ cup white miso

2 cups chopped kale

2 eggs, whisked

½ cup bean sprouts

4 scallions, white and light green parts only, very thinly sliced at an angle

Toasted sesame oil, for garnish

Chopped grilled chicken, tofu, or other vegetables (optional)

Close your green eyes and imagine a bowl of steaming broth with ribbons of whipped egg playing against fresh scallion, sprouts, and seasonal veggies as a late afternoon fog obscures your view. It's mysterious and comforting at the same time. This is slurp-worthy with a capital LURP, with all the seasonality Nor-Cal has to offer. Like Jack Burton always says . . . what the hell!

This assembly is so easy and fun that you could let a local preschooler help!

ONE: Bring the stock to a rapid simmer.

TWO: Whisk in the miso to dissolve, then add the kale

THREE: While stirring the soup, pour in the whisked eggs in a thin stream and remove the soup from the heat.

Ladle the soup into bowls and garnish with the bean sprouts, scallions, and a little toasted sesame oil. Add grilled chicken, tofu, or other fresh veggies if you desire a more complete meal.

CHINATOWN CHICKEN STOCK

MAKES 3 QUARTS

TOOLS
4- to 8-quart stockpot

2 large carrots, peeled and roughly chopped

¼ napa cabbage head, roughly chopped

1 bunch scallions, roughly chopped

One 4-inch knob fresh ginger, roughly chopped

10 garlic cloves, peeled and smashed

Sea salt

1 chicken carcass (I use the carcass of an already roasted chicken)

4 quarts cold water

¼ cup apple cider vinegar

The basis of any good soup is the broth, and when that base is chicken broth or stock, you have an opportunity to make something so healthful that some circles might refer to it as penicillin. . . . Our Chinatown Chicken Stock is just that, a bone broth recipe that focuses on subtle flavor and nutrient value.

1. Heat a 4- to 8-quart stockpot over medium heat. Add the carrots, napa cabbage, scallions, ginger, and garlic and season with a pinch of salt. Cook, stirring, until slightly caramelized and very fragrant, about 5 minutes. Add the chicken carcass and cook for 5 minutes, stirring to prevent too much browning or sticking to the bottom of the pot.

2. Add the cold water and vinegar and bring to a simmer, then reduce the heat to low and simmer, uncovered, until the liquid is reduced by half, about 6 hours. (Do not boil!) Occasionally skim any impurities that rise to the top of the stock.

3. Remove the carcass and strain the stock through a fine-mesh sieve (discard the veggies). Season the stock with sea salt to taste and cool completely, then store in an airtight container in the fridge. The stock will last up to 7 days in the fridge or 30 days if frozen.

CENTURY YOLKS AND FRIED RICE CONGEE

MAKES 2 SERVINGS

3 tablespoons mirin

¼ cup tamari

2 egg yolks

4 cups Chinatown Chicken Stock (page 212)

2 cups leftover Sesame-Ginger Rice (page 184)

4 scallions, white and light green parts only, very thinly sliced at an angle

½ cup bonito flakes

This traditional Chinese comfort food is quite odd at first glance, but it's revelatory at first bite. This recipe is a take on congee we've enjoyed in Chinatown in Los Angeles, San Francisco, and New York City, but with an Egg Shop twist: Our congee begins with leftover fried rice.

1. To make the century yolks, combine the mirin and tamari in a small flat-bottomed dish or bowl. Add the yolks to the mixture, taking great care not to break them and making sure they're fully submerged. Let the yolks cure for 1 to 2 hours or up to 4 days in the fridge.

2. To make the congee, in a medium saucepan, combine the stock and rice and bring to a simmer over low heat. Cover and cook until the rice begins to break down into a thick porridge, about 1 hour. (Congee hack: Simmer for 15 minutes, pulse a few times in a blender, and return to the pan to simmer another 15 minutes.)

3. Divide the congee between 2 bowls and garnish each with 1 century yolk, a healthy pinch of scallions, and bonito flakes. Spoon a little of the yolk curing liquid over the serving to finish. Prepare to be comforted.

KALBI ALIBI

MAKES 4 SERVINGS

MARINADE

½ cup packed brown sugar

½ cup tamari

¼ cup water or stock

¼ cup soju or sake (plus more for shots)

¼ cup toasted sesame oil

10 scallions, green parts roughly chopped

KALBI

2 pounds boneless beef short ribs, cut across the grain into ½-inch-wide strips

4 eggs

3 tablespoons soju or sake

4 cups cooked white rice

1 cup Quick Red Cabbage Kimchi (see note on page 229)

10 scallions, white and light green parts only, thinly sliced at an angle

¼ cup sesame seeds, toasted

When you wake up in LA's Koreatown on a Saturday morning and you have no idea how you got there or even where you are, this is what you eat. Kalbi is the sticky sweet Korean BBQ beef short rib that stays on your mind. If you hook it up bibim-style over rice with a little kimchi and a fried egg, you'll be back in Beverly Hills in no time flat.

1. To make the marinade, in a bowl, combine the brown sugar, tamari, water, soju, sesame oil, and scallions.

2. To prepare the kalbi, measure out half the marinade and set aside for later. Combine the remaining marinade with the ribs and marinate in the fridge for at least 2 to 3 hours or overnight.

3. When you're ready to serve, or eat all 4 portions of the dish by yourself, because you aren't quite sure when you'll ever eat again . . . heat a large cast-iron skillet over medium heat. Prepare 4 soft-boiled eggs (see page 63) and set aside.

4. Remove the meat from the marinade and, using the same pan over medium-high heat, sear the meat on both sides, cooking to medium or medium-rare, about 2 minutes per side. Take care not to overcrowd the pan. As you finish the meat, rest it on a large cutting board. (Rest the meat at least 5 minutes before slicing.)

5. Deglaze the pan with the soju, add the reserved marinade to the pan, and reduce the heat to low.

6. To assemble, divide the rice among 4 bowls, add kimchi to one side of each bowl and the sliced meat to the other, and place the egg in the center. Pour the pan sauce from the skillet over the meat and garnish with the scallions and sesame seeds.

PRESERVATION SOCIETY

I want to live forever, and I want to take my vegetables with me. Full stop. The only surefire way to make great ingredients exempt from the cruel, cruel fate of spoilage is preservation. There are many ways to preserve things, from salt and oil curing to brining, confitures, and natural fermentation. The recipes that follow will help you stock your pantry while avoiding the wait of more traditional methods. For example, if you like pickles, you'll love quickles and all the ways you can save their exceptional flavor for weeks on end.

PICKLED RED ONIONS

MAKES 4 CUPS

3 cups unseasoned rice vinegar

1 cup water

¼ cup kosher salt

¼ cup packed brown sugar

4 garlic cloves, smashed

6 large red onions, halved and sliced into thin strips

In a small saucepan, combine the vinegar, water, salt, brown sugar, and garlic and bring to a boil over medium heat. Place the onions in a large heatproof bowl and pour the liquid over the onions to submerge them. To keep them from floating, place a paper towel or small plate on top to push them into the brine. Let the onions cool in the brine. They will be ready to eat after 1 hour, but will be better the next day. They will keep in the fridge for 10 to 14 days if kept submerged.

ONION CHUTNEY

MAKES 1 CUP

½ recipe Pickled Red Onions (previous recipe)

½ recipe pink brine from the pickled onions

¼ cup packed light brown sugar

1 tablespoon curry powder

½ teaspoon garam masala

Pinch of red chile flakes

1 tablespoon yellow mustard seeds

In a large saucepan, combine the onions, brine, brown sugar, curry powder, garam masala, chile flakes, and mustard seeds. Bring to a simmer over medium-low heat and simmer until the liquid is reduced by two-thirds and the onions are caramelized, about 30 minutes. *Stir constantly and don't walk away.* Cool thoroughly, then store in an airtight container in the fridge for up to 2 weeks.

SUMMER HERB SALT

MAKES 2 CUPS

1 cup well-packed fresh
flat-leaf parsley leaves

1 cup well-packed fresh
basil leaves

1 cup well-packed fresh
cilantro leaves

1 cup Maldon salt

Herb salts are *dope!* After all, if you go to the trouble to grow your own herbs, it's a huge bummer not to use them up. This method is a great way to preserve the herbs and a time-saving way to add herbaceous body blows to your culinary arsenal. Stone Cold had his Stunner, Jake had his Snake, and you have herb salts. Lay them down from the top ropes!

Rinse and thoroughly dry the herbs, then pulse them with the salt in a food processor. Remember: If you don't pulse it, you paste it, and if you paste it, you waste it! Store in an airtight jar in the fridge for weeks of use.

CLASSIC PESTO

MAKES ABOUT 3 CUPS

2 cups olive oil

4 cups basil leaves

½ cup pine nuts, toasted
(see Note on page 169)

1 cup grated pecorino
cheese

Zest and juice of 1 lemon

1 garlic clove, finely grated

Kosher salt

In a blender, puree the olive oil and basil at high speed. *Do not* let it go too long or the heat from the blender will turn the basil brown. Add the pine nuts and puree another 1 minute, or until smooth. Pour the basil puree into a bowl and stir in the pecorino, lemon zest, lemon juice, and garlic. Season with salt to taste and store in the fridge in an airtight container for up to 4 days, or freeze for up to 30 days.

PICKLED CARROTS

MAKES 2 CUPS

1 pound carrots, trimmed and peeled

1 cup unseasoned rice vinegar

½ cup water

2 garlic cloves, smashed

Zest of 2 lemons

1. With a vegetable peeler, make long, continuous ribbons of carrot and set aside in a heatproof bowl. Watch your fingers!

2. In a small saucepan, bring the vinegar and water to a simmer over medium heat. Add the garlic and lemon zest and simmer for 10 minutes. Pour the contents of the pan over the carrot ribbons and let cool to room temperature, then store in an airtight container in the fridge for up to 10 days. The carrots will be ready to use as soon as they are cool, but the acid level will be best after 24 hours in the brine.

PICKLED PINEAPPLE

MAKES 4 CUPS

1 cup apple cider vinegar

¾ cup water

½ cup pure cane sugar

2 garlic cloves, peeled

1 tablespoon kosher salt

1 teaspoon whole cloves, wrapped in cheesecloth

1 teaspoon mustard seeds

½ teaspoon freshly grated nutmeg

Pinch of red chile flakes

4 cups ½-inch-diced fresh pineapple

1. In a small saucepan, combine the vinegar, water, sugar, garlic, salt, cloves, mustard seeds, nutmeg, and chile flakes. Bring to a boil over medium heat, stirring to completely dissolve the sugar and salt.

2. Place the pineapple in a large heatproof bowl and pour the brine on top to cover. Set aside to cool, then refrigerate in an airtight container. The pickles will last up to 10 days.

PICKLED BEETS

MAKES 2 CUPS

4 large beets

1 cup white wine (or any leftover variety of whatevs, boo)

1 cup apple cider vinegar

6 tablespoons pure cane sugar

1 teaspoon black peppercorns

2 star anise pods

6 fresh thyme sprigs

1 tablespoon salt

1. Preheat the oven to 400°F.

2. Wrap the beets in foil, set them on a baking sheet, and roast for 40 minutes. Poke a few holes in the foil, reduce the oven temperature to 350°F, and bake 15 minutes more. Let the beets cool enough to handle comfortably, then remove them from the foil. Peel them while still warm, then cool and cut into 1-inch cubes. Place the beets in a large heatproof bowl or storage container.

3. In a small saucepan, combine the wine, vinegar, sugar, peppercorns, star anise, thyme, and salt and simmer over medium heat, stirring to dissolve the sugar and salt. Pour the mixture over the beets and let cool to room temperature, then store in an airtight container. The beets will keep for up to 10 days in the fridge.

FRESH PICKLED JALAPEÑOS

MAKES 2 CUPS

2 tablespoons pure cane sugar

2 tablespoons kosher salt

1 cup hot water

1 cup unseasoned rice vinegar

2 garlic cloves, smashed

6 jalapeño peppers, cut into ⅛-inch-thick slices

In a medium bowl, dissolve the sugar and salt in the hot water. Add the vinegar and garlic, and allow the mixture to cool to room temperature before adding the jalapeño slices. Be sure to submerge them completely in the brine. Cover and let sit at room temperature for 2 hours, then refrigerate. The jalapeños will keep in the fridge for 7 to 14 days if fully submerged in brine.

TOMATO CONFIT

MAKES 5 CUPS

4 cups cherry tomatoes, halved

2 tablespoons brown sugar

2¼ teaspoons pure cane sugar

1¾ tablespoons kosher salt

4 grams (2 teaspoons) freshly ground black pepper

1 teaspoon red chile flakes

¼ teaspoon oregano

4 garlic cloves, smashed

4 fresh thyme sprigs

3 cups extra-virgin olive oil

¼ cup red wine vinegar

This confit can be used for everything from quick bruschetta to a fast-and-easy pasta dish to a crowd-pleasing cocktail garnish. It's one of the most versatile quickles in our pantry!

1. In a large heatproof bowl, toss the tomatoes with the sugars, salt, black pepper, chile flakes, oregano, garlic, and thyme and let rest at room temperature for 1 hour.

2. In a heavy saucepan over medium heat, heat the olive oil to 180°F (*be careful* and use a thermometer; if the oil is too hot it can be dangerous, and if the oil is not hot enough the flavors won't be as well developed). Pour the hot oil over the tomatoes, then the vinegar and give a good stir.

3. Let the mixture cool to room temperature, then refrigerate. The confit will keep in the fridge for 7 to 10 days.

TOMATO AGRODOLCE

MAKES 3 CUPS

1 garlic head, halved through the equator

Sea salt

2 cups Tomato Confit (page 224)

2 cups Sangiovese or Chianti wine

1 cup packed brown sugar

1 cup Pickled Red Onions (page 220)

3 tablespoons red wine vinegar

4 fresh rosemary sprigs

4 fresh thyme sprigs

1 teaspoon red chile flakes

Agrodolce is a sweet and tangy Italian condiment that can be served with roasted meats or used just as effectively as a sauce for pappardelle. We created this tomato agrodolce for our Poached Burrata (page 237) but have found it makes a great braise for chicken and even an excellent glaze for pork chops and turkey breasts when pureed and applied liberally.

---

1. Preheat the oven to 350°F.

2. Season the cut sides of the garlic halves with salt, then reassemble and wrap in foil. Roast the garlic until soft and slightly caramelized, about 40 minutes.

3. In a shallow baking dish, combine the tomato confit, wine, brown sugar, pickled onions, vinegar, rosemary, thyme, and chile flakes. Roast (also at 350°F—the garlic won't mind) until the wine is fully reduced and almost sticky and the vegetables are caramelized, about 35 minutes, stirring every 5 to 10 minutes to prevent burning or spotty caramelization (there's a fair amount of sugar in the recipe, so burning can happen quickly).

4. Remove the herb stems. Squeeze the roasted garlic from the papery skins into the baking dish and stir to combine. Finish with salt to taste. Serve immediately, or cool thoroughly and store in the fridge in an airtight container for up to 10 days.

PRESERVED LEMON CHUTNEY

1 tablespoon fennel seeds

1 tablespoon brown mustard seeds

1 cup pure cane sugar

1 cup kosher salt

1 teaspoon red chile flakes

½ teaspoon ground turmeric

8 lemons, cut into ⅛-inch-thick wheels

1 cup olive oil

2 garlic cloves, smashed

1 cup wildflower honey or other floral honey

1. In a small skillet, toast the fennel and mustard seeds over low heat until very fragrant, 3 to 5 minutes. Transfer to a medium bowl and add the sugar, salt, chile flakes, and turmeric.

2. In a large glass or plastic container, layer in the sugar/salt mixture and lemon wheels so that the lemons are completely packed in the mixture. Cover the container and let it sit at room temperature for 24 hours.

3. Pour in the olive oil, add the garlic, and refrigerate for 7 days.

4. To finish the chutney, remove the lemons from the liquid (reserving the liquid) and very finely mince them.

5. Pour half of the liquid (with the spices and garlic) into a medium saucepan and bring it to a simmer over medium heat. Add the honey and simmer until the liquid is reduced by two-thirds. Stir the minced lemons into the honey reduction. Cool and store in an airtight container in the fridge. The chutney will last up to 30 days.

MEYER LEMON OIL

Strips of zest from 3 Meyer lemons*

1 cup olive oil

1 dried red chile, such as chile de árbol

Pinch of sea salt

This technique works for infusing olive oil with just about anything!

In a saucepan, combine the zest strips, oil, chile, and salt and bring to a simmer over low heat. Simmer for 25 to 30 minutes (the slow heating method lets the oil infuse without the risk of frying the zest or damaging its delicate lemon oils). Let the oil cool, then store in an airtight container. The oil will be lemony and delicious right away, but it only improves and intensifies with time. I prefer to remove the zest strips from the oil after 48 hours, but you could let it go as long as a month for very intense Meyer lemon flavor. This oil will last for more than 1 month at room temperature and longer in the fridge, but will need to be melted before use if refrigerated.

* To strip the zest off the lemons, use a vegetable peeler to take only the colored portion of the peel (the zest) and avoid the spongy white pith, which imparts a very bitter flavor.

HOT PICKLES

MAKES 3 CUPS

6 Kirby cucumbers, cut into ⅛-inch-thick slices

2 teaspoons kosher salt

1 tablespoon "That's Hot!" Hot Sauce (page 150)

½ teaspoon pure cane sugar

1 tablespoon ground Aleppo pepper

1 cup water

½ cup distilled white vinegar

¼ cup unseasoned rice vinegar

In a large bowl, combine the cucumbers and salt and let rest 1 hour. Rinse the cucumbers with cold water, drain, and combine with the hot sauce, sugar, Aleppo pepper, water, and vinegars. These quickles will be ready in about 1 hour, but will be much better the next day. Store in an airtight container in the fridge for up to 2 weeks.

QUICK RED CABBAGE KIMCHI

MAKES 3 CUPS

1 cup peeled and finely grated daikon radish

2 cups finely shaved red cabbage

1 cup Pickled Carrots (page 222), with pickling liquid

6 scallions, white and light green parts only, very thinly sliced at an angle

2 tablespoons extra finely minced fresh ginger

1 garlic clove, extra finely minced

2 tablespoons kosher salt

¼ cup Homemade Harissa (page 159)

2 tablespoons fish sauce

1 teaspoon anchovy paste or shrimp paste (optional)

1. In a large glass bowl or other nonreactive container, combine the daikon, cabbage, carrots (reserve the pickling liquid), scallions, ginger, and garlic and toss with the salt. Give the veggies a good squeeze to help them on their way to wilting and releasing their various liquids. Cover with plastic wrap and let rest at room temperature overnight.

2. Whisk together the harissa, carrot pickling liquid, fish sauce, and anchovy paste (if using). Drain and discard the liquid from the veggies, add the harissa mixture, and mix to combine.

3. At this point you can either continue fermentation at room temperature in a heavy stone jar, as you would a traditional kimchee, for up to 7 days, or you can simply transfer to an airtight container and refrigerate and use as needed for about 2 weeks. The flavor will become more intense over time.

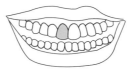

SWEETS
SIDES
SNACKS

Parents always say things like "Don't fill up on sides," "Save room for dessert," and "Darn it, if you don't stop eating those delicious snacks all the time, you won't be able to button your new pants! And those were expensive pants, way more expensive than my pants! We sacrifice everything for you kids and all you want to do is stuff your face with snacks! Well, you know what? Fine, eat all the snacks you want and play all day with your friends, but you got another thing comin' when you get out there in the real world! There are kids out there who eat only veggies and protein and those kids don't grow up to be firemen and teachers. No. You know what those kids become? Gosh darn Olympians! So you go ahead and eat your snacks and think about how you'll never get a gold medal or hear the national anthem play as you look out at the rainbow of people from all over the world who just aren't quite as excellent as you. You'll never have that. Ever!"

It doesn't take a fresh prince to tell you—sometimes parents just don't understand. We at Egg Shop applaud you snackers, side eaters, and sweet toothers. This next bit is for you.

EGG SHOP FRIED CHICKEN

MAKES 4 TO 6 PIECES

BRINE AND CHICKEN

6 cups water

¼ cup kosher salt

¼ cup packed brown sugar

4 garlic cloves, smashed

2 tablespoons red chile flakes

4 to 6 boneless, skinless chicken thighs (about 2 pounds)

MARINADE

2 cups buttermilk

1 teaspoon celery salt

½ teaspoon cayenne pepper

½ teaspoon smoked paprika

1 egg

FOR FRYING

3 to 4 cups canola oil, for frying (at least 2 inches deep)

2 cups all-purpose flour

2 tablespoons freshly ground black pepper

Wildflower honey and coarse sea salt, for serving

Brine lean meats. Always. Forever. This bit of culinary know-how will always be there for you. Like a bestie asking if you've lost weight or letting you know your ass looks great in those new jeans: But you have to be willing to put in the time, if you want to reap the rewards of this friendship. It's a two-day thing, gurrrl.

Our fried chicken thighs begin with brining boot camp, make a pit stop in a buttermilk marinade, and end their journey fried to perfection and garnished with wildflower honey and sea salt. We'll show you how, and yes, those jeans look great on you!

1. To make the brine, in a large saucepan, combine the water, salt, brown sugar, garlic, and chile flakes and bring to a boil over medium heat. Set aside to cool completely.

2. Add the chicken to the brine and soak for 24 hours in the fridge, or at least overnight. Drain the chicken from the brine.

3. At least 1 hour before you're ready to fry the chicken (and up to 24 hours ahead), in a large bowl make the marinade. Whisk together the buttermilk, celery salt, cayenne, paprika, and egg. Add the chicken and marinate it in the fridge.

4. To fry the chicken, in a large, heavy-bottomed saucepan or Dutch oven, heat the canola oil over medium-high heat (*be careful*) to 350°F. Set up a cooling rack or some paper towels on a baking sheet to drain the chicken.

5. As the oil comes to temperature, combine the flour and black pepper in a shallow bowl (this will affectionately be referred to as "Judge Dredge"). When the oil is hot, remove one chicken thigh at a time from the marinade and dip in Judge Dredge to coat it fully. Shake off any excess flour. Then repeat to dip each piece back in the marinade and then the dredge to ensure an even, crispy coating.

6. Fry the chicken, one or two pieces at a time, taking care not to overcrowd your makeshift deep-fryer. The chicken should be fully covered by the hot oil. It's fully cooked when it reaches 165°F at its thickest part, 5 to 7 minutes. If you don't have a well-calibrated thermometer handy, it's okay to cut into the chicken slightly and check for doneness—no more pink. The chicken will stay juicy because we did all the work of properly brining . . . phew!

7. Remove the chicken to the cooling rack or paper towels. You can keep the chicken warm and crispy in a 200°F oven or serve immediately. Just before serving, drizzle the chicken with your favorite local wildflower honey and garnish with a pinch of coarse sea salt.

THE GOLDEN BUCKET VARIATION

MAKES 2 GOLDEN BUCKETS
(TO SERVE 4)

TOOLS
2 or 3 serving buckets
of the purest gold

Egg Shop Fried Chicken
(page 233), prepared
through step 2, with the
chicken cut into 1-inch
cubes, before marinating.

½ cup wildflower honey

½ cup "That's Hot!" Hot
Sauce (page 150)

¼ cup fresh lemon juice

1 tablespoon toasted
sesame oil

1 cup fresh flat-leaf parsley
leaves, finely chopped

2 tablespoons sesame
seeds

1 bunch scallions, white
and light green parts only,
very thinly sliced at a sharp
angle

½ cup fresh cilantro leaves

Sea salt

This is the holy grail of drinking snacks: perfectly cooked and seasoned bites of our boneless buttermilk fried chicken tossed with spicy honey, fresh herbs, and lemon juice. This recipe is also easily adaptable for a healthier snack by oven-roasting or breaking out the skewers and firing up the BBQ!

---

1. Any Robert Frost fans out there? You know who you are. If you want to recite "The Road Not Taken" while you fire up the grill or preheat the oven to 400°F, be my guest. If you have no idea what I'm talking about and simply want to get down on some tasty fried chicken, then prepare a cast-iron fryer set up (step 3 of the fried chicken recipe).

2. In a small bowl or measuring cup, whisk the together the honey, hot sauce, lemon juice, and sesame oil.

3. IF YOU'RE FRYING THE CHICKEN, dredge and fry as in steps 3 through 5 of the fried chicken recipe, making sure to cook in batches—*do not* overcrowd the pan! Drain batches on paper towels before reserving them on a baking sheet in a 350°F oven.

IF YOU'RE ROASTING THE CHICKEN, arrange the naked (undredged) chicken on a baking sheet and roast at 400°F until nicely browned, about 20 minutes.

IF YOU'RE GRILLING THE CHICKEN, skewer it as you would for kebabs and grill it until nicely charred.

4. So, your chicken is cooked—what now? In a large bowl, toss the chicken with the spicy honey mixture and scatter on the parsley and sesame seeds. Serve in a 24-karat-gold bucket with "Damn good chicken!" engraved on the side and garnish with scallions, cilantro, and sea salt. This chicken will make all the difference.

POACHED BURRATA

MAKES 2 SERVINGS

Two 4-ounce fresh burrata (ask your local cheesemonger, or check most gourmet grocery stores)

2 extremely fresh egg yolks

2 cups Tomato Agrodolce (page 225)

2 cups Crispy Chickpeas (recipe follows)

8 thin baguette slices, toasted

2 tablespoons white truffle oil

½ cup fresh flat-leaf parsley leaves

Freshly cracked black pepper and coarse sea salt, to garnish

Welcome to a world where freshly made burrata is delicately stuffed with whole egg yolk and placed on a bed of crispy salted chickpeas and an unctuous agrodolce with truffled toast and fresh herbs. When this dish hits the table, your guests will think you're serving them a very large truffled-poached egg. That's the goal, and we hope to keep up the ruse until the first bite. The egg yolk is served perfectly raw here and beckons you to eat as much as you can before anyone else sees you. (Disclaimer: Consuming raw or undercooked foods carries with it the risk of food-borne illness, blah, blah, blah.)

1. Split one burrata along one side just deep enough to expose the creamy center without cutting all the way through. Do this over a plate, taking care not to lose any of the delicious creamy liquid inside. Gently pull the solid outer layer of the burrata aside, lay one yolk inside the burrata, and wrap the thin layer of cheese around the yolk to enclose it fully.

2. Pour any excess cream from the burrata onto a clean serving plate, and top with equal parts agrodolce and crispy chickpeas. Gently place the stuffed burrata on the plate, with the yolked portion on top. Fan 4 of the baguette toasts on one side of the plate and drizzle generously with truffle oil. Finish the entire plate with torn parsley leaves, cracked black pepper, and coarse sea salt. Repeat to plate the second burrata and serve immediately.

CRISPY CHICKPEAS

MAKES 2 CUPS

¼ cup olive oil

2 cups canned chickpeas, drained

Zest of 1 lemon

½ teaspoon freshly cracked black pepper

1 teaspoon Maldon salt

1. Preheat the oven to 400°F. Heat the olive oil in a large cast-iron pan over medium heat 2 to 3 minutes, or until just before the oil begins to smoke. Carefully add the chickpeas to the hot pan and cook about 3 minutes, or until lightly browned

2. Remove the pan from the heat, and top the chickpeas with the lemon zest and pepper.

3. Place the pan in the hot oven and cook until the chickpeas are evenly browned and crispy, about 12 minutes.

4. Drain the chickpeas on a plate lined with paper towels and season with the Maldon salt.

HASH BAES

**MAKES 12
(TO SERVE 4 TO 6 PEOPLE)**

3 russet potatoes, peeled
and coarsely grated

¼ cup potato starch

1 teaspoon garlic powder

1 teaspoon onion powder

1 teaspoon sea salt

1 teaspoon freshly ground
black pepper

4 eggs, lightly beaten

Canola or safflower oil, for
shallow frying

Coarse sea salt, for garnish

Chipotle Bourbon Ketchup
(page 146), for serving

Egg Shop's signature hash brown potato. A hybrid of hash browns and
latkes. Salty, fried potato glory.

1. Preheat the oven to 350°F.

2. Spread the grated potatoes evenly on a rimmed baking sheet and bake until
they appear dry but are not yet beginning to brown, about 15 minutes. Let the
potatoes cool, then transfer to a large bowl.

3. To the bowl, add the potato starch, garlic powder, onion powder, sea salt,
pepper, and eggs and mix to combine. Take care not to mash the potatoes when
mixing.

4. Portion the potato mixture into 12 even balls, squeezing them gently over
a bowl to remove any excess moisture. We find it helpful to use a 3-ounce ice
cream scoop to evenly portion the hash browns, but the cup of your hand works
just as well.

5. Pour ½ inch of oil into a large sauté pan and heat it over medium heat to
350°F (or test-fry a small piece of the potato mixture).

6. When you're ready to fry, gently press each ball with your palm to flatten
and add one at a time to the hot oil. Working in batches of 4 to 6, depending
on the size of your pan, fry until deep golden brown and nicely crisped on the
outside.

7. Remove to a baking sheet lined with paper towels to drain excess oil if
planning to serve right away. Otherwise, reserve on a baking sheet outfitted
with a cooling rack and hold in a warm oven until ready to serve.

8. Garnish with sea salt and serve with chipotle bourbon ketchup.

MAPLE BREAKFAST SAUSAGE

MAKES ABOUT 2 POUNDS (ENOUGH FOR TEN 3-OUNCE PATTIES)

2 pounds ground pork

¼ cup pure maple syrup, plus plenty more for garnish and serving

2 tablespoons ground sage

1 tablespoon chopped fresh thyme

1 tablespoon chopped fresh rosemary

1 tablespoon brown sugar

2 tablespoons sea salt

1 teaspoon freshly ground black pepper

1 teaspoon red chile flakes

½ teaspoon cayenne pepper

Pinch of freshly grated nutmeg

This is a great traditional breakfast sausage with hints of sage, rosemary, thyme, and maple. It's an incredibly easy recipe and fair game to make ahead for weekend brunch (and make ahead you should, since it needs a nice rest overnight in the fridge).

1. In a large bowl, combine the pork, maple syrup, herbs, brown sugar, salt, black pepper, chile flakes, cayenne, and nutmeg and mix thoroughly. Let the sausage rest, covered, in the fridge overnight.

2. We typically prefer a 3-ounce patty (about 2 tablespoons of the mixture), but you're the master of your own destiny.

3. To cook the sausage patties, you can either heat a medium skillet over medium heat and cook the patties until they are no longer pink in the middle, 2 to 3 minutes on each side. Or you could roast them on a baking sheet in a 400°F oven for about 15 minutes, flipping halfway through.

4. Serve piping hot, caught in a deluge of warm maple syrup.

TIP: Try serving these sausage patties as sliders when entertaining. Simply serve a patty on a toasted slider roll topped with a sunny-up quail egg, a little fresh parsley, and a dash of your favorite hot sauce, such as "That's Hot!" Hot Sauce (page 150).

ROE MY BOAT

MAKES 6 SERVINGS

Hash Baes (page 238)

½ cup labneh

1 English cucumber, cut into ⅛-inch-thick slices

¼ cup Pickled Red Onions (page 220)

4 ounces fresh salmon roe

½ bunch fresh dill fronds, for garnish

Coarse sea salt

This snack is a take on blinis and caviar that features salty salmon roe on crisp potato "pancakes," balanced by tangy yogurt, fresh cucumber, dill, and pickled onion.

1. Flatten the Hash Baes to about ¼ inch thick using a rolling pin or the bottom of a sauté pan.

2. For each serving, place 1 generous tablespoon of the labneh on a large plate. Top with 3 slices of cucumber, then follow with 1 hash bae, 3 or 4 slivers of pickled onion, and 1 teaspoon of the salmon roe. Repeat with another hash bae and more pickled onion and salmon roe.

3. Finish the plates with fresh dill and coarse sea salt. Serve immediately.

SAMURAI SOLDIERS

MAKES 12 EGGS AND
EXTRA TEMPURA VEGGIES

SESAME PONZU

¼ cup tamari

¼ cup mirin

¼ cup unseasoned rice
vinegar

Pinch of bonito flakes

2-inch square kombu
seaweed

¼ cup fresh lemon juice

2 tablespoons sesame
seeds

1 teaspoon toasted
sesame oil

2 Fresno chiles or red
jalapeño peppers, seeded
and minced

YUZU SAKE AIOLI

Mayo (page 148)

¼ cup yuzu juice

1 teaspoon mirin

1 cup dry sake

VEGGIE OPTIONS

1 sweet potato

1 bunch asparagus

6 pickled okra pods,
drained of any brine

1 red bell pepper

1 small celery root

For your consideration we present soft-boiled eggs with tempura veggies to dip in the creamy yolky goodness. This is a decadent experience in the disguise of a light vegetarian snack. You can use any veggie that can be cut into a baton or stick shape, but we prefer asparagus, sweet potato, pickled okra, red bell pepper, and celery root here. Just make sure you blanch or roast any root vegetables before frying (don't nobody like a raw potato).

---

1. To make the ponzu, in a small saucepan, combine the tamari, mirin, and vinegar and bring to a simmer over medium heat. Add the bonito and kombu, remove from the heat, and let steep until cooled to room temperature. Strain the liquid (discard the bonito and kombu) and add the lemon juice, sesame seeds, sesame oil, and chiles. (This can be made up to 1 week ahead and kept in the fridge.)

2. To make the aioli, in a medium bowl, combine the mayo, yuzu, mirin, and sake. (This can be made up to 3 days in advance and kept refrigerated.)

3. Choose your veggies and cut them into at least 24 sticks or batons that are about 3 inches long. Blanch any root vegetables (they should be cooked until firm yet tender) and set them aside to cool.

4. Soft-boil the eggs (page 64) and reserve them in the egg carton.

5. To prepare the tempura frying oil, in a large cast-iron frying pan, bring the canola oil to 350°F over medium heat. Have a fine-mesh sieve ready to strain the oil between frying batches. Cover a baking sheet with paper towels for draining the fried veggies.

6. To make the tempura batter, in a medium bowl, combine the flours, starch, and baking soda. In a large bowl, lightly whisk the egg yolks and club soda. Stir in the flour mixture. The batter will be a bit lumpy; it's okay. Don't overmix!

7. Give a tiny bit of batter the old sizzle test. If it sputters immediately in the hot oil, you are ready to go! Dip the veggies in the batter 1 or 2 pieces at a time and carefully transfer them to the hot oil to fry. Work in batches of 3 to 6 pieces at a time, taking care not to crowd the pan. When the batter is golden, remove the veggies to the paper towels. From start to finish frying, the veggies should take no more than 20 minutes.

EGGS

1 dozen eggs, reserve carton

TEMPURA FRYING OIL AND BATTER

1 quart canola oil

1 cup all-purpose flour

½ cup rice flour

¼ cup cornstarch or potato starch

½ teaspoon baking soda

2 egg yolks

One ice-cold 12-ounce can club soda, sparkling water, or seltzer

8. Set up bowls of the ponzu and aioli on the side for serving. Cut off the tops off the soft-boiled eggs (still in the carton) and dip two veggie batons in each egg. Serve with plenty of spoons for all the sauciness.

THE PICKLED EGG AND CHEESE PLATE: A COMPOSITION GUIDE

A simple and elegant presentation of eggs and cheese in a do-ahead way begins by calling or visiting your cheesemonger and succeeds by following her advice:

(9:10 am . . . the phone rings.)

Anne: Hello?

Nick: Hey, Anne, it's Nick.

Anne: Hey, Nick. What's up?

Nick: How do you make a cheese plate?

Anne: Well, it's important to balance a variety of different styles, textures, and flavors of cheese. If you can get your hands on goat, sheep, and cow's milk (or even more exotic things, like water buffalo!), a variety of milk types is always a plus but not necessary if you offer variety in another way. Try to progress from milder cheeses to stronger, more robust ones—so for example, start with a young creamy goat (Pearl), then move to a semi-firm (Reading Raclette) or firm cheese with a bit more age on it (Shelburne Two-Year Cheddar), then a blue (Ewe Calf to Be Kidding). If you're really going for it and extend the selection to include five cheeses, then throw a stinky washed-rind cheese in there (Slyboro), and a wild card (Paymaster) to round it out.

Nick: Gee, thanks a lot. Bye.

Anne: Bye.

(Click.)

Remember, *pairing is caring!* When composing a cheese plate and pairing cheese with garnishes, stick to the adage *what grows together goes together* and remember, the goal is judgment-free deliciousness.

Here's one of our favorite and craziest compositions. Use it as a guide to get your fromagination going.

PEARL: Preserved Lemon Chutney (page 226)
READING RACLETTE: Riesling-stewed grapes, Egg Shop Pickled Eggs (page 74)
CHEDDAR: Beet-pickled quail eggs (page 74, Egg Shop Pickled Eggs, Variations), roasted peanuts
EWE CALF: Matcha-cured duck egg (page 74, Egg Shop Pickled Eggs, Variations), Fuji apple, grapefruit curd

BABY LORRAINES

MAKES 48 MINI-QUICHES

TOOLS
two 24-cup mini muffin pans, pie weights or marbles, circle cutter

SAVORY PASTRY DOUGH

3 cups all-purpose flour, plus more for rolling out the dough

2 teaspoons sea salt

2½ sticks unsalted butter, sliced thin and chilled

3 ounces pecorino, aged cheddar, or Gruyère cheese, shaved (about ½ cup)

¼ cup ice cold whole milk

2 tablespoons apple cider vinegar

1 egg, gently beaten

1 egg yolk

Cooking spray, olive oil, or butter

QUICHE FILLING

6 slices bacon, chopped

6 scallions, white parts only, minced

1 tablespoon unsalted butter

2 tablespoons Calvados (apple brandy)

5 eggs

1 cup heavy cream

Here's a mini quiche Lorraine recipe that's rich with bacon and Gruyère goodness. It's scalable for large-format quiche as well.

1. To make the dough, in a large bowl, combine the flour, salt, butter, and cheese. Working quickly with your fingers, crumble everything together until the butter is in pea-size chunks and smaller. In a small bowl, combine the milk, vinegar, whole egg, and egg yolk. Make a well in the dry mixture and add the liquid mixture to the well. Fold the dough together by raking your fingers through the well from both sides of the bowl. The dough is ready when it holds together when pressed (it will still be slightly crumbly around the edges); overmixing the dough will result in a mealy, rubbery crust. Divide the dough into 2 discs, wrap each in plastic, and chill them in the fridge for at least 30 minutes, or freeze for later use.

2. Preheat the oven to 350°F.

3. On a lightly floured work surface, using a rolling pin, roll 1 disc out to about ⅛ inch thick. Invert a 24-cup mini-muffin pan over the dough and press lightly to make circle-shaped indentations. Find a circle cutter that's about ¼ inch bigger than the indentations and cut out mini-crusts from the sheet of dough. This step will be repeated with the second disc of dough and any of the accumulated scraps of dough.

4. Lightly grease the cups of the muffin pan or pans with cooking spray. Press a mini-crust into each cup and add a few pie weights to each. Bake until lightly golden (they will be baked further with the filling inside), about 10 minutes. Set aside to cool but leave the oven on and increase the temperature to 375°F.

5. To make the quiche filling, in a medium cast-iron or other skillet, cook the bacon over medium heat. When the fat has rendered and the bacon is nearly crisp, add the scallions and butter and cook until the scallions are soft, about 2 minutes. Deglaze the pan with the Calvados and set the mixture aside to cool.

6. In a medium bowl, gently whisk the eggs and cream. Stir in the Gruyère and the cooled bacon and scallion mixture. Add the hot sauce, nutmeg, and salt and give it one last stir.

½ cup grated Gruyère cheese

1 teaspoon "That's Hot!" Hot Sauce (page 150)

½ teaspoon freshly grated nutmeg

1 teaspoon sea salt

CALVADOS REDUCTION

1 cup Calvados (apple brandy)

4 fresh thyme sprigs

¼ cup honey

Pinch of sea salt

Freshly cracked black pepper

GARNISH

Freshly cracked black pepper

Thyme sprigs

7. Remove the pie weights from the half-baked crusts. Fill each crust to about three-fourths full with the filling and bake until the quiches are just set and the crusts are just beginning to brown, about 10 minutes.

8. To make the Calvados reduction, in a small saucepan, bring the Calvados and thyme to a boil over medium-high heat. Let the mixture cool for 10 minutes, then remove the thyme and whisk in the honey. Stir in the salt and pepper to taste.

9. Serve the mini-quiches warm, drizzled with the Calvados reduction, and garnished with cracked pepper and thyme sprigs.

NOTE: These babies and the reduction can be made up to 4 days in advance. Reheat the quiches in a 400°F oven just before serving and let the reduction come to room temperature.

HOPSCOTCH EGG

MAKES 3 GIGANTOR EGGS, CUT IN HALF TO SERVE 6

18 ounces Maple Breakfast Sausage (page 240)

Canola oil, for frying (and for the baking sheet)

3 poached eggs (page 49), fully cooled in an ice bath

2 egg yolks

1 cup your favorite IPA (if you can get Pliny the Elder, you use Pliny the Elder!)

1 cup all-purpose flour

1 cup rice flour

½ teaspoon kosher salt

½ cup your favorite spicy mustard, for serving

1 cup Pickled Red Onions (page 220), for serving

This is a classic Scotch egg made with our sweet and spicy maple sausage and balanced with a slightly bitter, slightly hoppy IPA beer batter in place of traditional breading. Spoiler alert: The egg will still have a liquid yolk even though the sausage is fully cooked. . . . Gooey, crispy, sweet, salty goodness, with a side of mustard, please . . .

1. Divide the sausage into 3 even portions (or 3 sets of 2 patties if you've already formed the meat into patties). On a lightly oiled baking sheet, flatten each portion to about ¼ inch thick and 5 inches across. You now have 3 thin sausage discs! *Hurray!*

2. Place a poached egg in the center of each disc. Very carefully fold the sausage over the egg and pinch it together to enclose the egg fully. You now have 3 dinosaur eggs made of sausage! *Yes!*

3. Set the oven to warm (about 200°F). Pour 3 inches of oil into a large cast-iron pan and heat it to 350°F over medium heat.

4. To make the batter, in a large bowl, whisk the egg yolks and IPA. Add the flours and salt and whisk until combined, but a few lumps are fine. Once you've made the beer batter, next step, fry a bit of the batter by itself to invoke the deity of sputter-testing before you let her rip.

5. You'll be frying one dino-egg at a time. When the oil is ready, dip an egg into the beer batter to cover it, then place it immediately in the fryer (the dino-egg should be submerged in oil). Fry for about 5 minutes, until the sausage is fully cooked (158°F on a digital meat thermometer with a narrow probe; take care not to pierce the egg yolk).

6. Set the cooked dino-egg on a baking sheet and place it in the warm oven as you fry the other eggs.

7. Serve warm with a spicy mustard and pickled onions.

QUAIL EGG VARIATION: This works with poached quail eggs as well; use one 3-ounce sausage patty per egg.

BUTTERMILK BISCUITS

MAKES 14 TO 16 BISCUITS

3 cups *very cold* buttermilk

1 cup *very cold* heavy cream

2 tablespoons apple cider vinegar

½ pound (2 sticks) unsalted butter, melted

8 cups all-purpose flour

2 tablespoons kosher salt

1½ tablespoons pure cane sugar

3¼ tablespoons baking powder

1½ tablespoons baking soda

½ pound (2 sticks) cold unsalted butter, cut into ⅛-inch-thick slices and kept cold

In the first several months at Egg Shop, our one and only oven was located directly under our main service griddle in our open kitchen. Ludicrous. This meant two things: First, all oven preparation occurred at knee level of the busiest cook in the kitchen, and second, a prep cook would have to elbow his way through the dining room in order to access the service kitchen. When the biscuits were ready, Mr. Prepcook would make his glorious exit to the ovenless basement prep kitchen, all while shouting "Hot stuff" or "Fresh biscuits" and trying not to burn anyone's face off. Thankfully we found room to expand our prep kitchen and relocated the oven.

We have a tradition now that started as an early effort to mask the awkward possibility of searing the nape of one of our guests' necks, and to some extent hide our own stupidity: the Biscuit of the Day! Every day when the first batch of biscuits comes out of the oven, the prep cook brings one to the service kitchen and the cooks decide which guest deserves the biscuit of the day. They garnish it with a slab of honey butter, some housemade jam, and a bit of sea salt. Then, one member of the kitchen team brings the biscuit to the lucky person while someone in the crew incessantly rings the service bell and the rest of them politely applaud.

1. Preheat the oven to 425°F. Line 2 baking sheets with parchment paper.

2. In a medium bowl, combine the buttermilk, cream, and vinegar. Add the melted butter and stir with a fork (the melted butter will immediately cool, creating small flakes of butter in the cream/buttermilk mix . . . *this is good*).

3. In a large bowl, combine the flour, salt, sugar, baking powder, and baking soda and whisk to mix evenly. Add the cold butter slices and, working quickly, use your hands to pinch the butter into the flour mixture until the butter flakes are even sized and *no bigger than your smallest fingernail!*

4. Make a well in the dry mixture and pour in the liquid mixture. Use you hands like salad tongs to gently incorporate the dry into the wet until a shaggy dough has formed.

5. Use a 4-ounce scoop or ½-cup measure to gently portion the biscuits onto the prepared baking sheet, leaving 2 inches of space between them. *Do not pack or overwork the dough.*

6. Immediately bake the biscuits until nicely browned and craggy, about 15 minutes. Let cool (if you can wait at all) and serve.

VARIATIONS

EVERYTHING BISCUITS

1. Mix equal parts sesame seeds, poppy seeds, dried onion flakes, and garlic flakes and season with a few pinches of celery salt.

2. Prepare an egg wash with 1 egg and ½ cup cold water.

3. Twelve minutes into the baking, use a pastry brush to sweep the egg wash onto the biscuits, then sprinkle generously with the everything seasoning. Bake for 3 to 4 minutes more.

CHEDDAR-JALAPEÑO BISCUITS, AND MORE . . .

Add fun features (grated cheese, chopped jalapeños, or whatever your heart desires) during the final mixing process. You can sprinkle the biscuits with additional cheese or seasonings at the 12-minute baking mark and return to the oven until perfectly delisherous.

CLOCKWISE FROM LEFT: Tutti Frutti (page 253), Welcome to Savory Sandwich Land (page 256), and Cheese It Up (page 255)

FRENCH TOAST

It's easy to take this dish for granted, but it's also easy to mess it up. Getting it right involves three Bs: batter, basting, and bread. A good French toast batter has a fair amount of cream but enough milk that it will fully saturate the bread, and it should be not too sweet or heavy on the spices; the bold flavors should come in the garnish. A good basting technique enters later, to develop a crisp, buttery outer crust. And when it comes to choosing bread for French toast, it's about using what you have in house, as day-old bread always works best. If you have a crusty sourdough, either cut off some crust or soak the bread in the batter a little longer to soften it up. If you have a soft, sweet bread, cut down the sweetness in the batter and make sure the soak is quick enough to avoid sogginess. If you're left with savory bread like rye or walnut raisin, or even focaccia, the same rules apply, and embrace the opportunity to get weird with your garnish choices!

5 TIPS FOR TRICKING OUT YOUR FRENCH TOAST

French toast is not for breakfast purists. Those folks can go sit in the corner with their noses in the air muttering their particular *voulez vous* and *pain perdu* all day long. French toast is for that kid in you who wants to eat a big-ass slice of birthday cake in the shower and leave the house wearing a pink tutu and rain boots. Here are our favorite tips for getting weird on our basic recipe. We hope they help you catch a respite from all that adulting.

CHEESE IT UP

Burrata, ricotta, chèvre, and triple crème are the jam when it comes to French toast. This idea is also pretty mainstream if you think about it—who doesn't think of whipped cream as an acceptable topping for French toast? Change up the dairy game with something more interesting. **GO TO: DOUBLE CREAM RICOTTA (PAGE 137) WHIPPED BY HAND WITH FRESH CRACKED BLACK PEPPER AND THYME**

TUTTI FRUTTI

Little Richard is a weird dude, but he's never been afraid of breaking the rules. Take a cue from the man when choosing fruit garnishes for French toast. Who ever said French toast had to be garnished with the same tired-ass triple-berry mix (blue-, rasp-, straw-)? Get weird on it, and stick with the seasons as much as possible. Try red wine–roasted pears, preserved apricots, fresh husk cherries, cherries both sweet and sour, pineapple, mango, quince, and *wop boppa loo bop a wop bam boom!* **GO TO: GRILLED STONE FRUITS, SUCH AS PEACHES, APRICOTS, NECTARINES, AND SOUR CHERRIES**

SHE'S A SAUCY ONE

Here in 'Murrica, land of the free, French toast and maple syrup just go together like a couple of crazy kids on date night at the malt shop. But if you want to ride your hot rod into the greasy heavens of breakfast bliss, we suggest branching out with bold sauces, fruit purees, and honey-and-syrup infusions. After all, "never change" is for yearbook captions and variety is the sauce of life. **GO TO: WHISKEY-SPIKED CARAMEL (PAGE 264) OR ADD A FEW SLICES OF JALAPEÑO TO OUR RHUBARB SYRUP (PAGE 309) FOR A REAL KICK IN THE PANTS**

SPICE IT OR SPIKE IT!

A wee dram of the whisk' or pull of the hooch has been known to cure all ills, just as a healthy dose of chile heat or pronounced dried spice flavors has aided many a yogi on the path to nirvana. Try adding these things to your batter or sauce game to keep things interesting. **GO TO: CHAI FRENCH TOAST BATTER! USE CHAI CONCENTRATE (PAGE 31) IN PLACE OF THE SUGAR AND CHOCOLATE CREAM IN THE SOAKING MIXTURE IN THE MAIN RECIPE (PAGE 257)**

WELCOME TO SAVORY SANDWICH LAND

McGriddles are gross—sorry, Ronald. But there's genius to be found everywhere. The idea of sweet/savory breakfast combos is a great idea, and it's an even better idea when executed with quality real-food ingredients! So be proud—romp in the ball pit of bacony sweet stuffs, play in the place of chicken and waffles—but don't feel the need to compose these into microwavable bite-size sandwiches. Geesh. **GO TO: ROASTED ALMOND BUTTER WITH FRIED CHICKEN AND HOT SAUCE**

CHOCOLATE MILK FRENCH TOAST

MAKES 3 HEALTHY SERVINGS

SOAKING MIXTURE

1 cup whole milk

1½ cups heavy cream

4 ounces (½ cup) dark chocolate chips

4 eggs

½ cup packed light brown sugar

1 teaspoon pure vanilla extract

1 teaspoon ground cinnamon

Pinch of salt

TOAST

6 slices challah or brioche bread (the Panini Roll on page 13 works well, too!)

2 tablespoons unsalted butter

Pure maple syrup, for serving

Our jumping-off point at Egg Shop is a basic batter with a little cinnamon and vanilla that has its own fun by replacing milk with chocolate cream and finishing with seasonal fruit and of course high-quality maple syrup.

The soaking mixture is a great make-ahead; it can be kept in the fridge for up to 2 days, just waiting for that French toast hunger to strike.

1. To make the soaking mixture, in a small saucepan, heat the milk and cream until just simmering (about 180°F). Place the chocolate in a heatproof medium bowl and pour the milk-cream mixture over the chocolate. Let it rest for about 10 minutes, then stir until evenly melted and combined.

2. In a medium bowl, whip the eggs gently, then stir in the brown sugar, vanilla, and cinnamon. Add 1 cup of the chocolate-cream mixture and stir until combined, then pour the egg mixture back into the original chocolate mixture. (This is called tempering, and it prevents the cold eggs from cooking in the warm liquid by gradually raising the temperature of the eggs in two stages.)

3. To make the French toast, heat a large cast-iron pan over medium heat while you dunk the bread in the egg mixture a few slices at a time. Be sure to saturate the bread fully, especially if using day-old bread. Add a bit of the butter to the pan and swirl to coat the pan. Shake off any excess soaking mixture and cook the toast in the butter. For extra points, add more butter and use your new-found basting technique (page 77) to make the toast nice and crispy on the outside! Serve drizzled with maple syrup.

CHOCOLATE MOUSSE

MAKES 6 TO 8 SERVINGS

1 cup heavy cream

3 eggs

10 ounces extra dark chocolate (90 to 100% cacao)

¼ cup hot water

¼ cup pure cane sugar

½ cup Biscuit Crumble Topping (page 260)

¼ cup Smoky Sugar (page 260)

This mousse maintains the flavor of good chocolate like no other. It's quick, simple, and something special when given a little crunch and a bit of heat. We combine hot and sweet with our smoked sugar–ground chipotle garnish and add a bit of butter crunch with our buttermilk biscuit crumble topping. This is how we do it at Egg Shop, and with any luck, how you'll want to do it from now on.

1. Get ready to whisk like you've never whisked before and fold with the best of them! In a large bowl, whip the cream to full volume and set aside. Or take a short cut and use an electric mixer at medium-high speed.

2. Heat water in a saucepan to make a double boiler.

3. Separate the egg yolks and whites into 2 clean, heatproof bowls. The yolks bowl should fit over the double boiler saucepan without hitting the water and the whites bowl should be big enough to whip the whites.

4. Place the chocolate in a microwave-safe container and melt it in the microwave, 20 seconds at a time, checking often so that it doesn't burn.

5. In a small saucepan, combine the hot water and sugar and cook over low heat to make a syrup, stirring until the sugar is dissolved.

6. Set the bowl with the yolks over the double boiler and whisk the yolks until light and frothy, adding the sugar syrup little by little. Whip the yolks into sabayon (see page 52), remove from the heat, and stir in the melted chocolate. (This bowl will ultimately hold all the components, so swap it for a bigger one now if need be.)

7. Using a very clean whisk or a mixer, whip the egg whites to medium peaks.

8. Alternate folding the whipped cream and whipped whites into the chocolate-yolk mixture in three stages. Gently transfer to your desired serving vessel (coffee mugs and mason jars work well, or throw back to 1992 and use a stemmed martini glass) and chill in the fridge until ready to serve, or at least 40 minutes. The mousse will hold up in the fridge for 3 or 4 days.

9. To serve, top each mousse with 1 tablespoon of the biscuit crumble, and serve the smoky sugar on the side for guests to consume at their own chosen speed.

BISCUIT CRUMBLE TOPPING

MAKES 1½ CUPS

1 Buttermilk Biscuit
(page 252), crumbled

2 tablespoons brown sugar

2 tablespoons olive oil

The topping can be used on fresh fruit, yogurt, ice cream, or anything you see fit. It will keep for about 1 week.

---

1. Preheat the oven to 350°F.

2. In a bowl, combine the crumbled biscuit, brown sugar, and olive oil. Spread on a baking sheet and bake until toasted, about 15 minutes.

SMOKY SUGAR

MAKES ½ CUP

1 dried chipotle pepper, stemmed

½ cup pearl sugar

In a food processor or a mortar and pestle, grind the chipotle with the sugar until the mixture is finely ground, but with some larger flakes of chipotle remaining.

SALTED CARAMEL BACON BREAD PUDDING

MAKES ONE 9 X 13-INCH PAN
(TO SERVE 4 TO 6)

SEA SALT CARAMEL SAUCE

2 cups pure cane sugar

¼ cup water

¼ pound (1 stick) unsalted butter

1 cup heavy cream

½ teaspoon sea salt

BACON BREAD PUDDING

7 eggs

1 cup packed light brown sugar

2 cups heavy cream

1 teaspoon pure vanilla extract

8 day-old Panini Rolls (page 13), cut into 2-inch cubes

¼ cup finely chopped cooked bacon, plus 4 to 6 strips cooked thick-cut bacon, for garnish

A few pinches of sea salt

Bread pudding is all about simplicity of flavor and great texture. Salt and caramelized sugar should always be at the forefront, and the pudding should be nearly as moist and tender as a panna cotta. Everything else is just a garnish. At Egg Shop our garnish of choice is bacon. Are you surprised? And can you blame us?

1. To make the caramel sauce, in a heavy-bottomed saucepan with a lid, combine the sugar and water. Stir gently until the mixture is the consistency of wet sand. Cover and cook over medium heat for 10 minutes. At this stage the sugar mixture will appear to be simmering rapidly, as if it were simply a pan of water, but you will notice it quickly becoming more viscous, and the simmering bubble will begin to slow down. Uncover, reduce the heat to low, and cook until the sugar begins to caramelize and takes on the color of a dark honey.

2. Remove from the heat and stir in the butter using a long-handled whisk (this will keep your skin away from spattery sugar and burning steam). When the butter is fully melted, stir in the heavy cream and finish with the sea salt. Let the sauce cool for 20 minutes before tasting or using. (This caramel sauce will last for up to 30 days in the fridge in an airtight container—if you don't eat it by the spoonful.)

3. To make the bread pudding, in a large bowl, whisk the eggs, brown sugar, cream, and vanilla until complete combined. Add the bread cubes and chopped bacon and toss to let the bread soak up the egg mixture. Lightly press the bread mixture into the bowl. Cover the surface of bread mixture with plastic and set it aside to rest for 30 minutes.

4. Preheat the oven to 350°F.

5. Have ready a 9 x 13-inch baking pan (metal preferred). Spread ¼ cup of the caramel sauce on the bottom of pan, followed by half the bread mixture, then ¼ cup of the caramel sauce, a pinch of sea salt, then the rest of the bread mixture, and another pinch of sea salt. Drizzle ¼ cup of the caramel sauce on top.

7. Cover the pan with foil and bake for 30 minutes. Remove the foil and bake until the top is a deep brown, 30 minutes longer. *Cool completely before cutting!*

8. To serve, either microwave for 2 or 3 minutes or cover with foil and reheat in a 350°F oven for 15 minutes. Cut into 4 x 4 inch cubes in the pan, then cut each diagonally into wedges. Garnish each wedge-shaped serving with a strip of cooked thick-cut bacon and plenty of caramel sauce.

BRUNCHKINS

MAKES 24 'KINS

2 cups canola oil

Several 3 x 4-inch wedges of leftover Salted Caramel Bacon Bread Pudding (page 263), cut or broken into 1-inch cubes

1 cup milk (or chocolate milk for thrill seekers)

2 cups superfine sugar

2 tablespoons ground cinnamon

¼ cup bourbon (we use Bulleit or Knob Creek Smoked Maple)

1 cup Sea Salt Caramel Sauce (steps 1 and 2 of Salted Caramel Bacon Bread Pudding recipe, page 263)

I had a pet squirrel once. I kept him in my pocket. His name was Jeff. Jeff was my BFF. Then one day Jeff was gone. I was sad, and I wondered if somewhere Jeff was sad, too. . . .

So here's a recipe about how to turn our bread pudding into delicious bite-size doughnuts! I hope they bring you the never-ending joy of having your best friend right there in your pocket. Miss ya, Jeff. Love ya!

(DISCLAIMER: Repeated consumption of tiny doughnuts has been known to cause rapid mental regression and overwhelming childlike euphoria followed by feelings of guilt and loss. Please dial 311 on yourself immediately, as playing pop music at high volumes will likely occur. Brunchkins are extremely dangerous when accompanied by alcohol and opportunities to use emojis.)

1. In a medium saucepan, heat the oil to 350°F over medium-high heat.

2. In a large bowl, soak the bread pudding cubes in the milk for 2 minutes, then use your hands to round each cube into a small meatball shape. Squeeze gently, taking care not to make the brunchkins too dense.

3. Combine the sugar and cinnamon and set aside.

4. Simmer the bourbon briefly over medium heat to evaporate the alcohol, about 1 minute. Stir in the caramel sauce and set aside.

5. Working in batches as needed, fry the brunchkins until golden brown on the outside, about 3 minutes. Use a wire skimmer to remove them from the oil to the cinnamon-sugar mix and turn to coat evenly. I dare you to let these cool!

6. Enjoy warm with the whiskey-spiked caramel, but be warned.

MILE-HIGH BLACK BOTTOM PIE

MAKES 1 PIE

TOOLS
pastry torch

CHOCOLATE GRAHAM CRACKER CRUST

3 cups very finely crumbled chocolate graham crackers

3 tablespoons pure cane sugar

¼ pound (1 stick) unsalted butter, melted

FILLING AND TOPPING

1 tablespoon unflavored gelatin

¼ cup water

2 ounces unsweetened baking chocolate (either bar or disc form)

½ cup plus ⅓ cup pure cane sugar

¼ cup cornstarch

2 cups whole milk

4 egg yolks plus 3 egg whites

1 tablespoon pure vanilla extract

¼ teaspoon cream of tartar

Italian Meringue (page 106), made with 6 egg whites

Variations of this rich chocolate custard pie date back to the 1920s, and this version is an expansion on my grandmother Betty's recipe. It's a chocolate lover's dream. With a chocolate graham cracker crust filled with a layer of dark chocolate, a layer of vanilla custard, and a mountainous topping of toasted Italian meringue, it's everything a custard pie should be, and taller!

1. To make the crust, preheat the oven to 350°F.

2. In a food processor, pulse the graham crackers and sugar to fine crumbs, then add the melted butter and process. When the mixture will hold a shape when pressed, transfer to a 9-inch pie plate and press to distribute evenly in a single uniform layer on the bottom and sides. Bake until the crust is firm, but not dry or fissured, 15 to 20 minutes. Set aside to cool.

3. To make the filling, in a small dish, sprinkle the gelatin over the water and set aside.

4. In the microwave or over a double boiler, melt the chocolate, stirring until smooth and being careful not to scorch it. Set aside to cool.

5. In a heavy saucepan, whisk ½ cup of the sugar and the cornstarch, then slowly whisk in the milk. In a medium bowl, beat the egg yolks until foamy, then whisk them into the milk mixture, stirring until no yellow streaks remain. Bring to a simmer over medium heat stirring constantly (alternate using a whisk and spoon to prevent lumps). Simmer for another minute or so, taking care not to curdle the custard or scorch on the bottom of the pan.

6. Add 1 cup of the custard mixture to the melted chocolate and stir until smooth. Spread this mixture carefully over the crust and refrigerate for at least 1 hour.

7. Meanwhile, prepare a large bowl of ice water. Add the softened gelatin to the remaining hot custard mixture and stir or whisk until smooth. Place the pan into the ice water to cool completely, then stir in the vanilla. Set aside until cool, then remove from the ice.

8. In a large bowl, beat the 3 egg whites with the cream of tartar to medium peaks, then beat in the remaining ⅓ cup sugar, 1 teaspoon at a time until you have firm peaks. Fold the beaten egg whites into the cooled custard a little at a time, very gently, so as not to lose the incorporated air.

9. Spoon the mixture evenly over the chocolate mixture in the pie shell. Chill, well covered, for at least 1 hour.

10. Make the Italian Meringue (see page 106 for tips) and spread it on top of the pie. Make the meringue as tall as humanly possible and brûlée the peaks with the pastry torch before serving to toast the meringue and unlock the marshallowy sumpin-sumpin you've been looking for all these years.

11. Cut into wedges with a hot knife to serve. This pie will keep in the fridge for up to 2 days, and makes for one of the guiltiest breakfasts you could ever imagine.

VARIATION: KEY LIME PIE

MAKES 1 PIE

4 egg yolks

One 14-ounce can sweetened condensed milk

½ cup fresh key lime juice (or 50/50 regular lime and Meyer lemon juice)

1 baked Chocolate Graham Cracker Crust (page 267, steps 1 and 2)

Italian Meringue (page 106), made with 6 egg whites

If you're pressed for time or find the Mile-High Black Bottom Pie intimidating, try this one on for size. This is great with the chocolate cookie crust, and a sprinkle of ground chipotle powder on the crust before you fill the pie adds yet another dimension.

1. Preheat the oven to 350°F.

2. In a large bowl, whisk together the egg yolks, sweetened condensed milk, and lime juice. Pour the mixture into the prepared pie crust and bake until fully set in the realm of a firm Jell-O shot (you know what I mean, don't lie), about 20 minutes. Cool in the fridge for about 1 hour.

3. Top with the Italian Meringue and torch as in step 10 of the Mile-High Black Bottom Pie.

GIANT MERINGUE (PAVLOVA GIGANTATA)

MAKES ONE 12-INCH
PAVLOVA

**MEZCAL STRAWBERRIES
AND TOASTED COCONUT**

2 cups strawberries,
quartered

3 tablespoons mezcal

Zest and juice of 1 lime

3 tablespoons pure cane
sugar

Pinch of sea salt

1 cup dried shaved coconut

PAVLOVA GIGANTATA

1 cup pure cane sugar

¼ cup packed light brown
sugar

¼ cup potato starch

4 large egg whites, at room
temperature

Pinch of sea salt

2 tablespoons cold water

2 tablespoons fresh lemon
juice

WHIPPED CREAM

1 cup ice-cold heavy cream

1 tablespoon powdered
sugar

A crisp meringue gives a unique eating experience, as you feel it crunching and melting simultaneously. A perfect meringue dessert, with its fissures and epic swirls, also presents a beautiful landscape for garnishes. If you were able to shrink yourself to approximately one inch tall, this dessert would be the gnarliest surf breaks frozen in time. While we know this is impossible, we can always live vicariously through the myriad fruits, nuts, purees, and whips of the world as they garnish our Pavlova Gigantata. Turn on, tune in . . . eat Pavlova. (It's easy, too, because you already know how to make French Meringue, page 106.)

1. To make the mezcal berries, in a medium glass bowl, combine the berries, mezcal, lime zest, lime juice, pure cane sugar, and salt. Let the berries rest at room temperature for 2 hours.

2. Preheat the oven to 350°F. Line a baking sheet with parchment paper. While the oven is preheating, spread the coconut shavings on the baking sheet and toast until golden, about 5 minutes. Transfer the coconut to a bowl, but keep the lined baking sheet for the Pavlova.

3. To make the Pavlova, in a food processor, pulse the sugars and potato starch until uniformly combined and substantially more fine. Sift the sugar-starch mixture and set aside.

4. In a large bowl with an electric mixer or in a stand mixer, whip the egg whites with the salt to stiff peaks, add the water and whip 1 minute. Add the sugar mixture little by little—a tablespoon at a time—while continuing to whip the meringue. When you've added half the sugar mixture, add the lemon juice. Keep whipping and adding the sugar mixture. When all the sugar is incorporated, whip another 2 or 3 minutes, until you have stiff, glossy peaks.

5. Taking care not to deflate the meringue, form one giant mass of meringue in the center of the parchment-lined baking sheet. Using a spatula, gently work the meringue closer to the sides of the baking sheet into whatever amorphous shape suits your fancy. After all, perfect circles are for squares, man. As you work, be sure to pull straight up with the end of the spatula to create interesting shapes and curls of meringue.

6. When you are finished with your edible art project, reduce the oven temperature to 300°F and place the masterpiece in the oven. Bake for 30 minutes, then reduce the oven temperature to 250°F (keep the oven door shut!) and bake another 20 minutes. Turn the oven off and let the meringue rest another 10 minutes, then open the oven door and let the Pavlova cool for another hour or so.

7. To make the whipped cream, using an electric mixer (or a whisk and some elbow grease), whip the heavy cream with the powdered sugar until light and fluffy.

8. To serve, carefully peel the parchment away from the Pavlova (or better yet, serve on the paper to aid in clean up) and garnish as you see fit with heaping spoonfuls of whipped cream, the berries, and the toasted coconut. This is a grab-and-grub scenario, so don't even bother slicing it—just provide plenty of napkins and scold people who don't wash their hands before digging in!

PROFITEROLES WITH DARK CHOCOLATE SAUCE

MAKES 12 PROFITEROLES

TOOLS
stand mixer fitted with a paddle attachment (unless your arms are very strong), piping bag fitted with a medium round tip

PÂTE À CHOUX

1¾ cups all-purpose flour

6 or 7 egg yolks

2 cups water

3 tablespoons pure cane sugar

Pinch of salt

5 tablespoons unsalted butter

SAUCE AND FILLING

1 cup dark chocolate chips

1 tablespoon unsalted butter

2 tablespoons agave or honey

¼ cup water

Montauk Frozen Custard (page 277)

Now that you're egg obsessed, you'll find that making all those meringues, reformers, and egg white scrambles has left you swimming in a pool of yolky goodness. You've made mayo and aioli, and you've even cured yolks in tamari, *but you still have more yolks!* Here's another yolk destroyer for your arsenal.

This versatile egg-based pastry is a staple of most pastry kitchens. Pâte à choux (*pat-uh-shoe*) is the basis of the most delicious things in life: cream puffs, éclairs, gougères, and profiteroles. For puffs, éclairs, and profiteroles, simply pipe this recipe into the appropriate shape, bake, and fill to your heart's content. For gougères, fold in shredded Gruyère or cheddar at the end and top with a bit more cheese for the final bake.

As Kanye said to me one time after I presented a five-course meal at a dinner party, "Well, *damn*, son! Voilà!"

Voilà indeed, Yeezy. Voilà indeed.

1. To make the pâte à choux, sift the flour and set aside. Keeping them intact, place the egg yolks in a bowl and set aside.

2. In a medium saucepan, combine the water, sugar, salt, and butter and bring to a boil over medium-high heat. When the butter is fully melted, add the flour to the pan all at once, remove from the heat, and stir it with a heavy wooden spoon. This dough will fight back as you stir and stir to incorporate the flour evenly and use the residual heat from the pan to gelatinize the starch (you're so clever). You're near the finish line when the dough forms a shiny, uniform ball, clearing the sides of the pan, and is free from any visible lumps of flour.

3. Transfer the dough to a stand mixer fitted with a paddle attachment (you can do this next step by hand with the wooden spoon, but it's a workout). Mix the dough on medium speed until there is no visible steam rising from the bowl. Begin to add the egg yolks, one or two at a time, as the mixer keeps going. The dough has reached the right consistency when you can dip the paddle into the dough and pull up to reveal a long, narrow V shape clinging to the point of the paddle. Some days the dough may be ready with 6 yolks, some days it may take all 7. Absorption is weird. This test will help: You should be ready to go about 5 minutes after you add the first yolk!

4. Preheat the oven to 375°F. Line a baking sheet with parchment paper and fill a piping bag fitted with a medium round tip with the pâte à choux.

5. Carefully pipe onto the baking sheet a spiral of dough that's 2 to 3 inches in diameter and climbs into a tiny mountain with 3 turns around the circle and a pointy top. As you pipe, count slowly to yourself—one, two, three—and when you say three, stop squeezing and gently pull straight up. Practice makes perfect—repeat to make 11 more pastries.

6. Dip your finger in cold water and use it to gently round the pointy tops over. Bake the pastries until golden brown, about 20 minutes. *Be very careful not to slam the oven door shut, or to open and close it while baking.* Let the pastries cool without being jostled. Pastry can tend to deflate. (Once cooled, these profiteroles will last for 2 days in an airtight container stored at room temperature, or pop them in the freezer for up to 2 weeks and simply toast them in a 350°F oven for 10 to 12 minutes.)

7. To make the sauce, melt the chocolate chips, butter, agave, and water in a medium bowl, either over a double boiler or in the microwave. Stir the chocolate sauce to make it smooth, then set aside in a warm place.

8. To serve, cut the pastries in half horizontally and fill each with a scoop of frozen custard. Drizzle with chocolate sauce and enjoy without delay.

MONTAUK FROZEN CUSTARD

MAKES 4 CUPS

TOOLS
candy thermometer, ice-cream maker

One 12-ounce can plus half a 12-ounce can Montauk Summer Ale or your favorite light ale, cans reserved for serving

¾ cup pure cane sugar

3 cups heavy cream (the higher quality, the better)

9 egg yolks

When I was in the seventh grade, I checked myself into the little-known Gerald Ford Clinic. Unlike his wife Betty's lauded treatment centers for drug abuse and addiction, Jerry's clinic focused on something simpler, something sweeter. I had an ice cream problem, and it was time to face it. What had I been looking for at the end of the pint? It was tough, but once I hit bottom I was able to start on the rocky road to recovery. It wasn't until recently, decades later, that I could sit on the beach in the summer without even a passing thought of all the mint chips, Cherry Garcias, or moose tracks in this one sweet world. I had finally arrived, and on that day I cracked open a different kind of cold one to celebrate.

Infused with the delicious yeasty notes of my favorite beach beer, this frozen sweet cream custard is a lasting reminder of the struggles that led to that moment. Please enjoy responsibly.

---

1. In a small saucepan, simmer the 12 ounces of Montauk Summer Ale over medium-low heat until reduced by half (about ¾ cup), about 30 minutes. Meanwhile, let the remaining 6 ounces Montauk Summer Ale go flat at room temperature.

2. Prepare an ice bath.

3. In a heavy saucepan, whisk the sugar, cream, and egg yolks. Bring the custard to 175°F (just below a simmer) while stirring constantly with a wooden spoon or silicone spatula. Strain the custard through a medium-mesh sieve into a bowl and cool the bowl in the ice bath immediately.

4. When the custard has cooled to room temperature (or roughly 70°F), stir in the beer reduction and the degassed beer.

5. Cool the custard in the fridge overnight with a layer of plastic pressed gently against the surface to prevent any kind of skin from forming (and to keep out any rogue fridge aromas). Do not skip this step; it is very important that the custard rest and cool for at least 4 hours. This balances the custard, making it uniform and thoroughly cold.

6. Spin the custard mixture in an ice-cream maker according to the manufacturer's instructions. Be sure to store in an airtight container in the freezer for at least 2 hours before digging in. This gives the ice cream time to firm up a bit and really improves the texture and scoopability.

7. Serve in beer cans with the tops carefully removed or in your favorite frosty beer mug.

DRUNKEN EGGS

Having a drink with friends is essential, and over eggs, it's simply devotional. Whether that drink is a mimosa, a black coffee, a craft cocktail, or a fresh juice, the experience is of the utmost importance. Bev Life: It's about snacking and relaxing (snack-a-laxing!) with friends at any point in the day, at any proof. But, if you want to go pro you have to get that bev game tight. We break it down like this: Chilling, Pairing, Batching.

FROM LEFT TO RIGHT: In Love with the Coco (page 291), Orange Juju (page 291),
Ms. Michelada (page 284), Tequila Honey Bee (page 285), Just Another Tequila Sunrise (page 286),
P.Y.T. (page 283), Point Break (page 290), Rosemary Negroni (page 293), Hot Pants (page 297).

IN LOVE WITH THE COCO

5 lime wedges

4 mint leaves, plus 1 sprig for garnish

¼ ounce agave

2 ounces Sagatiba cachaça

1½ ounces Coconut Puree (see Note)

3 brandied cherries, for garnish

This is a beach drink, light but not too sweet. It was inspired by a semi-obscure hip-hop song and my best dog friend (Coconut the English bulldog). It's a take on a caipirinha that substitutes fresh coconut puree for sugar, but otherwise keeps it real with fresh lime and Sagatiba cachaça. Go ahead.

Muddle the lime wedges in a cocktail shaker or pint glass. Add the the mint, agave, cachaça, coconut puree, and ice. Shake vigorously and pour dirty (without straining). Garnish with the brandied cherries on a sword and a healthy mint sprig.

TO MAKE MANY COCKTAILS

Follow this ratio: 4 parts lime juice, 1 part agave, 2 parts cachaça, 1 part coconut puree. Use mint as the variable here. Begin by combining the agave, lime, and mint in a pitcher or serving vessel. Stir until the agave and lime juice are evenly combined. Add the cachaça and coconut puree and stir until well combined. Fill the pitcher with ice and stir until well chilled. Garnish with lime wheels, mint sprigs, and brandied cherries.

NOTE: To make coconut puree, puree fresh or frozen coconut in a blender using 2 parts coconut to 1 part water.

P.Y.T. (PRETTY YOUNG THANG)

2 ounces Espolón tequila blanco

1 ounce grapefruit juice

¾ ounce agave

¾ ounce fresh lime juice

½ ounce beet juice, or to taste

Lime wheel, for garnish

This cocktail is very now, very next, very Insta. It's like a Sea Breeze but with tequila, served upside-down with fresh beet juice instead of cranberry. Like, hello . . . it's literally actually so pretty.

In an ice-filled pint glass, build the cocktail by adding the tequila, grapefruit juice, agave, and lime juice. Shake, strain into an ice-filled Collins glass. Float the beet juice on top and garnish with the lime wheel.

TO MAKE MANY COCKTAILS

Follow this ratio: 2 parts tequila, 1 part grapefruit, then balance with equal parts agave and lime juice. For large batches it's best to make this in a pitcher over ice and give it a good stir, then top with beet juice and garnish with a few lime wheels.

MS. MICHELADA

MAKES 1 COCKTAIL

Tajín Clásico seasoning

2 ounces Michelada Cutter Mix (recipe follows)

1 Tecate beer

1 lime wedge, for garnish

The michelada is huge part of our brunch lives. If a toddy cures a cold, then Ms. Michelada is your homegirl for hangovers. We start with Worcestershire and Clamato juice spiced with "That's Hot" Hot Sauce, add a little fresh lime, top with Modelo Especial and serve in a glass rimmed with plenty of Tajín seasoning (the quintessential Mexican garnish made of dehydrated lime powder, ground dried chiles, and salt).

Rim a pint glass generously with Tajín and fill it with ice. Pour the michelada cutter mix over the ice and top with beer to your taste. Stir once, garnish with the lime, and enjoy your visit with Ms. Michelada.

TO MAKE MANY COCKTAILS

The most enjoyable way to make a bunch of Micheladas is to prepare all of the glasses on a rimmed tray (Tajín rims, fill with ice, add 2 ounces of cutter mix to each). Get everyone together, open the Tecates at the same time, and fill all the glasses as fast as you can. It's like that volcano science project from third grade . . . except full of beer!

MICHELADA CUTTER MIX

MAKES 4 CUPS (ENOUGH FOR 16 TO 20 MICHELADAS)

¼ cup Worcestershire sauce

4 cups (32 ounces) Clamato juice

¼ cup "That's Hot!" Hot Sauce (page 150)

¾ cup fresh lime juice

2 teaspoons Tajín Clásico seasoning

Whisk the ingredients together and store in an airtight container in the fridge. Use as needed for up to 30 days.

TEQUILA HONEY BEE

MAKES 1 COCKTAIL

¼ ounce mezcal

1 ounce Cardamom-Honey Syrup (recipe follows)

1 ounce fresh lemon juice

2 ounces añejo or reposado tequila

Dash of Angostura bitters

Lemon twist, for garnish

Possibly one of the simplest cocktails we serve, the Tequila Honey Bee is a take on the typical vodka and rum Honey Bee cocktail. We use a green cardamom–infused honey syrup, añejo tequila, and fresh lemon for a cocktail that's as easy to drink as a margarita but less sweet and more complex.

Give an old-fashioned glass a mezcal rinse. In an ice-filled cocktail shaker, combine the honey syrup, lemon juice, tequila, and bitters and shake. Strain into the glass over ice and garnish with the lemon twist.

TO MAKE MANY COCKTAILS

This is one of the easiest ratios to remember: 2 parts tequila, 1 part lemon juice, and 1 part cardamom-honey syrup. Use mezcal and Angostura bitters as the variables to adjust the aromatics and smoke to your liking. This tastes great frozen, just blend with ice and serve. Otherwise pour it over crushed ice as you would a julep.

CARDAMOM-HONEY SYRUP

MAKES 2 CUPS

1 cup wildflower honey

1 cup piping hot water

10 green cardamom pods

Combine the honey, hot water, and cardamom pods and stir to combine. Let steep for 24 hours. Strain out the cardamom pods, or leave them in the syrup for a more intense flavor. Store in the fridge in an airtight container for up to 2 weeks.

JUST ANOTHER TEQUILA SUNRISE

MAKES 1 COCKTAIL

1 ounce Chipotle Sherry Grenadine (recipe follows)

2 ounces reposado tequila

3 ounces fresh orange juice

1 ounce fresh lime juice

Orange slice, for garnish

Maraschino cherry, for garnish

Pomegranate seeds, for garnish

I was admittedly obsessed with the 1970s growing up, and this drink is an homage to a simpler time. A time when California cowboys and polyester swingers gathered around their enormous American cars to talk about new concepts like smog and equal pay. Here's to you and your sweet fruity Mexican screwdriver, Don Henley!

Pour the grenadine into a Collins glass. In an ice-filled cocktail shaker, combine the tequila and juices, shake briefly to chill, and pour slow and dirty (without straining) into the glass. Garnish with an orange slice, maraschino cherry, a few pomegranate seeds and as many umbrellas or plastic swords as you can find.

TO MAKE MANY COCKTAILS

Add 1 recipe Chipotle Sherry Grenadine to a pitcher or punch bowl and fill with ice. In another pitcher, combine 24 ounces each of the tequila and juices over ice and stir to chill. Add the juice/booze mixture to the pitcher or bowl with the ice. Tip: Finish with Champagne for a peaceful, easy feelin'.

CHIPOTLE SHERRY GRENADINE

MAKES 3 CUPS

2 cups organic pomegranate juice

½ cup fresh lemon juice

½ cup Brandy de Jerez

1 cup pure cane sugar

1 dried chipotle pepper

In a medium saucepan, combine the juices, brandy, sugar, and pepper and simmer over medium heat for about 10 minutes, stirring constantly. Be careful not to burn the sugar! Let the grenadine cool to room temperature, then either remove the chipotle for a mild, less spicy and smoky grenadine or store with the pepper for a more pronounced smoke flavor. This grenadine will keep for 1 month or more in the fridge in an airtight container.

DRINKS WITH WHITES: BLINDED BY THE LIGHTS, DIZZY NEW HEIGHTS

We found it nearly impossible to tend bar for even an hour at Egg Shop without a guest asking for drinks with eggs. While we stay away from fringe fest cocktail freakshows that involve egg yolks (enter the Golden Fizz . . . yikes!), we do love using just the whites to make classics and to update more obscure drinks that may call for heavy cream by substituting a well-shaken white. With a few tips you can easily use egg whites to fluff and foam yourself into the annals of cocktail history!

THE MUSTACHE RYE'D: HOW TO MAKE A PROPER WHISKEY SOUR

The craft of the whiskey sour is that of blending water, whiskey, lemon, and sugar to create a cocktail that is balanced, frothy, and attractive in the glass. While the oldest sour recipes do not call for egg white, bartenders have been using them to improve the balance, texture, and presentation of the cocktail for the last ninety years. To that end, when cocktail enthusiasts ask for an egg drink at Egg Shop, it's usually the whiskey sour. (Note: If you ask for a Ramos Gin Fizz anywhere outside New Orleans, a bartender will likely spit in your drink, not think you're knowledgeable and cool.)

There are numerous variations of the whiskey sour, each named for their oft-disputed place of origin. Purists argue that the basic egg white whiskey sour is a Boston sour. Topping a Boston sour with a red wine float makes it a Greenwich sour, and so on and so forth. At Egg Shop we like to experiment with the sour elements of the drink, exchanging tart cherry, blood orange, or yuzu juice for the lemon juice, and even kaffir lime–infused pineapple and ginger juice from time to time. Whatever the variation or disputed place of origin, the "proper" whiskey sour is the best platform for discussing how to work with egg whites when mixing an exceptional cocktail.

MUSTACHE RYE'D

MAKES 1 COCKTAIL

1 egg white

1 ounce fresh lemon juice

½ ounce simple syrup (see Note, page 317)

2 ounces Bulleit rye whiskey

Dash of Angostura bitters, lemon twist, and maraschino cherry, for garnish

1. Add the egg white to an empty cocktail shaker and shake vigorously until the white is foamy but still loose, about 10 seconds.

2. Fill the shaker with ice and build the cocktail in the shaker. Shake vigorously for 10 to 15 seconds.

3. Strain into a coupe if serving up or a Collins glass if on the rocks.

4. Garnish the pristine white foam on top of the cocktail with a tiny dash of bitters, a generous lemon twist (use a peeler and make a twist about ½ inch wide by 2 inches long), and because we don't take ourselves too seriously, a bright red maraschino cherry, or a fresh local cherry if they are in season. (Rainier cherries are the best if you find yourself out west.)

SOUR VARIATIONS

To get the perfect flavor profile in a sour, it's all about balancing the sweetness levels of the whiskey and juice, and adjusting with simple syrup—or just try these interesting ideas:

Yuzu juice + Yamazaki Japanese whisky + 1 ounce simple syrup

Tart cherry juice + Old Overholt rye + ½ ounce simple syrup

Blood orange juice + Elmer T. Lee bourbon (no simple syrup)

Fresh lime juice + Amrut aged single malt + ½ ounce kaffir lime or ginger simple syrup

POINT BREAK

1 egg white

2 ounces grain vodka (we use Ketel One)

½ ounce fresh lemon juice

½ ounce fresh lime juice

2 ounces pineapple juice

¼ orgeat syrup

2 drops of John D. Taylor Velvet Falernum (traditional liqueur in tiki cocktails)

1 ounce blue Curaçao

Brandied cherry and pineapple wedge, for garnish

The point break is a take on a classic tiki-style cocktail: the Blue Hawaiian. The Egg Shop Point Break is much lighter than the original recipe, trading egg whites for heavy cream and fresh juices for an artificial sour mix. There were a lot of good things about the 1950s, but artificial flavors, preservatives, and processed foods aren't our favorites. This vibrant seafoam-blue drink is out there; think Keanu Reeves skydiving with Patrick Swayze in Hawaii.

1. Add the egg white to an empty cocktail shaker and shake vigorously until the white is foamy but still loose, about 10 seconds.

2. Fill the shaker with ice and build the cocktail in the shaker. Shake vigorously for 10 to 15 seconds.

3. Strain into a highball glass over ice. Garnish with a brandied cherry and a pineapple wedge.

ORANGE JU-JU

MAKES 1 COCKTAIL

1 egg white

2 ounces vodka

3 ounces fresh orange juice

½ ounce fresh lemon juice

½ ounce agave

½ teaspoon bourbon vanilla extract

Orange twist, for garnish

We are kids from the 1990s. This drink reminds of all of those hours spent posting up in a food court broadcasting our starter jacket brand of cool, reeking of Drakkar Noir, and dreaming of having a driver's license one day. Slurp this down and remember how easy life used to be before Al Gore invented the interwebs.

1. Add the egg white to an empty cocktail shaker and shake vigorously until the white is foamy but still loose, about 10 seconds.

2. Fill the shaker with ice and shake again vigorously. Build the cocktail and shake again.

3. Pour dirty (without straining) into a Collins glass. Garnish with a wide orange twist.

ALONE TIME

These drinks are best made one or two at a time. Use these recipes as your survival guide when mercury is in retrograde or it's too cold to go to the beach. Stir and sip your woes away. . . .

ROSEMARY NEGRONI

MAKES 1 COCKTAIL

½ ounce Campari

½ ounce Amaro Nonino

1 ½ ounces Tanqueray gin

1 ounce Rosemary-Infused Vermouth (recipe follows), plus ¼ ounce for rinse

Orange twist and rosemary sprig, for garnish

Living in Southern California provides access to fresh herbs and produce in the most bizarre places. In LA it's not uncommon to see rosemary bushes used as shrubbery. This drink reminds me of old Hollywood with its booze-stirred-over-ice framework showcasing rosemary outside of its typical wintry context. Light but strong, refreshing, classic.

1. Fill two old-fashioned glasses with ice. Measure the Campari, amaro, and gin into one glass and stir gently for about 30 seconds.

2. Discard the ice from the second glass. Add ¼ ounce of the rosemary vermouth and twist the glass to coat the inside of the glass. Add the 1 ounce of vermouth to the stirred cocktail.

3. Strain the stirred drink into the prepared glass and garnish with the orange twist and rosemary sprig.

ROSEMARY-INFUSED VERMOUTH

MAKES 16 OUNCES

16 ounces sweet vermouth (Carpano Antica Formula)

2 large rosemary sprigs

Combine the vermouth and rosemary and let infuse for 48 hours, then strain. It's perfectly fine to strain out just the quantity you need and let the infusion continue for the long haul, but the rosemary flavor will become more and more intense.

RUM MANHATTAN
(AKA RYE 'N GOSLING'S)

1½ ounces Gosling's Old Rum

1 ounce Rittenhouse rye

¼ ounce Punt e Mes

3 dashes Regans orange bitters

3 brandied cherries, for garnish

Orange twist, for garnish

Our take on the classic is a balancing act that features aged dark rum, a punchy rye, and mélange of bittersweet flourishes. You know—a little of this, a little of that, stirred and strained.

1. Build the cocktail in a pint glass, add ice, and stir well, about 10 seconds. We prefer this cocktail served up in an old-fashioned glass, but it's also good on the rocks.

2. Garnish with the brandied cherries and be sure to make a big show of squeezing an orange twist before dropping it in the drink. This is your time to shine.

MAPLE BOURBON TODDY (AKA THE BROADCASTER)

MAKES 1 COCKTAIL

2 ounces Knob Creek
Maple Bourbon

½ ounce pure maple syrup

1 ounce fresh lemon juice

5 ounces hot water (196° to
205°F)

Lemon twist, for garnish

This is the only known cure for the common cold. The sweetness of maple syrup and maple-infused bourbon are balanced with fresh lemon juice and hot water in this quick and easy remedy. If we were hosting a talk show this would be in our desk mug every night.

1. Add the bourbon, maple syrup, and lemon juice to your mug of choice. Add the hot water and stir briefly to distribute the syrup and bourbon evenly.

2. Garnish with a lemon twist, being sure to squeeze the fragrant lemon oil into the mug before dropping the twist into the drink.

HERR SCHUTZ'S MULLED WINE

MAKES 1 PIPING HOT MUG
OF YULETIDE GLORY

1 ounce Calvados

4 ounces light-bodied red
wine (such as Burgundy or
Blaufränkish)

2 ounces Chai Concentrate
(page 31)

½ ounce fresh lemon juice

½ ounce simple syrup
(page 317)

Orange twist, for garnish

Cinnamon stick, for garnish

Herr Schutz (aka our friend and business partner Florian) is a big part of
Egg Shop's success. His Germanic love of efficiency helps maintain a high
standard of cleanliness and productivity. But Herr Schutz longs for the cold
nights of his motherland from time to time, and in those moments he asks
that we serve this long-steeped, cinnamon and clove scented mulled wine.
Of course we oblige, but, sometimes we just can't wait for the steeping
required in the old family recipe, and we cheat a little. . . .

1. Measure the Calvados into a mug or heatproof glass. Heat the wine, chai,
lemon juice, and simple syrup in a kettle or saucepan until it begins to simmer,
then pour it into the prepared mug.

2. Squeeze an orange twist into the mug to release all the aromatic orange oil.
Stir with a cinnamon stick until the wine is cool enough to drink without burning
your tongue.

HOT PANTS

MAKES 1 COCKTAIL

Apple cider, enough to almost fill your mug

¾ ounce lemon juice

2 ounces Knob Creek Maple Bourbon

¼ ounce Amaro Nonino

¾ ounce Sea Salt Caramel Sauce (steps 1 and 2 of Salted Caramel Bacon Bread Pudding recipe, page 263)

Cinnamon stick, for garnish

Freshly grated nutmeg, for garnish

Fresh local apple cider is a true luxury of autumn in the Northeast. Sweet and crisp with a well-rounded apple flavor, good cider is only better when served piping hot with a bit of quality bourbon and Sea Salt Caramel Sauce.

Bring the cider to a simmer as you would if making water for coffee and tea about 196° to 205°F. Measure the lemon juice, bourbon, and amaro into a mug. Add the cider, then drizzle in the caramel sauce while stirring with the cinnamon stick. Finish the drink with some nutmeg.

PAIRING IS CARING: A DISPATCH FROM THE LAND BEYOND MIMOSA

My adventures in wine began in Sonoma County several years ago with the phrase "breakfast wine." Excuse me, what did you say, dude? Apparently breakfast wine is a thing. Granted, under first consideration the idea conjures a baby wombat–size moral dilemma. It's nine a.m.: To drink, or not to drink, that is the question. Whether 'tis nobler in the mind to suffer the slings and arrows of an outdated temperance movement, or to raise up a glass with your soft scramble, and by pairing end them. To drink, to sip . . .

All silliness aside, how can we give these "breakfast" foods and egg dishes their due as a complete meal unless we offer serious beverage pairing? Breakfast is at its best when elevated, expertly balancing sweet and savory components. These important foods can transcend their morning station when given a thoughtful pairing.

So we call upon our ally in the fight, a homie from way back, Bev-Life pro Carla Rzeszewski, to be our tour guide to the *land beyond the mimosa*!

Carla began her career in the service industry fifteen years ago as it ought to have begun: as a silverware polisher. After holding virtually every front-of-the-house job imaginable, she wrangled the position of wine director for April Bloomfield's Spotted Pig, the Breslin, and the John Dory Oyster Bar in New York City. Eventually she and her partner, Richard Betts, chose to become winemakers, and their first wine, Sucette, hails from ancient Grenache vines grown in the deep sands of Vine Vale in the Barossa. Carla has been regularly featured in the mainstream and wine media and was dubbed the Queen of Sherry by the *Village Voice.* There's simply no better human to turn you on to wine and beer pairings. Yo, Carla . . .

WHERE DO WE START?

First, curate a space where people feel comfortable rather than judged, where you and your guests are willing to relax into whatever your idea of a great meal is, regardless of time of day. The dusty, moral-spined ideals of "how to drink" are outdated. Toss all that out the window and do what makes you happy! Above all, it *must* be fun. You cannot eat and drink surgically, and without joy. You've gotta throw yourself into the game and let yourself be seduced by the yum. . . .

Next, drink! Drink as much as you can! Find out what *you* like:

› Taste blind with friends in order to eliminate the intimidation factor. Don't taste blind to "get it right," taste blind so you can approach the drink without preconception.

› Ask your local wine shop staff or favorite sommelier what *they* like and take a chance. If it turns out you don't dig it, no worries! That means you've narrowed your field of possibilities, and you know what *not* to order next time.

› Take notes, or use a wine app, or simply take photos with your phone. Do whatever you can to remember what you drink and what you think.

SO, YOU GET NO KICK FROM CHAMPAGNE . . .

First, it's worth asking yourself, *Am I actually drinking Champagne?* Champagne comes from France, specifically from the Champagne region, and offers a uniquely yeasty and occasionally nutty complexity. Sparkling wines are made all over the world with a similar technique to true Champagne, but they can have very different profiles. It may be that you have been served an Italian Prosecco, or a Spanish Cava, or a California Brut. Regardless of the style of sparkling wine, it's important to *pinpoint what is not pleasing* to your palate. Is this wine too sweet? Is it too fruity? Too floral? Too acidic?

It could also be that you have only experienced the gratis "Champagne" found at the brunch buffet or a "ballers on a budget" birthday bonanza. Chances are very good that you have been subjected to the lowest of the low in terms of what the region has to offer. Sometimes you've got to *pay to play* . . . opt for spending a bit more to buy a bottle and see if a little more complexity doesn't help you see the light.

If your hang-up with Champagne is that it's too sweet, you should search out a drier style, of which there are plenty. *Pro Tip: Look for bottles labeled "non-dosage" or "brut nature," which have no additional sugars added. These are bone dry.*

HOW WE APPROACH PAIRING

You are now entering our zone. You can be you. Go ahead. Everyone else, they can deal with the fact that we are going to do exactly what we do, whenever we want to do it. —Gandhi

Most "traditional" pairings are based on the classic adage, *what grows together, goes together.* You can follow regional gastronomic tradition to make foolproof pairings, or simply mimic the flavor profile and ingredients of any dish with wine or beer that hails from the same region. There are plenty of books and pairing guides out there that lay the ground rules for traditional pairing success, but who wants to eat and drink by rules? Life is too short. Just remember this:

What you're drinking should be delicious with what you're eating!

SWEET SOMETHINGS: A.M. DESSERT, OR P.M. DAWN?

Eggy breakfast sweets, whether consumed first thing in the morning or late at night, tend to have a few things in common:

1. They provide a rich, almost custard-like eating experience.
2. They are typically balanced by a salty, nutty ingredient.
3. They are always improved by a little fresh fruit.

A **MOSCATO D'ASTI** provides the fresh fruit-forward match with super-pretty orange blossom and ripe peach notes in a range from off-dry to sweet depending on your preference, and all with lower alcohol (5.5% ABV). It's a guilt-free guzzler! A good **BELGIAN TRAPPIST BEER** matches the custard fattiness with malty richness, while the bubbles in the beer help to cut through the cream, ending in pure refreshment. Both choices allow the salty, nutty component to shine and complete the dish without being overwhelmed by acid or minerality.

TRY THESE:

> › Chai French Toast Variation (page 256) with Goji Açai Butter (page 79)
> › Basted Eggs (page 76) with Mocha Bacon Butter (page 81)
> › Mile-High Black Bottom Pie (page 267)
> › Brunchkins (page 264)

- › Chocolate Milk French Toast (page 257)
- › Profiteroles (page 273) with Montauk Frozen Custard (page 277)

WITH THESE:

- › Moscato d'Asti or Belgian Trappist Beer (Rochefort 10)

CHEESY, SAVORY RICHNESS: WE WANT THE FUNK

Soft-scrambled eggs topped with caviar go extremely well with **BLANC DE NOIRS**, a full-bodied Champagne that can handle the funk of tangy, earthy, oceanic caviar and provide balance with its toasty, yeasty complexity. Can you say Liquid Blini?

While a **SINGLE-MALT SCOTCH FROM THE ISLE OF SKYE** (a sister to Islay, that home of the super-peated beauties) may seem like a bit of a stretch upon waking, pour a glass for brunch alongside smoked salmon or breakfast sausage or corncob-smoked bacon and we guarantee that your mind will be blown. Try **TALISKER,** which gives you just enough delicate smoke to grab onto the smoked salmon or bacon but doesn't bludgeon you with peat as Islay's whiskies are wont to do. All trepidation about "morning drinking" is swiftly silenced by one of the greatest whisky pairings ever!

TRY THESE:

- › Eggs Caviar (page 61)
- › Eggs Foie (page 59)
- › Pepper Boy! (page 122)
- › Hangtown Fry (page 209)
- › Lobster Roll Benedict Variation (page 51)
- › Norwegian Benedict Variation (page 51)

WITH THESE:

- › Blanc de noirs or single malts from Isle of Skye

SPICY HOTS AND MEATY MEATS:
THAT SWEET, SWEET HEAT

If you're feeling frisky (which we usually are) and you've made a super-savory, meaty, or spicy breakfast (which we usually do), it's likely you're not in the headspace to overthink a beverage pairing. Keep it simple and reach for the most thirst-quenching beer in your immediate vicinity. A **LITTLE KINGS CREAM ALE**, at just 7 ounces, is the perfect beer for a little hair of the dog, and the refreshing malt-forward, light lager qualities can also help take some heat off the tongue.

If the frisk factor extends to your drink of choice (as we hope it will), a totally underrated but applicable wine choice would be a low-alcohol, off-dry (aka slightly sweet) sparkling red from France or California. Seek out a **BUGEY-CERDON** (named for its region in France) from Patrick Bottex. Or, try the California version of a Bugey-Cerdon, **LA VIE EN BULLES** from Bellus Wines, to attain full frisk consciousness. You are a pop of the cork and flick of the wrist from mouthwateringly juicy red fruits and just enough sweetness to counteract the spice! Pop. Flick.

TRY THESE:

› Shakshuka (page 177)

› El Camino (page 163)

› Steak and Egg (page 118)

› The Chorizone (page 96)

› My Shorty (page 143)

› The Beast (page 111)

› Egg Shop Fried Chicken (page 233)

WITH THESE:

› Little Kings Cream Ale or Patrick Bottex, Bugey-Cerdon, or Bellus, La Vie en Bulles

ADULT MOVES:
THE KEY TO THE KINGDOM FROM THE QUEEN HERSELF

We all experimented a bit in college, sure. Maybe you did some things you regret, maybe you found some things that felt so right they could never be wrong.

After all, we've been on quite a journey together over the last few pages, haven't we? We outed you on the whole Champagne thing. We drank Scotch together at nine a.m. Like beer and Brunchkins or steak and rosé, pairing can help you be you! But, as the days go by and you venture away from the nest of this book and the safety of these suggestions please remember this one thing, and enjoy your newfound adulthood:

SHERRY IS QUEEN. It's Carla's personal favorite and our number one Bev-Life pro tip! Yes, it takes a brave soul to call out "Sherry!" for breakfast. But, we aren't talking about a sweet, syrupy raisin bomb from the musty bubbleguts of Aunt Doris's liquor stash. That's a cream sherry. We want that dry, crisp, sea-salt stuff that makes you think of translucent ribbons of jamón and dancing to sounds of Paco de Lucia. Whether the dish is sweet, rich, meaty, salty, or spicy, a *copita* of Manzanilla is enough to show the world you are now a Bev-Life Pro. You know what's up. You make adult moves. (Q.E.D., *drop the mic.*)

First, a special adage for sherry pairing:

If it swims: Fino/Manzanilla
If it flies: Amontillado
If it runs: Oloroso

Next, sherry for the win!

LA GUITA MANZANILLA—The ultimate juicy-juice sherry. Incredibly light and chuggable, with a fantastic chalky spine. Great on its own, or with a lighter style egg/tomato/cured ham dish. An Egg Shop B.E.C. (page 115), perhaps?

ARGÜESO SAN LEÓN MANZANILLA—Slightly less fruity than the La Guita, but no less drinkable. If you prefer the salty kick to the fruity profile, choose the San León. Both the San León and the La Guita would be great with oysters, fried fish, or ceviche-style fresh seafood as well.

FERNANDO DE CASTILLA FINO EN RAMA—If you like it a little earthier, a little fuller, maybe even slightly more serious? Go for this *en rama* or "raw" style of Fino. (Fino is very similar to Manzanilla in style, and for our purposes here, just know that either of these bone-dry white wines will fix your craving for dry, salty, food-friendly a.m. options.) You'll find the same supersalty,

beautifully chalky deliciousness of the La Guita in the San León, but with a bit more meat on the bones.

BARBADILLO PRÍNCIPE AMONTILLADO—Amontilado is a Manzanilla/Fino taken to the next level . . . still bone dry, but because of a bit of oxidation from aging, you'll find all the saline yum here of Manzanilla/Fino, with a wonderful layer of nutty richness. Try it with fried chicken or pork shoulder!

GUTIERREZ COLOSIA "SANGRE Y TRABAJADERO" OLOROSO—So you like it rich? And I don't mean sweet; all of these sherries are bone dry. But with the Oloroso style, you combine the richness of a fuller-bodied sherry with the dried-fruit nuttiness of the Amontillado style. You're definitely moving into meats and fuller, more savory dishes here (this sherry *loves* anything with mushrooms, gravies, porky sauces, or sausage).

COCKTAILS AND CHILL: LEGIT COCKTAIL AND PUNCH RECIPES WITHOUT THE FUSS-STACHE!

There are many schools of thought on what makes a quality cocktail menu. For the longest time, "craft" and "classic" cocktails have been all the rage. After all, there's an air of legitimacy to every hair of the moustache. Though handlebar moustache-sporting anti-prohibitionists do make great drinks, they, like rum runners from the days of yore, are primarily nocturnal. So too is the culture of mixing and serving craft cocktails.

At Egg Shop, our cocktail menu has to cover more ground, featuring cocktails that not only pair well with eggs and lighter brunch/lunch fare but also enhance the culture of our restaurant, both at brunch and in the wee small hours. How did we do it? One word: *fun.* We wanted to make drinks that carried with them a sense of whimsy rather than the usual moody sex appeal. So we set out to create drinks that could easily be prepared in a larger format, like a punch or a pour-and-go scenario on our busiest of days, to make life super chill behind the bar. This idea makes most of our cocktails extremely adaptable for party settings and takes the pressure off the host, no matter how perfect his or her moustache (and thereby bartending skills) may be.

As is the case with every Egg Shop recipe, our cocktails take things a little further. We pride ourselves on using premium spirits; infusions with roots, herbs, and spices; freshly muddled ingredients; fresh fruit juices and purees, and quality syrups (see Setting Up Your Home Bar, page 317, for a list of our spirits and equipment of choice), Cocktails are for cocktail hour, and cocktail hour starts during brunch service on Elizabeth Street.

LARGE-FORMAT DRINKS FOR PARTY-TIME: BABY GOT BATCH

Oh my God, Becky, look at her batch. It is soooo big. It looks like one of those rap guy's beverages. But who understands those rap guys anyway. They only mess with drinks that are easy, okay? I mean, look at it. The batch is sooo big. I can't believe it serves so many people, and it's just out there. It's just sooo . . . batched!

I like big batches and I cannot lie. The following recipes were built for expanding for party times. The most important aspect of expanding a cocktail recipe is staying true to the balance and experience of the single drink. Here we offer the single-serving recipe along with our large-format serving instructions, so you can make sure everything checks out before you go all-in on pouring an entire bottle of premium booze into the Bermuda punch bowl.

GIN RUMI

MAKES 1 COCKTAIL

Three ⅛-inch-thick cucumber slices, plus 1 slice for garnish

2 ounces Turmeric-Infused Gin (page 307)

½ ounce St-Germain elderflower liqueur

¼ ounce rose water

1 ounce Passion Fruit Puree (page 307)

½ lime

3 fresh mint leaves, plus 1 sprig for garnish

Club soda (or Champagne, optional)

Stop acting so small. You are the Universe in ecstatic motion.

—Rumi

The best advice inspires the best summer cocktails. This poetic and dynamic gin drink is a take on a gin spritz that incorporates exotic floral elements to complement the verdant notes of quality gin. Rose water, St-Germain, and fresh passion fruit puree help make this the most romantic cocktail in our repertoire.

Muddle the cucumber in a mixing glass. Build the cocktail, adding ingredients in the order listed, ending with the mint. Fill the glass with ice. Stir the cocktail with a long bar spoon and strain it into a highball glass over ice. Top with club soda (or Champagne if you are balling out of control). Garnish with a healthy sprig of mint and a cucumber wheel.

TO MAKE MANY COCKTAILS

Slice an English cucumber into chunks, pulse it briefly in a blender or food processor, and pour it into a pitcher or punch bowl. Add the ingredients in the following ratio: 4 parts infused gin, 1 part St-Germain, 1 part lime juice, 2 parts passion fruit puree. Use the rose water as a variable and add to your liking (the drink should be floral and exotic but not taste like cheap perfume). Add ice, stir to chill, and just before serving, add Champagne or club soda and garnish with cucumber and mint. The same rule applies here: Champagne makes the world go round, but club soda can keep your head on straight.

TURMERIC-INFUSED GIN

MAKES 24 OUNCES

One 700 ml bottle Martin Miller's gin or your favorite London dry-style gin

2 pieces turmeric root 3 inches long and the diameter of a pencil, peeled

Knob of fresh ginger the same size as the turmeric, peeled

2 green cardamom pods

In the bottle of gin, combine the turmeric, ginger, and cardamom. Let infuse for 24 hours, then strain out the solids for a subtle flavor or continue to infuse for more intensity.

PASSION FRUIT PUREE

MAKES 2 CUPS

2 cups passion fruit pulp

1 cup water

¼ cup pure cane sugar

It's relatively difficult to find fresh passion fruit, but frozen pulp is easily found.

In a blender, puree the passion fruit pulp, water, and sugar. Pass the mixture through a fine-mesh sieve, using a spoon to get every last bit through. Only fibrous seeds should be left in the sieve. This puree does well in the freezer and can last up to 1 month; we suggest freezing in an ice cube tray and thawing as needed.

RHUBARB RYE JULEP

MAKES 1 COCKTAIL

1 large mint sprig

1 ounce Mint Extract
(page 309)

1 ounce rye whiskey

½ ounce Rhubarb Syrup
(page 309)

¼ ounce lemon juice

A good mint julep is hard to find. My father, a resident of Louisville, Kentucky, and a bourbon lover, taught me the art of the julep one Derby Day a long time ago. At Egg Shop, we keep our juleps seasonal with house-made syrups such as rhubarb, nectarine, blueberry, or apricot. Part of the fun in incorporating an additional flavor profile is finding a particular whiskey to fit. This is our most popular springtime version, done with Bulleit rye and rhubarb syrup.

Shake enough ice vigorously in a cocktail shaker to fill a julep cup or rocks glass. Pour the chipped ice into your glass and garnish with a large sprig of mint. Add the rest of the ingredients and stir with the ice for about 10 seconds, then strain into the glass.

TO MAKE MANY COCKTAILS

In a large pitcher, combine 1 recipe Mint Extract, 16 ounces rye whiskey, 8 ounces Rhubarb Syrup, 4 ounces fresh lemon juice, and 2 cups ice. Stir until the ice is fully melted. Refrigerate until ready to pour. To serve, fill a julep or rocks glass with crushed ice and pour, then garnish with a big sprig of fresh mint.

MINT EXTRACT

MAKES 2 CUPS

Leaves from 1 bunch mint
(about 1½ cups)

16 ounces rye whiskey
(about half a 1-liter bottle)

1. Soak the mint leaves in the whiskey for 20 to 30 minutes.

2. Strain out the leaves and gather them in a clean kitchen towel or cheesecloth. Wring them out gently into the whiskey.

3. Place the towel/leaf setup back in the whiskey. Soak 10 minutes.

4. Repeat this last step twice more, then discard the mint. Refrigerate until needed.

RHUBARB SYRUP

MAKES 4 CUPS

2 cups chopped fresh
rhubarb

2 cups pure cane sugar

2 cups water

In a medium saucepan, combine the rhubarb, sugar, and water and simmer over medium heat until the rhubarb is tender and the sugar is completely dissolved, about 10 minutes. Cool, then strain out the rhubarb. Store the syrup in the fridge; it's also great over soft cheese or French toast.

WHATTA MARG! OUR WATERMELON MARGARITA

2 ounces tequila blanco

½ ounce fresh lime juice

4 pieces watermelon
(1-inch cubes)

½ ounce agave

This little pink number is unbelievably fresh and so light it almost tastes like a bite of the real thing soaked in premium tequila. Simple, refreshing, and not too sweet. It's a little ridiculous but with a plastic spigot and a little DIY you can serve this on tap out of a hollowed-out watermelon, just sayin' . . .

In an ice-filled cocktail shaker, combine all the ingredients. Shake hard and pour dirty (that is, to pour the entire contents of the shaker into the glass, without straining). Salted rims are optional, but this one is great with a Tajín rim as well. (Tip: For a more tropical experience use blue Curaçao in place of the agave—pink becomes purple.)

TO MAKE MANY COCKTAILS (FOR PEOPLE GATHERED AROUND A WATERMELON IN YOUR BACKYARD GETTING DRUNK)

Cut one end of the watermelon off and reserve. Using a large spoon, scoop out the inside of the watermelon and puree it in a blender. Strain out any seeds. Cut a small slice from the opposite (still round) end of the watermelon to create a flat base. Be careful not to cut into the red part! Using an apple corer, cut a hole for the spigot about 3 inches up from the base of the watermelon on the long side. Insert the spigot and stand your DIY watermelon apparatus upright on a large round plate for extra stability.

Here's the ratio for a big batch: 4 parts tequila, 1 part lime juice, 4 parts watermelon puree, and 1 part agave. In a large pitcher, stir the mixture with plenty of ice until well chilled and pour it directly into the open end of the watermelon. Immediately fend your guests off with a stick while you serve yourself first. (Use the same ratio for frozen margaritas, but they won't pour well from the spigot, so try serving three- or four-person frozen Whatta Margs! with large straws in cute little baby watermelons that have been hollowed out in the same manner.)

THAT HOUSE LEAN

MAKES 1 COCKTAIL

2 ounces tequila blanco

¾ ounce Bauchant orange liqueur

¾ ounce fresh lime juice

½ ounce agave

2 dashes "That's Hot" Hot Sauce (page 150)

Lime wedge, for garnish

At its core That House Lean is a spicy margarita. What makes it our "lean" is the floral heat of our habanero-based "That's Hot" Hot Sauce and Bauchant orange liqueur used in place of triple sec. Rest assured the drink contains no jolly ranchers, or cough syrup.

Build the cocktail in a cocktail shaker adding ingredients in the order listed. Add ice and shake hard. Pour dirty (that is, pour the entire contents of the shaker into the glass, without straining) into a rocks glass (a salt rim is optional) and garnish with the lime wedge.

TO MAKE MANY COCKTAILS

Just follow this ratio: 4 parts tequila, 1½ parts Bauchant, 1½ parts lime juice, 1 part agave. Adjust the "That's Hot" Hot Sauce at the end to your desired heat level. If serving in a pitcher, add ice last and stir until well chilled. For a frozen drink, blend with the ice and serve.

EGG SHOP BLOODY MARY

MAKES 1 DRINK

Bacon Salt (see Note)

2 ounces vodka, bourbon, or tequila

¼ ounce fresh lemon juice

6 ounces Egg Shop Bloody Mix (page 314)

2 dashes "That's Hot" Hot Sauce (page 150), for an extra spicy Bloody Mary

1 lime wedge

1 lemon wedge

1 pitted martini olive

One 6-inch celery stalk

1 seasonal pickled vegetable (okra is our favorite, but use whatever pickle you dig)

The Bloody Mary can be quite personal; everyone seems to prefer it their own way. At Egg Shop our Bloody is offered as a fully customizable cocktail, centered on a standout base bloody mix. It's done pub-style, as we call it, with a little Guinness, plus spicy mustard added for body. The mix is balanced with the goal of making it adaptable for different spirits and heat preferences. This recipe is great for entertaining and allows you to create a totally streamlined Bloody Mary bar for any occasion. Just don't forget the "That's Hot" Hot Sauce and give the people what they want: bacon-salted rims and pickled seasonal veggies.

1. Rim a glass (a pint glass, mason jar, or 11-ounce Collins glass is a good choice) with bacon salt.

2. Add your booze of choice to a cocktail shaker. Top with ice, the lemon juice, and Bloody mix, a dash of the hot sauce and shake briefly. Pour dirty into the glass (that is, pour the entire contents of the shaker into the glass, without straining). Stab your garnishes on a cocktail pick, plastic sword, umbrella, or whatever suits your mood and serve.

NOTE: For bacon salt, pulse equal parts Maldon sea salt and chopped extra crispy bacon in a food processor until well combined. Will keep in the fridge for months, becoming only more bacony and delish.

EGG SHOP BLOODY MIX

MAKES ENOUGH FOR 12 DRINKS

1 cup Guinness

1 cup red wine

¼ cup Colman's mustard powder

2 teaspoons brown sugar

7 cups organic tomato juice

½ cup fresh lemon juice

3 tablespoons plus 1 teaspoon "That's Hot!" Hot Sauce (page 150)

2 tablespoons plus 1 teaspoon finely grated horseradish

2 teaspoons kosher salt

2 teaspoons freshly ground black pepper

1 teaspoon celery salt

Here's your key to the city, and the first step in being DTB (down to brunch). This recipe can be doubled for parties or cut in half to make just a few drinks—up to you, just please make it a staple in your fridge, and never, ever buy the shelf-stable stuff again. Frankly, you can tell Mr. & Mrs. T, whoever they are, to go F themselves after you make this mix!

---

1. In a container with a cover, whisk the Guinness, wine, mustard powder, brown sugar, and 1 cup of the tomato juice. Cover and rest overnight in the fridge. (This step flattens the Guinness and mellows out the mustard powder.)

2. To finish, add the remaining 6 cups tomato juice, the lemon juice, hot sauce, horseradish, kosher salt, pepper, and celery salt and stir to combine. Store in the fridge in an airtight container. Just make sure the mix is nice and cold before serving. This mix will keep for up to 10 days if using purchased tomato juice and 4 days if you are juicing your own tomatoes.

TO MAKE 1 COCKTAIL: Go to the Egg Shop Bloody Mary (page 313).

TO MAKE MANY COCKTAILS: Mix 1 part vodka with 2 parts Bloody Mix in a large pitcher full of ice and stir to combine. Simply pour into prepared glasses and garnish as you see fit.

CRYSTAL BLOODY VODKA

One 750 ml bottle vodka

One 6 x 1-inch piece horseradish root, peeled

1 slice smoky pepper bacon

10 sun-dried tomatoes

1 habanero pepper, halved

Zest of 1 lemon

1 teaspoon black peppercorns

1 teaspoon yellow mustard seeds

1 teaspoon celery seeds

½ teaspoon coriander seeds

½ teaspoon cumin seeds

1 heirloom tomato

This is a total reversal of the flavorful bloody mix + booze = excellent Bloody Mary formula. The Crystal Bloody is a more refined, almost martini-like take on the Bloody Mary that involves infusing the vodka with all the outstanding flavor components of a good Bloody mix and keeps the tomato pure and simple.

In a bowl or pitcher, combine the vodka, horseradish, bacon, sun-dried tomatoes, habanero, lemon zest, spices, and tomato. Cover and steep at room temperature overnight. Strain before serving if you are going for the element of surprise; otherwise strain as you mix drinks for presentational flair (the mixture will last for up to 1 month, strained and refrigerated).

TO MAKE 1 COCKTAIL: Shake 2 ounces infused vodka over ice with 1 roughly chopped large heirloom tomato and serve strained straight up in a chilled coupe or martini glass. Garnish as you see fit.

TO MAKE MANY COCKTAILS: Puree 8 heirloom tomatoes roughly chopped in a blender with 1 cup cold water and a pinch of sea salt, and strain through a fine-mesh sieve. Discard the tomato pulp and mix 3 parts tomato water to 1 part Crystal Bloody Vodka. Chill thoroughly and serve in an equally frosty glass.

GREEN JUICE BLOODY MIX

1 English cucumber diced

5 tomatillos, husked and halved

½ cup baby kale

½ cup fresh cilantro

1 jalapeño pepper, stemmed

1 cup cold water

Zest and juice of 2 limes

2 ounces olive juice

Your morning health ritual, optimized.

In a blender, combine the cucumber, tomatillos, kale, cilantro, jalapeño, water, lime zest, lime juice, and olive juice and puree on high. This mix can be made up to 3 days ahead and stored in the fridge in an airtight container. *We recommend citrus garnishes and spiced salt rims for this one.*

TO MAKE 1 COCKTAIL: Shake 2 ounces of your choice of vodka, tequila blanco, or mezcal (if you nasssty) with 6 ounces Green Juice Bloody Mix and pour dirty.

TO MAKE MANY COCKTAILS: Fill a pitcher with ice and mix 1 part you-choose booze with 3 parts Green Juice Bloody Mix and stir.

ON GARNISH GAMES AND BLOODY BARS

You now have at your disposal everything you need to offer brunch guests an exceptional custom Bloody Mary experience. But, there's more fun to be had here with a full-on "choose your own adventure" Bloody bar experience! Anyone can put fancy spirits and Bloody mix on a cute table with all the expected garnishes, but that sucks because it's just not *fun*. We ask one thing of you: *Don't be boring!* Give the people variety and, most important, give the people *skewers,* and let them build their own Technicolor tower of social media greatness. Trust me, if you want to see adults turn into drunken third-graders, offer all three of these Bloody variations, along with ridiculous and exciting garnishes to play with . . .

SKEWER GAME ON POINT

Experiment with these categories and you can't miss.

INFUSED SALTS AND SUGARS: Bacon Salt (page 297), Smoky Sugar (page 260), Summer Herb Salt (page 221)

COOKED STUFFS: fried chicken, deviled eggs, sliders, head-on prawns!

PICKLEY STUFFS: jalapeño, onion, carrots, eggs, olives

FRESH STUFFS: citrus, fruits, crunchy whole veggies, herbs that poke up your nose

SETTING UP YOUR HOME BAR

When people talk about their "home bar" they usually mean their local watering hole. The kind of place where Ted Danson tries to remember your name is not, however, what we have in mind. When we say "home bar" we're talking about a kick-ass bar that you create in your own home. A great home bar starts with a few pro-level tools, the most important of which are the Japanese jigger and a quality shaker combo.

All the recipes in this book are listed in ounce measurements because that's how a jigger works! Much as a scale is necessary for a bread baker, a jigger is the tool of the trade for tending bar. We specifically recommend a Japanese-style jigger because it includes ¼- and ¾-ounce marks in addition to the 1- and 2-ounce marks.

When it comes to shakin' it, we prefer to have 18- and 28-ounce weighted tin shakers on hand, along with a tempered pint glass. The pint glass is a versatile part of this combination, as it can be used as half of a shaker or as a vessel for making stirred cocktails that require you to pay attention to the visual cue of ice melting in balance to spirits and bitters.

When you're ready to build your bar, start small and start with what you like! There's no need to overspend on things you'll never drink or to stock "just in case" spirits on the off chance you make friends with some weirdo that only drinks Benedictine sours.

PRO TOOLS: Shaker, pint glass, stir spoon, strainers (julep and Hawthorne), muddler, and Japanese jigger (we dig www.cocktailkingdom.com).

GLASSWARE: We try to avoid stemware as much as possible to save space and avoid breakage. A solid rocks glass and an elegant highball/Collins glass will do the trick for cocktails, spirits, and beer. If you love wine, consider starting with a high-quality, all-purpose glass that's neither too large for the bubble structure of your Champagne nor too small to get some air into a full-bodied red.

NICE ICE: If you love stirred cocktails, please invest in silicone ice cube trays to make solid 1½-inch cubes. You and your guests will appreciate the gesture, as they watch the cube slowly melt and combine perfectly without watering down the spirit.

MIXERS, SYRUPS, AND JUICES: Please only use fresh juice, not the kind that comes in the little citrus-shaped squeezy bottle. When using carbonated mixers, buy the smallest bottles available so you never have to worry about them going flat. Never buy simple syrup, that's seriously lazy.

NOTE: To make simple syrup, just combine 1 part sugar to 1 part piping-hot water and stir to dissolve the sugar, then let cool before using.

GARNISH: Buy a lemon, lime, and orange and a bunch of mint whenever you go shopping and you'll never be out of garnishes. If you haven't used these things for cocktails within a couple days, simply slice and put in a pitcher in the fridge for a batch of infused water . If you have more exotic garnish tastes for your drinks, try to stick to high-quality garnishes in small quantities. The big jar of maraschino cherries will haunt you every time you open the fridge. . . .

APERTIF/DIGESTIF/AMARO: This is the bartender's choice, and these bottles are usually beautiful on the bar but very slow to be consumed. So buy your favorites and get weird when you want to, but no need to overstock these things. Our favorites are Campari, Fernet-Branca, green Chartreuse, and Amaro Nonino.

BITTERS AND TINCTURES: Angostura bitters are an absolute must! Beyond that, take your pick of other varieties (Peychaud's, Regans, Fee Brothers) We also like to have some weird stuff on hand for spritz and giggles (rose water, orange blossom water).

BOURBON AND RYE: While these two whiskies have similar uses and flavor profiles, one is made from corn mash and the other a mix of corn and rye. If you're a fan of the category, you might want to collect a range of bourbons and ryes for sipping, but when it comes to mixing, we prefer classics that are neither too strong or too sweet (Old Overholt rye and Evan Williams, and Bulleit bourbon).

GIN: Gin falls into two categories for us: dry or highly botanical. A more traditional dry gin will have some essence of juniper and a higher ABV (alcohol by volume), while a highly botanical gin may have a lower ABV and carry a wide range of flavor profiles. We recommend stocking a quality dry/London-style gin as your go-to and expanding with a more botanical gin as you see fit.

SCOTCH: If you love Scotch whisky, you'll stop at nothing to increase your collection. Good on you. We believe in limiting ourselves to our favorite styles of single malt and single-maltish things. For easy drinking we go to Glenlivet 12 for a Speyside, for smoky complexity we choose Islay and Laphroiag 10, and for intellectual curiosity we sip Nikka Coffey Grain Whisky.

RUM: Rum exists in three main categories for our purposes: light, dark, and premium/aged. There's a huge variance within each category, so it's really about choosing one bottle based on what you love to drink. If you like tropical mixed rum drinks but hate rum flavor, maybe substitute a more subtle cachaça or an elegant Brugal. If you dig a dark and stormy, then stock Goslings. If you have pirate goals, sip on Diplomático Reserva.

TEQUILA/MEZCAL: No longer the official drink of adolescent hangovers! We love the stuff and highly recommend stocking a quality tequila blanco (such as Espolón) and either a reposado or añejo (Herradura). Mezcal is tequila's smoky friend, and much like Scotch whisky, it can be either subtle or overwhelming. We recommend stocking a very subtle mezcal (Los Amantes) along with a more complex single-village mezcal (del Maguey).

VERMOUTH: Look for a quality sweet vermouth (Carpano Antica Formula) and a quality dry vermouth (Boissiere Bone White). Red or sweet vermouth is a key component of a good Negroni, and balancing a perfect martini truly depends on the quality of your white/dry vermouth.

VODKA: Vodka is about both subtlety and marketing. Recognizing the name doesn't guarantee quality! If you're a vodka fan, stock a potato vodka (Tito's) and a grain vodka (Ketel One) and stand by your choices. When choosing between a potato or grain vodka for a cocktail, remember that potato vodkas are luxurious, thick, and great for savory applications; wheat/grain vodkas are crisp, clean, and occasionally have citrus notes, making them a perfect match for fruit juices and other sweet mixers.

ACKNOWLEDGMENTS

THANK YOU TO:

All of the Egg Shop family, past, present, and future. It's by the hands of many that something is "made by hand." This is your work, your place, and a book about you.

Sarah and Demetri, for never giving up on your love of the perfect egg sandwich, and being the dearest of partners and friends. I owe you the world in an egg.

Florian, for being a great ally, resource, partner, and friend. You've given me a new definition of hospitality.

Dado and Steve at Folio Lit. You saw a book in a breakfast bowl, and championed what Egg Shop is all about.

Cassie Jones and her team at William Morrow, for letting my voice be heard and never standing in the way of creativity.

Lauryn Tyrell, David Malosh, and all of the supercool doods that styled and shot these photos. Stay cool, doods.

Anne, Benoit, Carla, Cesar, Helvia, Pino, Leo, and Sal for sharing your words, your craft, and your tremendous talents. It's a tasty world because you are in it.

Leigh Nelson and everyone at LMNOP Creative, for getting our face on straight from day one. May our smiles always be dotted with gold and all our eggs have legs!

Our purveyors of quality goods, everyone at Mi Barrio, Pain D'Avignon, Sohha Savory Yogurt, and Di Palo's. Sorry we raised our voice that one time and keep texting you in the middle of the night.

My family and friends, especially my parents, my brothers, and the Luginbills. You made me weird(er).

Thanks to the City of New York, for always being yourself; too unkind to be great, but great enough to help us see the good, the try-harder place where we fell in love, again, because we finally could.

UNIVERSAL CONVERSION CHART

OVEN TEMPERATURE EQUIVALENTS

250°F = 120°C   350°F = 180°C   450°F = 230°C

275°F = 135°C   375°F = 190°C   475°F = 240°C

300°F = 150°C   400°F = 200°C   500°F = 260°C

325°F = 160°C   425°F = 220°C

MEASUREMENT EQUIVALENTS

Measurements should always be level unless directed otherwise.

⅛ teaspoon = 0.5 ml

¼ teaspoon = 1 ml

½ teaspoon = 2 ml

1 teaspoon = 5 ml

1 tablespoon = 3 teaspoons = ½ fluid ounce = 15 ml

2 tablespoons = ⅛ cup = 1 fluid ounce = 30 ml

4 tablespoons = ¼ cup = 2 fluid ounces = 60 ml

5⅓ tablespoons = ⅓ cup = 3 fluid ounces = 80 ml

8 tablespoons = ½ cup = 4 fluid ounces = 120 ml

10⅔ tablespoons = ⅔ cup = 5 fluid ounces = 160 ml

12 tablespoons = ¾ cup = 6 fluid ounces = 180 ml

16 tablespoons = 1 cup = 8 fluid ounces = 240 ml

INDEX

Note: Page references in *italics* indicate photographs.

YOU HAVE EGG ON
YOUR FACE.

NO, REALLY,
YOU DO.